S0-BOT-921

Classic Designs

ARCO PUBLISHING, INC.
New York

Editor Mary Devine
Designer Gordon Robertson
Production Richard Churchill

Published 1985 by
Arco Publishing, Inc.
215 Park Avenue South
New York, NY 10003

© Marshall Cavendish Limited 1985

Library of Congress Cataloging in Publication Data
Main entry under title:

Classic designs.

1. Sweater.   I. Arco Publishing.
TT825.C63   1985   746.9′2   84–28446

ISBN 0–668–06506–0

Printed and bound in Hong Kong by
Dai Nippon Printing Company

Introduction

Beautiful knitwear is as popular today as it has always been, but good quality garments are now so expensive that you cannot always afford the kinds of sweaters and cardigans you like. So why not knit your own?

We have compiled an exclusive collection of timeless classics that will appeal to everyone who appreciates exquisite woolens. If you are a newcomer to knitting, our Know How section will bring this delightful skill to your fingertips. All the basic knitting stitches and methods are given in an easy-to-follow, step-by-step style, so it won't be long before you are knitting with confidence. Then you can put your new skills to the test by simply choosing a pattern from our stylish collection.

There's a superb range of women's casual sweaters in bright colors and bold designs. Knit yourself a light and lacy summer top, a luxurious mohair or angora sweater for special occasions or a cozy shawl and sweater set to keep out winter chills. Then, for the evening, try a dazzling off-the-shoulder style; wear it alone, or teamed with an eye-catching cardigan.

For classic men's knitwear, our rugged sweaters are hard to beat. Who can resist traditional Guernsey or Fair Isle—so easy to knit and so comfortable to wear—they look just as good on women too!

And we haven't forgotten the smaller members of the family as we've also included a selection of patterns that can be made up in both big *and* small sizes, to keep everyone happy.

Each design is accompanied by superb color photographs so you can see exactly how attractive and professional the finished garment will look, and throughout, there are handy diagrams and tips to make sure you don't go wrong.

So if you love beautiful, high quality woolens, start right away and knit your own collection of classic designs.

Contents

Cozy Shawl Set

Wear this attractive shawl sweater on the coldest winter's days. Two layers are worn together to give extra warmth. The body is worked in two sections with a center front and back seam. Work a bright shawl and attach onto the neckband.

BEFORE YOU BEGIN
Only the right section of the shawl has been charted. To work the left section of the shawl follow as for the right section to the center dotted line, reversing all the shapings and working a mirror image of the pattern.

Sizes
Bust   32[34:36]in
Length   25¼in
Sleeve seam   15½in

Note: Instructions for larger sizes are in brackets [ ]; where there is one set of figures it applies to all sizes.

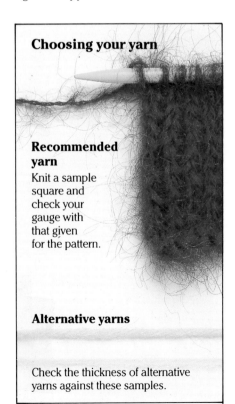

Choosing your yarn

Recommended yarn
Knit a sample square and check your gauge with that given for the pattern.

Alternative yarns

Check the thickness of alternative yarns against these samples.

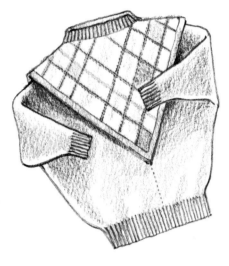

Gauge
22 sts and 28 rows to 4in over St st on size 6 needles.

Materials
☐ Approx 11[12:13]oz of lightweight mohair yarn in main color (m.c.)
☐ Approx 4oz in contrast color (a)
☐ Approx 2oz in each of 2 contrast colors (b and c)
☐ 1 pair each sizes 3 and 6 needles
☐ 1 stitch holder

INSTRUCTIONS
1 Back
Using size 3 needles and m.c., cast on 88[94:100] sts. Work 4in in K1, P1 rib.
Next row: Rib 13[9:16], * rib 3[4:4] M1 (by picking up the loop which lies between the next st on the left-hand needle and knitting through the back of it), rep from * to last 9[5:12] sts, rib to end.
Sl last 55[57:59] sts onto a st holder for left half of back.
Cont on first set of sts for right half of back. Change to size 6 needles.
Commencing with a P row, work in St st, casting on 2 sts at beg of every foll alt row until there are 97[99:101] sts on the needles.
Now cast on 3 sts on every alt row at same edge until 118[120:122] sts are on the needles, ending with a WS row. Mark this point with a colored thread. Now work 4 rows in St st. Inc 1 st on the same edge on the next and every foll 4th row 7 times in all. (125[127:129] sts.) Work a further 3 rows in St st. Mark this point with a colored thread.
Next row: (RS) Bind off 3 sts at beg of row.
Now bind off 3 sts on every foll alt row until 29[31:33] sts rem, ending with a WS row.
Place these sts on a st holder.
Left half of back
Rejoin yarn to the 55[57:59] sts on the st holder. Work across these sts to the end of the row. Now work as for the right half of back, reversing all the shapings.

2 Front
Work exactly as for the back.

3 Neckband
With RS facing, sl the 29 [31:33] sts on all 4 sections onto size 3 needles. (116[124:132] sts.)
Using m.c., work 20 rows in K1, P1 rib.
Bind off loosely.

4 Cuffs
Using size 3 needles and m.c., pick up and K 46[48:50] sts, from the colored markers on all 4 sections. Work in K1, P1 rib for 4in.
Bind off loosely.

5 Shawl
Using size 3 needles and m.c., cast on 210 sts. Work 8 rows in K1, P1 rib.
Dec 1 st at each end of 3rd, 5th and 7th rows. (204 sts.)
Change to size 6 needles and foll chart, reading odd rows K from right to left, and all even rows P from left to right. When chart is complete bind off the sts and fasten off the loose ends. Then fold shawl in half and join shaped shoulder edge for 2in. Work

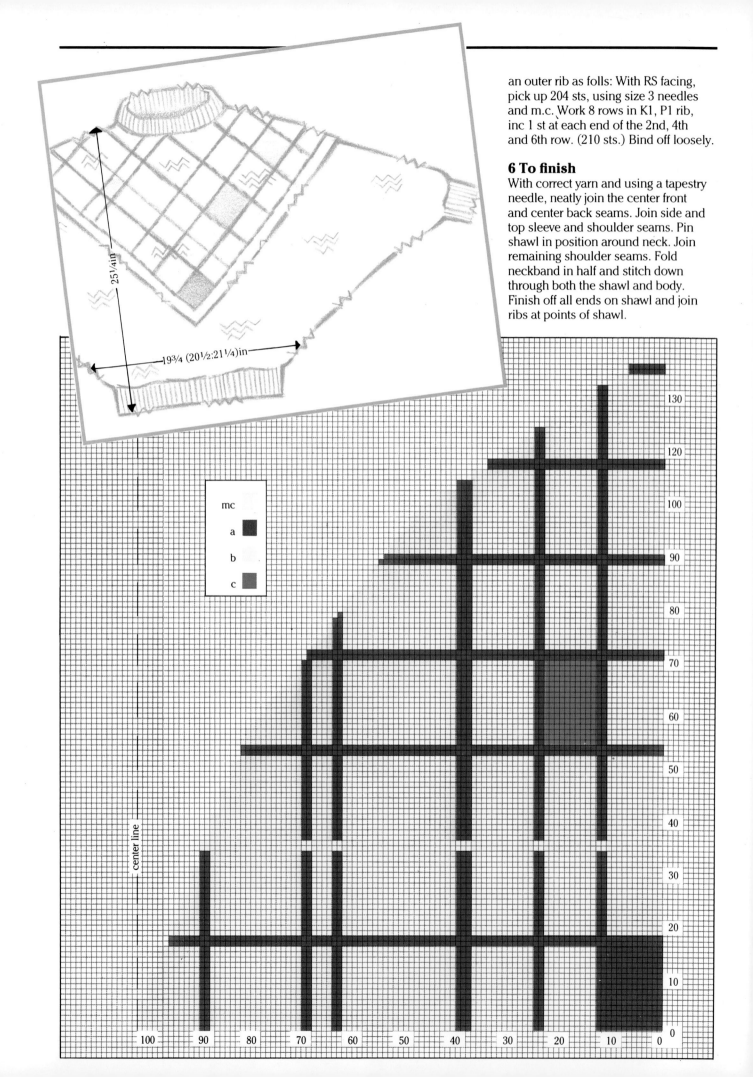

an outer rib as folls: With RS facing,
pick up 204 sts, using size 3 needles
and m.c. Work 8 rows in K1, P1 rib,
inc 1 st at each end of the 2nd, 4th
and 6th row. (210 sts.) Bind off loosely.

6 To finish

With correct yarn and using a tapestry
needle, neatly join the center front
and center back seams. Join side and
top sleeve and shoulder seams. Pin
shawl in position around neck. Join
remaining shoulder seams. Fold
neckband in half and stitch down
through both the shawl and body.
Finish off all ends on shawl and join
ribs at points of shawl.

25¼in

19¾ (20½:21¼)in

mc
a
b
c

center line

Cockleshell Patterned Sweater

Sizes

Bust	32[34:36:38]in
Length	24½[24¾:25¼:25½]in
Sleeve seam	15¾[16¼:16½:17]in

Note: Instructions for larger sizes are in brackets [ ]; where there is one set of figures it applies to all sizes.

Gauge

22 sts and 30 rows to 4in over St st on size 6 needles.

Materials

☐ Approx 16[18:20:22]oz of knitting worsted weight yarn in main color (m.c.)
☐ Small amounts in each of 3 contrast colors for embroidery
☐ 1 pair each sizes 3 and 6 needles

INSTRUCTIONS

1 Back

With size 3 needles and m.c., cast on 107(111:113:117] sts.

1st row: K1, * P1, K1, rep from * to end.

2nd row: P1, * K1, P1, rep from * to end.

Rep the last 2 rows for 4in, ending with a 2nd row and inc one st at end of last row on 1st and 3rd sizes only. (108[111:114:117] sts).

Change to size 6 needles and work in patt as folls:

1st row: (RS) K to end.

2nd row: * P17[18:19:20], K1, M2 – by bringing yarn to the front of the needle and wrapping it around the needle twice, P2 tog tbl, K13, P2 tog, M2, K1 rep from * to end.

3rd row: * K1, (K1, P1) into made st, K15, (P1, K1) into made st, K18[19:20:21], rep from * to end. ·

4th row: * P17[18:19:20], K21, rep from * to end.

5th row: As 1st row.

6th row: * P17[18:19:20], K1, (M2, P2 tog tbl) twice, K11, (P2 tog, M2) twice, K1, rep from * to end.

7th row: * (K1, (K1, P1) into made st) twice, K13, ((P1, K1) into made st, K1) twice, K17[18:19:20], rep from * to end.

8th row: P17[18:19:20], K25, rep from * to end.

9th row: * K6, (M2, K1) 14 times, K22[23:24:25], rep from * to end.

10th row: * P17[18:19:20], K1, (M2, P2 tog tbl) twice, M2, sl next 15 sts dropping extra sts to make 15 long sts, insert left-hand needle into the backs of the 15 long sts and P them all tog as one st, (M2, P2 tog) twice, M2, K1, rep from * to end.

11th row: * (K1, (P1, K1) into made st) 3 times, K1, (K1, (P1, K1) into made st, K1) 3 times, K17[18:19:20], rep from * to end.

12th and 13th rows: As 1st row.

14th row: K1, M2, P2 tog tbl, K13, P2 tog, M2, K1, P17[18:19:20], rep from * to end.

15th row: * K17[18:19:20], K1, (K1, P1) into made st, K15, (P1, K1) into made st, K1, rep from * to end.

16th row: * K21, P17[18:19:20], rep from * to end.

17th row: As 1st row.

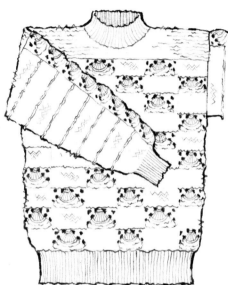

18th row: * K1, (M2, P2 tog tbl) twice, K11, (P2 tog, M2) twice, K1, P17[18:19:20], rep from * to end.

19th row: * K17[18:19:20], (K1, (K1, P1) into made st) twice, K13, ((P1, K1) into made st, K1) twice, rep from * to end.

20th row: * K25, P17[18:19:20], rep from * to end.

21st row: K17[18:19:20], K6, (M2, K1] 14 times, K5, rep from * to end.

22nd row: * K1, (M2, P2 tog tbl) twice, M2, sl next 15 sts dropping extra made sts to make 15 long sts, insert left-hand needle into the backs of the 15 long sts and P them all tog as one st, (M2, P2 tog) twice, M2, K1, P17[18:19:20], rep from * to end.

23rd row: * K17[18:19:20], (K1, (P1, K1) into made st) 3 times, K1, ((K1, P1) into made st, K1) 3 times, rep from * to end.

24th row: K to end.

Rep these 24 rows 4 times more. **

Cont in g st until back measures 23½[24:24½:24¾]in from beg, ending with a WS row.

Shape shoulders

Bind off 15(15:16:17] sts at beg of next 2 rows, then 16 sts at beg of next 2 rows. Leave rem 46[49:50:51] sts on a stitch holder.

2 Front

Work as given for back to **

Cont in g st for 6[10:14:18] rows.

Shape neck

Next row: K46[47:49:50], turn and leave rem sts on spare needle.

Bind off 4 sts at the beg of next row, 3 sts at beg of foll alt row, then 2 sts at beg of foll 2 alt rows.

Dec one st at neck edge on next and every foll row until 31[31:32:33] sts rem Cont even until front measures the same as back to shoulders, ending with a WS row.

Shape shoulder

Bind off 15[15:16:17] sts at beg of next row. Work 1 row then bind off rem 16 sts.

Shape second side of neck
Return to the sts on spare needle,
with RS facing, sl first 16[17:16:17] sts
onto stitch holder, rejoin yarn and K
to end.
Work to match first side reversing all
shapings.

3 Sleeves
With size 3 needles and m.c., cast on
51[53:55:57] sts and work in rib as for
back for 3¼[3½:4:4¼]in, ending with a
1st row.
1st size (Rib 2, M1) 24 times, rib to
end.
2nd, 3rd & 4th sizes (Rib 2, M1)
[11:10:9] times, (rib 3, M1) [3:4:6]
times, (rib 2, M1) [10:10:9] times, rib
to end. (75[77:79:81] sts.)
Change to size 6 needles and work in
patt as folls:
1st row: K to end.
2nd row: P28[29:30:31], K1, M2, P2
tog tbl, K13, P2 tog, M2, K1, P to
end.
3rd row: K29[30:31:32], (K1, P1) into
made st, K15, (P1, K1) into made st, K
to end.
4th row: P28[29:30:31], K21, P to
end.
5th row: As 1st row.
6th row: P29[30:31:32], (M2, P2 tog
tbl) twice, K11, (P2 tog, M2) twice, P
to end.
7th row: K28[29:30:31], (K1, (K1, P1)
into made st) twice, K13, ((P1, K1)

into made st, K1) twice, K to end.
8th row: P29[30:31:32], K23, P to
end.
9th row: K28[29:30:31], K6, (M2, K1)
14 times, K5, K to end.
10th row: P29[30:31:32], (M2, P2 tog
tbl) twice, M2, sl next 15 sts dropping
extra made sts to make 15 long sts,
insert left-hand needle into the backs
of the 15 long sts, P them all tog as
one st, (M2, P2 tog) twice, M2, P to
end.
11th row: K28[29:30:31], (K1, (P1,
K1) into made st) 3 times, K1, ((K1,
P1) into made st, K1) 3 times, K to
end.
12th row: K to end.
These 12 rows form the patt. Cont in
patt at the same time inc one st at
each end of the next and every foll
8th row until there are 95[97:99:101]
sts.
Cont in patt without shaping until
work measures approx 15¾[16:16½:
17]in from beg, ending with 12th patt
row. Bind off loosely.

4 Neckband
Join right shoulder seam.
With size 3 needles, m.c. and RS
facing, pick up and K20[21:22:22]
sts down left front neck, K front neck
sts inc 2 sts evenly across them, pick
up and K20[21:22:22] sts up right front
neck, K back neck sts inc one st in
center. (105[111:113:115] sts.)
Beg with a 2nd row work in rib as on
back for 3¼in.
Bind off loosely in rib.

5 To finish
Press lightly according to instructions
on ball band.
Join left shoulder seam and neckband.
Sew in sleeve. Join side and sleeve
seams.
Using the contrasting colors, oversew
around the outer edge of patt to form
a shell. Work two bullion knots in the
center of the shell.

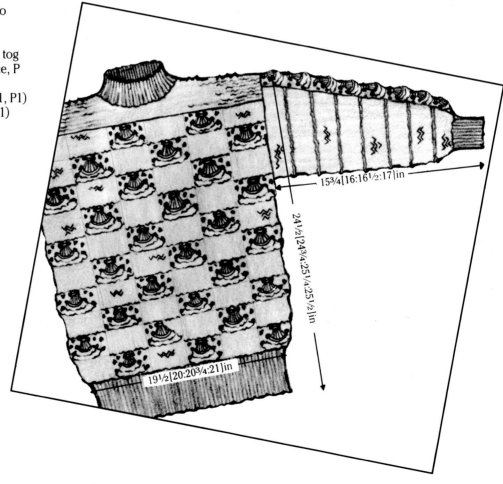

15¾[16:16½:17]in

24½[24¾:25¼:25½]in

19½[20:20¾:21]in

Bright Bobbled Sweater

K nit yourself this colorful bobble sweater, with a stripey yoke and a fun fringe. These multi-colored bobbles are knitted in afterwards to give a cheerful touch.

BEFORE YOU BEGIN

When making a garment with a yoke, using circular needles, always mark each round with a colored thread on every row. This is very important as all decreasing stitches are worked from the beginning of the round.

Sizes

Bust	32[34:36:38]in
Length	23[23:23½:24]in
Sleeve seam	17[17¼:18:18½]in

Note: Instructions for the larger sizes are given in brackets []; but where only one figure is given it applies to all sizes.

Choosing your yarn

Recommended yarn

Knit a sample square and check your gauge with that given for the pattern

Alternative yarns

Check the thickness of alternative yarns against these samples.

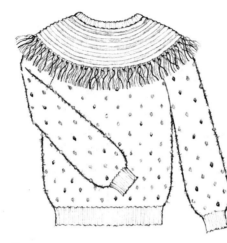

Gauge

23 sts and 28 rows to 4in over St st on size 3 needles.

Materials

- ☐ 14 [14:14:16]oz of Pingouin Confort in main color (m.c.)
- ☐ 2oz each of Pingouin Confort in contrast colors (a, b, c and d)
- ☐ 1 pair each sizes 2 and 3 needles
- ☐ Size 5 circular needle
- ☐ Crochet hook

INSTRUCTIONS

1 Back and front alike

Using size 2 needles and m.c., cast on 97 [103:109:115] sts and work in K1, P1 rib as folls:

1st row: K1, *P1, K1, rep from * to end.

2nd row: P1, *K1, P1, rep from * to end. Rep the last 2 rows for 2¼in, ending with 1st row.

Next row: Rib 1, * inc in next st, rib 15[16:17:18], rep from * to end. (103 [109:115:121] sts.)

Change to size 3 needles and work in St st, until work meas 16½[16½:17:17½]in from beg, ending with a WS row.

Shape armholes

Bind off 3 sts at beg of next 2 rows. Bind off 2 sts at beg of next 2 rows.

Shape yoke line

1st row: K2 tog, patt 30 [33:36:39]sts, turn work. Working on these 31

[34:37:40]sts only cont as folls:

2nd row: Bind off 4 [5:6:7] sts, patt to end.

3rd row: K2 tog, patt to end.

4th row: Bind off 6 sts, patt to end.

5th row: K2 tog, patt to end.

6th row: Bind off 6 sts, patt to end.

Work in patt dec 1 st at armhole edge on every foll 4th row, at the same time dec 1 st at neck edge on every row, until 1 st rem.

Break yarn and fasten off. With RS facing, st next 29 sts onto a piece of thread.

Rejoin yarn to rem 32 [35:38:41] sts, and cont as folls:

1st row: Bind off 4 [5:6:7] sts, patt to last 2 sts, K2 tog.

2nd row: Patt to end.

3rd row: Bind off 6 sts, patt to last 2 sts, K2 tog.

4th row: Patt to end.

5th row: Bind off 6 sts, patt to last 2 sts, K2 tog.

6th row: Patt to end.

Work in patt dec 1 st at armhole edge on every foll 4th row, at the same time dec 1 st at neck edge on every row, until 1 st rem. Break yarn and fasten off.

2 Sleeves

Using size 2 needles cast on 47 [47:47:49] sts and work in K1, P1 rib until cuff meas 2¼in, ending with a 1st row.

Next row: Rib 1, (inc in next st, rib 1) 8 times, (inc in next st) 11 [11:11:13] times, (rib 1, inc in next st) 9 times in all, rib 1. (75[75:75:79] sts.)

Change to size 3 needles and work in St st. Continue even until work meas 17½[17¾:18:18½]in from beg, ending with a WS row.

Shape cap

Bind off 5 [5:4:3] sts at beg of next 2 rows. Bind off 2 sts at beg of next 2 rows.

Dec 1 st at each end of every foll alt row until 43 [43:43:47] sts rem. Leave these sts on a thread.

3 Yoke

With RS of work facing, using a size 5 circular needle, and starting at the back, working from right hand side, pick up 29 [29:32:34] sts down right side of neck, K across the 29 sts on the thread, pick up and K 29 (29:32:34) sts up left side of neck, K across the 43 [43:43:47] sts from thread at top of 1st sleeve, pick up and K 28 [28:31:34] sts down left side of neck, K across the 29 sts from thread, pick up and K 28 [28:31:34] sts up right side of neck, K across the 43 [43:43:47] sts from 2nd sleeve. 258 [258:270:288] sts. Work in rounds always starting from the right side, mark end of rounds with a thread and move it up as every round is completed.

Work patt as folls:

1st round: Using m.c., P.
2nd round: Using m.c., K.
3rd round: Using a, K.
4th round: Using a, P.

Rounds 2-4 form the patt, cont working in patt using contrast colors a-d in sequence, at the same time work the shapings as folls:

10th round: *Patt 2 tog, work 4 sts, rep from * to end (215 [215:225:240] sts). Cont in patt for a further 11 [11:11:12] rounds.

Next round: *Patt 2 tog, work 3 sts, rep from * to end (172 [172:180:192] sts). Work a further 8 [8:8:10] rounds even in patt.

Next round: *Patt 2 tog, work 2 sts, rep from * to end (129 [129:135:144] sts). Work a further 2 [2:2:4] rounds even in patt.

Next round: *Patt 2 tog, work 4 sts, rep from * to end, ending 3 [3:3:0] sts. (108 [108:113:120] sts.)

4 Neckline

Change to size 2 needles and m.c., work in K1, P1 rib for 2¼in. Bind off loosely.

5 To finish

Press lightly on the WS with a warm iron over a dry cloth. Sew side and sleeve seams. Fold neckband in half and sew in place. Attach the first row of tassels to yoke, keeping colors in sequence. To place the bobbles, count 9 rows up and 5 stitches in from beginning of row. The first bobble row is worked in color sequence c, d, a and b, with 9 complete stitches between each bobble. Count a further 9 rows up and 10 stitches in and work bobbles in color sequence b, c, d and a.

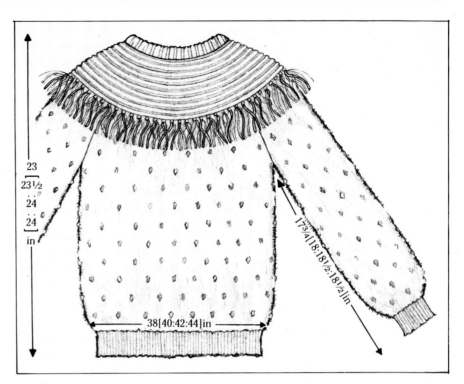

23
23½
24
24
in

38[40:42:44]in

1¾[18:18½:18½]in

HELPING HAND

Fringing

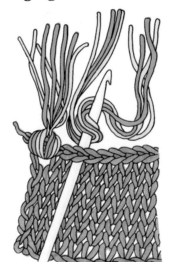

Bobbles

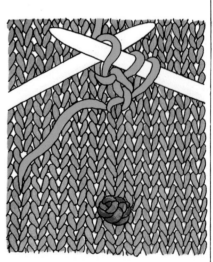

To make a tassel, cut a 6in length of yarn in each of the four contrast colors. Fold the length in half. With right side of work facing, insert crochet hook into the first row of the yoke and draw looped end of folded yarn through, pass cut ends through looped end and pull firmly, to form one tassel. In the same way make a second tassel ¼in away from first, then make tassels in the same way all around the yoke.

To make a bobble, with right side of work facing, insert a crochet hook into the center of chosen stitch. Wrap the yarn around the crochet hook and pull through to make a loop. Slip it onto a knitting needle, and hold in your left hand. Knit into the loop three times to make three stitches, turn, purl three stitches, turn and knit two stitches together, bind off one stitch and fasten off the remaining stitch. Darn in loose ends.

Casual Lacy Sweater

This lacy sweater is easy to make – just knit four rectangles without shaping. The picot edge neckband and sleeve trimming add to the delicate touch. It is worn short with an off-the-shoulder look.

BEFORE YOU BEGIN

Check your bust measurement against the chart's actual measurement before you commence the sweater. Choose the width first as this is a very loose style and more movement is given here compared with a classic style.

When working a mass increase, work into the front and back of the same stitch very loosely. Otherwise the stitches become too taut to work into on the following row.

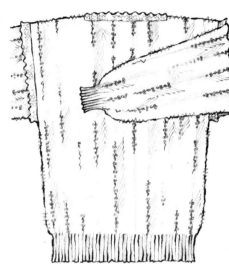

Sizes

Bust	32[35:38]in
Length	19¾[20:20½]in
Sleeve seam	19¾[20:20½]in

Note: Instructions for the larger sizes are in brackets [ ]; where there is only one set of figures it applies to all sizes.

Gauge

20 sts and 24 rows to 4in over patt on size 6 needles.

Materials

☐ Approx 14[16:16]oz of Pingouin Pingofrance
☐ 1 pair each sizes 3 and 6 needles

INSTRUCTIONS

1 Back and front alike

Using size 3 needles, cast on 91[101:109] sts.

1st row: K1,* P1, K1, rep from * to end.
2nd row: P1,* K1, P1, rep from * to end.
Rep the last 2 rows for 2¾in, ending with a 2nd row, inc 1 st at the end of row for

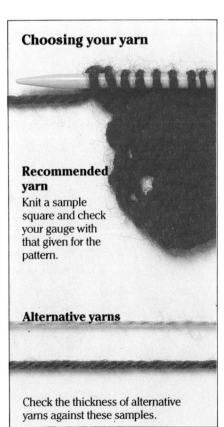

Choosing your yarn

Recommended yarn

Knit a sample square and check your gauge with that given for the pattern.

Alternative yarns

Check the thickness of alternative yarns against these samples.

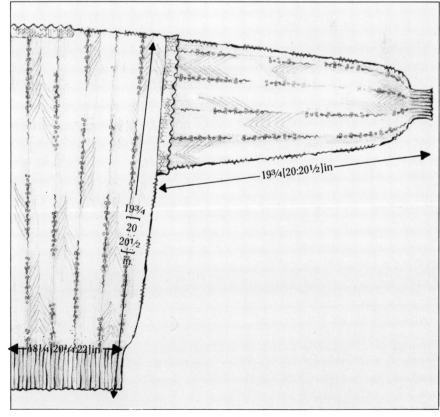

18¼[20¼:22]in

19¾
20
20½
in.

19¾[20:20½]in

4 To finish

Press lightly using a dry cloth with a warm iron.
Fold picot edge in half for the neckband and sew in place.
Stitch the picot edge down on the sleeves so it stands out. Using a flat stitch join shoulder seams. With a backstitch sew side and sleeve seams.

HELPING HAND

Picot edge

Picots are often used on babies' garments for hems instead of working a waistband. Cast on an odd number of stitches, using one size smaller needle than recommended. Starting with a knit row work an even number of rows in stockinette stitch. The eyelet holes form the foldline of the edge. To make the eyelet holes, start the row by * knitting two stitches together, yarn over needle, repeat from * to end of row, knitting the last stitch.

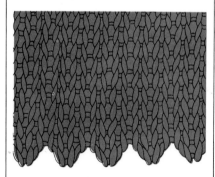

Starting with a purl row continue in stockinette stitch.
Once the edge has been made, change to the recommended needle size. When finishing turn the hem to the wrong side along eyelet hole row and sew in place.

1st and 3rd sizes only. (92[101:110] sts.)
Change to size 6 needles and work in patt as folls:
1st row: (RS) K1, * K1, yo, K2, sl 1, K1, psso, K2 tog, K2, yo, rep from * to last st, K1.
2nd and 4th row: P.
3rd row: K1,* yo, K2, sl 1, K1, psso, K2 tog, K2, yo, K1, rep from * to last st, K1.
Cont in patt until work meas 19¼ [19½:20]in from the beg, ending with a WS row. **

2 Neckband

Change to size 3 needles and work picot edge as folls:
1st row: K.
2nd row: P.
3rd row: Bind off 28 sts, K to end of row.
4th row: Bind off 28 sts, Pl[2:1], *

yo, P2 tog, rep from * to end of row.
5th row: K.
6th row: P.
7th row: Bind off very loosely.

3 Sleeves

Using size 3 needles, cast on 42[46:46] sts and work in K1, Pl rib for 2¼in, ending with a RS row.
Next row: K1,* inc into the next st by working in the front then the back, rep from * to end. (83[92:92] sts.)
Change to size 6 needles and work patt as for front and back from ** to **.
Change to size 3 needles and work picot edge for the top of sleeve.
1st and 3rd rows: K.
2nd row: P.
4th row: P1[2:2], * yo, P2 tog, rep from * to end of row.
5th, 7th and 9th rows: K.
6th, 8th and 10th rows: P. Bind off.

Apple Motif Sweater

Work one eaten apple amongst the many rows of delicious uneaten ones. All four pieces of the sweater are simple rectangular shapes which are quick and easy to make.

BEFORE YOU BEGIN
Knit a sample before starting the sweater, being careful not to pull the yarns too tightly across the back of the work. Once the sample is completed, pin out and press according to the ball band instructions. If the work is slightly puckered, work another sample with a looser tension. Pin and press as before.

Sizes
Bust   32-34[36-38]in
Length   26¾[27½]in
Sleeve seam   17½[18]in

Choosing your yarn

Recommended yarn
Knit a sample square and check your gauge with that given for the pattern.

Alternative yarns

Check the thickness of alternative yarns against these samples.

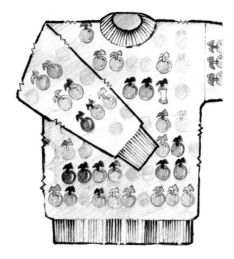

Note: Instructions for the larger size are in brackets []; where there is one set of figures it applies to both sizes.

Gauge
22 sts and 24 rows to 4in over patt on size 6 needles.

Materials
☐ Approx 11[13]oz of knitting worsted weight yarn in blue (m.c.)
☐ Approx 6oz of knitting worsted weight yarn in red (a)
☐ Approx 4oz of knitted worsted weight yarn in green (b)
☐ Approx 2oz of knitting worsted weight yarn in cream (c)
☐ Approx 2oz of knitting worsted weight yarn in yellow (d)
☐ 1 pair each sizes 3 and 6 needles

INSTRUCTIONS
1 Back
* Using size 3 needles and m.c., cast on 76[84] sts. Work in K1, P1 rib for 2¾[3½]in, ending with a RS row.
Inc row: * Rib 3, M1 (by picking up the bar that lies between the st just worked and the next st on left-hand needle and K into back of it), rep from * to last 1[3] sts, rib 1.[3] sts. (101[111] sts.) Change to size 6 needles and starting with a K row,

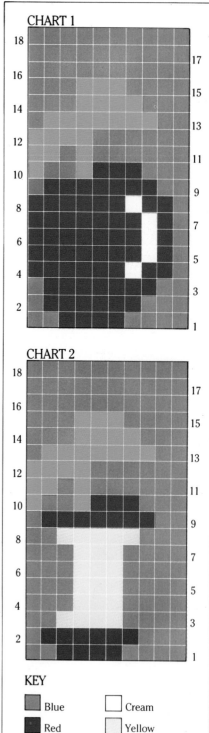

CHART 1

CHART 2

KEY
☐ Blue   ☐ Cream
☐ Red   ☐ Yellow
☐ Green

work 2 rows in St st. Now work from chart 1, work all the K rows from right to left and all P rows from left to right. Join in and break off colors when required. Strand the yarn loosely across back of work. For every K row, work across chart 10[11] times across row to last st, K1 m.c. For every P row, P1 m.c., work across chart 10[11] times across row. This sets the pattern of the apples. * Cont foll chart 1 until 8 complete patterns have been worked.
Bind off, marking center 33 sts.

2 Front
Work as for back from * to *. Cont foll chart 1 until 5 complete patterns have been worked.
Next row: Work 2 reps of chart 1, now foll 1st row of chart 2 for 3rd apple, work 7[8] reps of chart 1. K1 m.c. Cont working apples as before substituting chart 2 for 3rd apple for 1 repeat only. Cont until work meas 22[22¾]in, ending on a WS row.
Shape neck
Next row: Work 45[50] sts in patt, turn. Cont working on these sts only, dec 1 st at neck edge on next 11 rows. (34[39] sts.) Cont even until work meas same as back. Bind off.
Shape second side of neck
With RS facing, sl next 11 sts onto a stitch holder. Rejoin yarn to rem sts and work to end of row. Now work as for first side, reversing all the shapings.

3 Sleeves
Using size 3 needles and m.c., cast on 46[54] sts. Work in K1, P1 rib for 2¾[3¼]in.

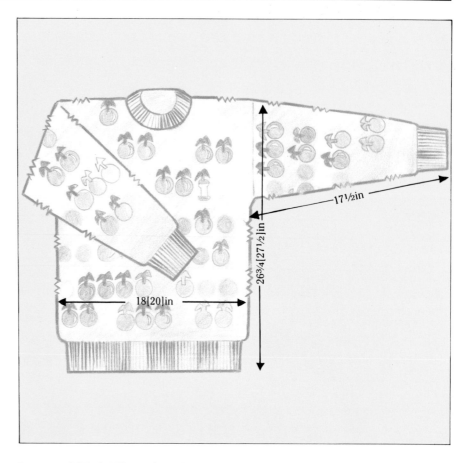

Inc row: * Rib 3, M1, rep from * to last 1[3] sts, rib 1[3]. (61[71] sts.) Change to size 6 needles, work 2 rows St st, work from chart as before, at the same time, inc 1 st at each end of the 5th and every foll 4th row until 101[111] sts are on the needles. Cont working even until 5 complete patts have been worked. Bind off.

4 Neckband
Join left shoulder seam. With RS facing, using size 3 needles and m.c., pick up and K 33 sts across back neck, 18 sts from side front neck, K across the 11 sts from the stitch holder then pick up and K 18 sts up front neck. (80 sts.) Work in K1, P1 rib for 3¼in. Bind off loosely.

To finish
Join shoulder seam and neckband. Fold neckband in half onto WS and slip stitch down. Sew sleeves in position. Join side and sleeve seams. Press seams lightly.

**HELPING HAND**

Alternative motifs
This sweater can be knitted using the cherry or banana motif. Alternatively design your own motif, but make sure that it is only 10 sts wide and 18 rows deep so that it fits correctly.

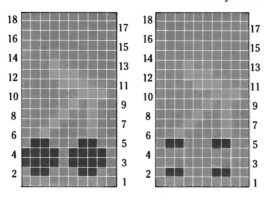

Cherries

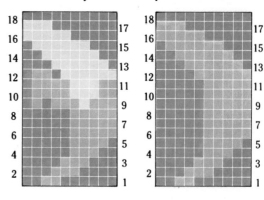

Bananas

Mohair Intarsia Sweater

K nit this stunning mohair sweater to wear on festive occasions. The intarsia pattern is named after a similarly decorative wood inlay design.

BEFORE YOU BEGIN
Use a small ball of each color for each motif, making sure to twist the yarns around each other to avoid holes forming when changing colors.

Size
One size only
Bust   36in
Length   25in
Sleeve seam 17¾in

Gauge
16 sts and 22 rows to 4in over St st on size 8 needles.

Materials
☐ Approx 5oz of medium weight mohair yarn in main color (m.c.)
☐ Approx 4oz of medium weight mohair yarn in each of 4 contrast colors (a, b, c and d)
☐ 1 pair each sizes 6 and 8 needles

Choosing your yarn

Recommended yarn
Knit a sample square and check your gauge with that given for the pattern.

Alternative yarns
Check the thickness of alternative yarns against these samples.

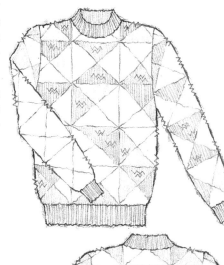

INSTRUCTIONS
1 Front
Using size 6 needles and m.c., cast on 75 sts.
1st row: K1, * P1, K1, rep from * to end.
2nd row: P1, * K1, P1, rep from * to end. Rep these 2 rows 8 times more. Change to size 8 needles and work in St st foll the chart for front, using small balls of wool for each triangle. Cont even until 74 rows have been worked.
Shape armholes
Keeping patt correct, bind off 2 sts at beg of next 2 rows. Dec 1 st at each end of next 6 rows until 59 sts rem. Cont working from the chart until the 104th row has been worked.
Shape neck
K21 sts and turn leaving rem sts on a spare needle.
Next row: Patt to end.
Dec 1 st at neck edge on next and every foll alt row until 15 sts are on the needles.
Work a further 4 rows on these sts.
Shape shoulder
Bind off 7 sts at beg of next row.
Work 1 row. Bind off rem 8 sts.
Shape second side of neck
Slip the next 17 sts onto a stitch holder. Rejoin yarn to rem sts and work as for the first side of neck reversing all the shapings.

2 Back
Work as for front, foll chart for back. When row 74 has been completed shape armholes as for front.
Cont from chart until row 120 has been worked and back matches the front to shoulder shaping.
Shape shoulders
Bind off 7 sts at beg of next 2 rows, then bind off 8 sts at beg of foll 2 rows. Leave rem 29 sts on a stitch holder for neckband.

3 Sleeves
Using size 6 needles and a (use b for second sleeve), cast on 39 sts.
1st row: K1, * P1, K1, rep from * to end.
2nd row: P1, * K1, P1, rep from * to end.
Rep these 2 rows 8 times more. Change to size 8 needles and work in St st, foll chart for sleeve.
Inc 1 st at each end of 5th and every foll 6th row until there are 59 sts on the needle. Cont in St st until row 78 has been worked and sleeve meas approx 17¾in from beg.
Shape cap
Cont working from chart.
Bind off 2 sts at beg of next 2 rows.
Dec 1 st at each end of next and every foll alt row until 23 sts rem.
Dec 1 st at each end of every row until 11 sts rem. Bind off.

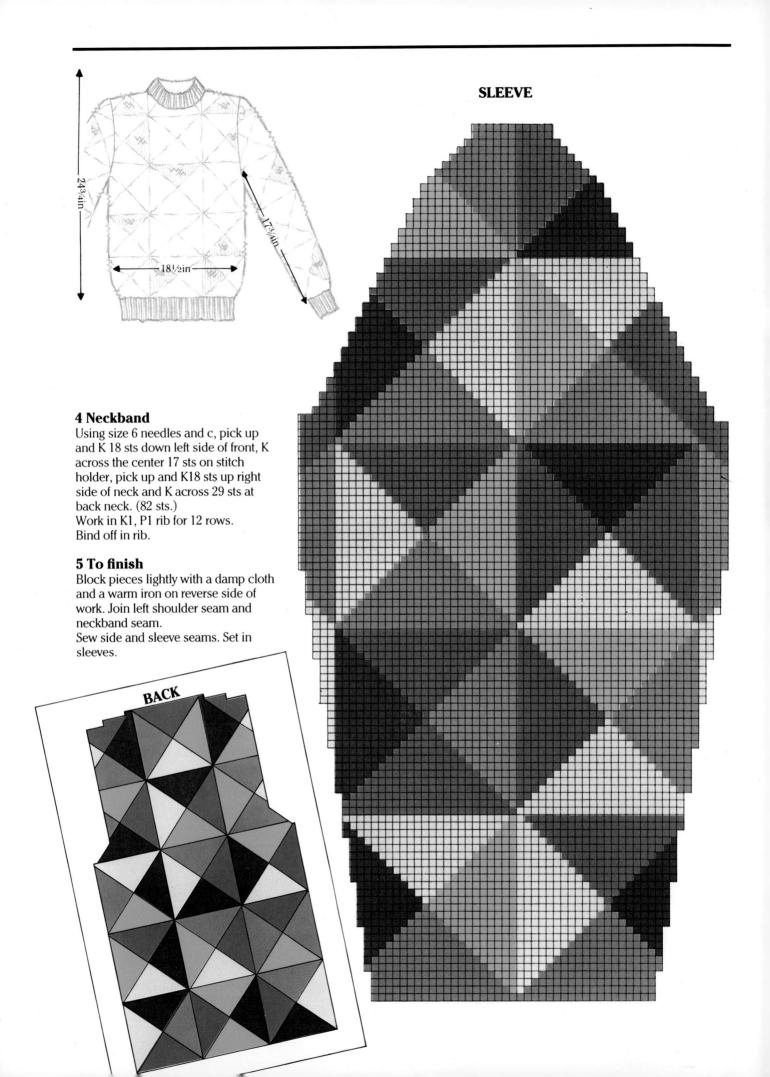

SLEEVE

4 Neckband

Using size 6 needles and c, pick up and K 18 sts down left side of front, K across the center 17 sts on stitch holder, pick up and K18 sts up right side of neck and K across 29 sts at back neck. (82 sts.)
Work in K1, P1 rib for 12 rows.
Bind off in rib.

5 To finish

Block pieces lightly with a damp cloth and a warm iron on reverse side of work. Join left shoulder seam and neckband seam.
Sew side and sleeve seams. Set in sleeves.

BACK

24¾in

18½in

17¾in

FRONT

m.c.

a

b

c

d

24

Sweater With Diamonds

This attractive sweater is easy to make. The raglans are the simplest of shapings to work and the diamonds and stripes are easily knitted, using only one color at a time.

BEFORE YOU BEGIN
When making up the sweater, match the stripes exactly at the seams. Pin at regular intervals, and join the seams by taking one stitch at a time from alternate sides, until the seam is completed.

Sizes
Bust   32[36:40]in
Length   23¼[24:25¼]in
Sleeve seam   17[17¼:17¼]in

Note: Instructions for larger sizes are in brackets []; where one set of figures is given it applies to all sizes.

Gauge
22 sts and 30 rows to 4in over St st on size 6 needles.

Choosing your yarn

Recommended yarn
Knit a sample square and check your gauge with that given for the pattern

Alternative yarns

Check the thickness of alternative yarns against these samples.

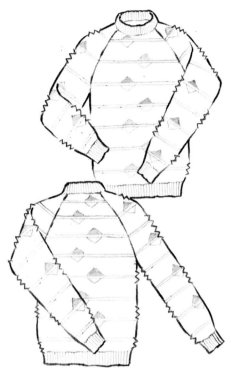

Materials
☐ Approx 14[16:18]oz of knitting worsted weight yarn in main color (m.c.)
☐ Approx 2oz each of knitting worsted weight in each of the 3 contrast colors (a, b and c)
☐ 1 pair each sizes 3 and 6 needles

INSTRUCTIONS
1 Back
Using size 3 needles and m.c., cast on 83[95:107]sts.
1st row: (RS) K1, * P1, K1, rep from * to end.
2nd row: P1, * K1, P1, rep from * to end.
Rep these 2 rows for 2¾in, ending with RS row.
Next row: Rib 5, M1 (by picking up the loop which lies between the next st on the left-hand needle and working into back of it), * rib 6[7:8], M1, rep from * 11 times, rib to end. (96[108:120]sts.)

Change to size 6 needles, starting with a K row, work 2 rows in St st. Join in and break off colors as required. Work from chart. When working in patt from chart, do not carry colors across WS of work, but use separate balls as required; twist yarns when changing colors to avoid a hole. Read all knit rows from right to left and all purl rows from left to right.
Place motifs as folls:
1st row: K37[43:49]m.c., work 22 sts, from 1st row of chart, K to end in m.c.
2nd row: P37[43:49] m.c., work 22 sts, from 2nd row of chart, P to end in m.c.
Cont working patt as set. Note all sts on the 7th, 8th, 27th and 28th row will be worked in c.
Cont working patt until back meas approx 14½in, ending with an 8th patt row.

Shape raglans
Keeping patt correct, bind off 2 sts at beg of next 2 rows.
Dec 1 st at each end of next row.
Work 3 rows.
Rep last 4 rows 1[0:0]more time.
Dec 1 st at each end of next and every alt row until 32[36:38]sts rem.
Work 1 row.
Leave rem sts on a spare needle.

2 Front
Work as for back, shaping raglan until 50[54:60]sts rem.
Work 1 row.
Shape neck
Keeping patt correct, cont thus:
Next row: K2 tog, patt 15[15:17], turn and leave rem sts on a spare needle.
Dec 1 st at neck edge on every row and at the same time cont dec 1 st at raglan edge as before until 7[7:9]sts rem.
Work 1 row.
Cont dec 1 st at raglan edge only as before until 2 sts rem.
Work 1 row.
Next row: K2 tog and fasten off.

Shape second side of neck
With RS of work facing, sl center 16[20:22]sts on a spare needle. Rejoin yarn to rem sts. Patt to last 2 sts, K2 tog.
Work to match first side, reversing all the shapings.

3 Sleeves
Using size 3 needles and m.c., cast on 43[45:47]sts, work in rib as on back for 2¾in, ending with RS row.
Inc row: Rib 3[4:5], M1, * rib 3, M1, rep from * 11 times, rib to end. (56[58:60]sts.)
Change to size 6 needles, rejoin and break off colors when required. Work from chart, placing motifs as folls:
1st row: K17[18:19]m.c., work 22 sts as 21st[17th:17th]row of chart, K to end in m.c.
2nd row: P17[18:19]m.c., work 22 sts as 22nd[18th:18th]row of chart, P to end in m.c.
Cont as set, working appropriate rows of chart. Note all sts on 7th, 8th, 27th and 28th will be worked in c. At the same time, shape side by inc 1 st at each end of the 9th and every foll 14th[12th:10th]row, until there are 70[74:80]sts, taking inc sts into stripe patt.
Work even until sleeve seam meas approx 17[17¼:17¼]in, ending with an 8th patt row.
Shape raglans
Keeping patt correct, bind off 2 sts at beg of next 2 rows.
Dec 1 st at each end of next row.
Work 3 rows.
Rep last 4 rows 2[3:5]times more.
Dec 1 st at each end of next and every alt row until 8 sts rem.
Work 1 row.
Leave these sts on a safety pin.

4 Neckband
Join raglans, leaving left back raglan open. With RS facing and using size 3 needles and m.c., K8 across left sleeve, pick up and K13[14:16]sts down left side of neck, K16[20:22]from front, pick up and K13[14:16]sts up right side of neck, K8 from right sleeve, then 32[36:38] sts from back. (90[100:108]sts.)
Work in K1, P1 rib for 2¼in, ending with a WS row.
Bind off loosely in rib.

5 To finish
Join left back raglan and neckband. Fold neckband in half to WS and stitch hem loosely in position. Join side and sleeve seams.

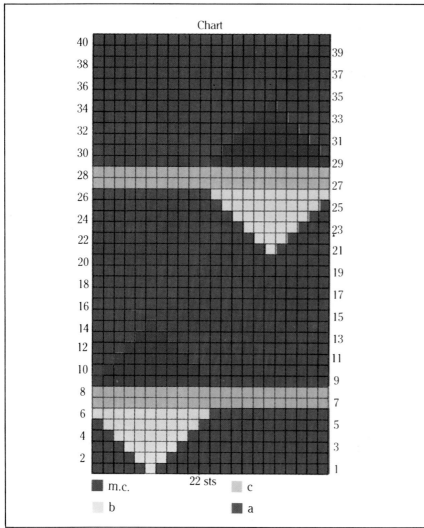

Chart

22 sts

■ m.c.   ■ c
■ b   ■ a

Gossamer Sweater

Using a soft mohair-type yarn, make this delicate lacy sweater. The lacy stitch is easy to follow and all four pieces require little shaping.

BEFORE YOU BEGIN
The rows on this lacy stitch read very similarly. Keep a careful check of all the pattern repeat rows. Use either a row counter or write down the rows on a piece of paper.

Sizes
Bust   32[34:36:38]in
Length   24½[24¾:25¼:25½]in
Sleeve seam 18½[18½:19:19]in

Note: Instructions for larger sizes are given in brackets [ ]; where only one set of figures is given it applies to all sizes.

Gauge
24 sts and 30 rows to 4in over patt on size 5 needles.

Choosing your yarn

Recommended yarn
Knit a sample square and check your gauge with that given for the pattern.

Alternative yarns

Check the thickness of alternative yarns against these samples.

Materials
☐ Approx 9[11:11:13]oz sport weight mohair-type yarn
☐ 1 pair each sizes 2 and 5 needles

INSTRUCTIONS
1 Back
Using size 2 needles, cast on 96[102:108:114] sts. Work in K1, P1 rib for 3¼in.
Next row: Rib 4[7:4:7], M1 (by picking up horizontal loop lying before next st and working into back of it), * rib 11[11:10:10], M1, rep from * to last 4[7:4:7] sts, rib to end. (105[111:119:125] sts.)
Change to size 5 needles and work in patt as folls:
1st row: (RS) K2[5:2:5], yarn to front of work to make a yo, sl 1 K-wise, yarn to back of work over top of right-hand needle to complete yo and then K2 tog, psso, yo, K1, * K2, K2 tog, yo, K1, yo sl 1 K-wise, K1, psso, K3, yo sl 1 K-wise, K2 tog, psso. yo, K1, rep from * to last 1[4:1:4] sts, K to end.
2nd and every alt row: P.
3rd row: K2[5:2:5], yo, sl 1 K-wise, K2 tog, psso, yo, K1, * K1, K2 tog, yo, K3, yo, sl 1 K-wise, K1, psso, K2, yo, sl 1 K-wise, K2 tog, psso, yo, K1,

rep from * to last 1[4:1:4] sts, K to end.
5th row: K2[5:2:5], yo, sl 1 K-wise, K2 tog, psso, yo, K1, * K2 tog, yo, K5, yo, sl 1 K-wise, K1, psso, K1, yo, sl 1 K-wise, K2 tog, psso, yo, K1, rep from * to last 1[4:1:4] sts, K to end.
7th row: K2[5:2:5], yo, sl 1 K-wise, K2 tog, psso, yo, K1, * K1, yo, sl 1 K-wise, K1, psso, K3, K2 tog, yo, K2, yo, sl 1 K-wise, K2 tog, psso, yo, K1, rep from * to last 1[4:1:4] sts, K to end.
9th row: K2[5:2:5], yo, sl 1 K-wise, K2 tog, psso, yo, K1, * K2, yo, sl 1 K-wise, K1, psso, K1, K2 tog, yo, K3, yo, sl 1 K-wise, K 2 tog, psso, yo, K1, rep from * to last 1[4:1:4] sts, K to end.
11th row: K2[5:2:5], yo, sl 1 K-wise, K2 tog, psso, yo, K1, * K3 yo, sl 1 K-wise, K2 tog, psso, yo, K1, rep from * to last 1[4:1:4] sts, K to end.
12th row: P.
These 12 rows form the patt.
Cont in patt until back meas 15¾in, ending with WS row.
Shape armholes
Keeping patt correct, bind off 14[16:19:21] sts at beg of next 2 rows. (77[79:81:83] sts.) Work even until armholes meas 8¾[9:9½:9¾]in, ending with WS row.
Shape shoulders
Bind off 6 sts at beg of next 4 rows then 5 sts at beg of foll 2 rows. Leave rem 43[45:47:49] sts on spare needle.

2 Front
Work as given for back until front is 28 rows shorter than back to start of shoulder shaping, ending with a WS row.
Shape neck
Keeping patt correct, patt 26 sts, work 2 tog, turn, leave rem sts on a spare needle.
Dec 1 st at neck edge on edge 6 rows then foll 4 alt rows. (17 sts.)
Work even until front meas same as back to start of shoulder shaping, thus ending with WS row.

Shape shoulder

Bind off 6 sts at beg of next and foll alt row.
Work 1 row.
Bind off rem 5 sts.

Shape second side of neck

With RS facing, sl centre 21[23:25:27] sts onto a spare needle. Rejoin yarn to rem sts, work 2 tog, patt 26. Work to match first side, reversing all shapings.

3 Sleeves

Using size 2 needles, cast on 50[50:52:54] sts and work in K1, P1, rib for 3¼in.
Next row: Rib 1[4:5:6], M1, * rib 4[3:3:3], M1, rep from * to last 1[4:5:6] sts, rib to end. (63[65:67:69] sts.)
Change to size 5 needles and work in patt as folls:
1st row: (RS) K23[24:25:26], yo, sl 1 K-wise, K2 tog, psso, yo, K3, K2 tog, yo, K1, yo, sl 1 K-wise, K1, psso, K3, yo, sl 1 K-wise, K2 tog, psso, yo, K23[24:25:26].
2nd and every alt row: P.
3rd row: K23[24:25:26], yo, sl 1 K-wise, K2 tog, psso, yo, K2, K2 tog, yo, K3, yo, sl 1 K-wise, K1, psso, K2, yo, sl 1 K-wise, K2 tog, psso, yo, K23[24:25:26].
5th row: K23[24:25:26], yo, sl 1 K-wise, K2 tog, psso, yo, K1, K2 tog, yo, K5, yo, sl 1 K-wise, K1, psso, K1, yo, sl 1 K-wise, K2 tog, psso, yo, K23[24:25:26].
7th row: K23(24:25:26], yo, sl 1 K-wise, K2 tog, psso, yo, K2, yo, sl 1 K-wise, K1, psso, K3, K2 tog, yo, K2, yo, sl 1 K-wise, K2 tog, psso, yo, K23[24:25:26].
9th row: K23[24:25:26], yo, sl 1 K-wise, K2 tog, psso, yo, K3, yo, sl 1 K-wise, K1, psso, K1, K2 tog, yo, K3, yo, sl 1 K-wise, K2 tog, psso, yo, K23[24:25:26].

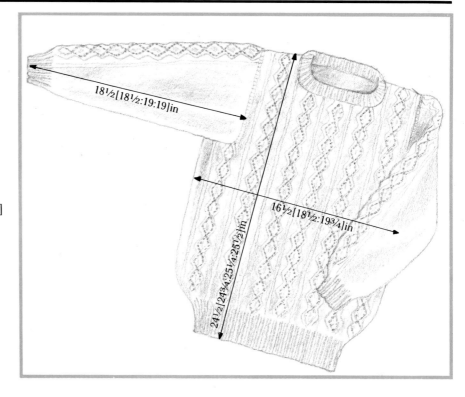

11th row: K23[24:25:26], yo, sl 1 K-wise, K2 tog, psso, yo, K4, yo, sl 1 K-wise, K2 tog, psso, yo, K4, yo, sl 1 K-wise, K2 tog, psso, yo, K23[24:25:26].
12th row: P.
These 12 rows form the patt.
Cont in patt, work 4[2:2:6] rows even. Keeping continuity of patt, inc 1st at each end of next and every foll 4th[4th:4th:3rd] row until there are 107[111:115:121] sts. Work even until sleeve seam meas 18½[18½:19:19]in from beg.
Mark end of last row with a colored thread to mark end of sleeve seam and beg of gusset. Work a further 18[20:24:26] rows even in patt for gusset. Bind off.

4 Neckband

Join right shoulder seam. With RS facing and using size 2 needles pick up and K24 sts down left side of neck, K21[23:25:27] sts across center front, pick up and K24 sts up right side of front, then 43[45:47:49] sts across back neck. (112[116:120:124] sts.)
Work in K1, P1 rib for ¾in.
Bind off evenly in rib.

5 To finish

Do not press. Join left shoulder seam and neckband. Placing center of sleeve to shoulder, sew bound-off edge of sleeves to armhole, sewing bound-off edge of armholes to gusset. Join side and sleeve seams. Fasten off ends securely.

Triangle Patterned Sweater

The triangle pattern on this attractive sweater is very simple to knit and looks very effective in four contrasting colors.

BEFORE YOU BEGIN
When working the triangle pattern, pass the colored thread loosely across the back of the work, to the next pattern repeat. Do not work too tightly otherwise the work may pucker and spoil the look of the fabric.

Sizes
Bust   34[36:38]in
Length   22[22½:23¾]in
Sleeve seam   17in

Note: Instructions for larger sizes are in brackets [ ]; where there is only one set of figures it applies to all sizes.

Gauge
24 sts and 30 rows to 4in over St st on size 6 needles.

Choosing your yarn

Recommended yarn

Knit a sample square and check your gauge with that given for the pattern.

Alternative yarns

Check the thickness of alternative yarns against these samples.

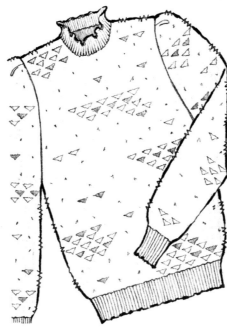

Materials
☐ Approx 11[13:13]oz of sport weight yarn in main color (m.c.)
☐ Approx 2oz of sport weight yarn in each of 3 contrast colours (a, b and c.)
☐ 1 pair each sizes 3 and 6 needles.

INSTRUCTIONS
1 Back
Using size 3 needles and m.c., cast on 97[103:109] sts.
1st row: K2, * P1, K1, rep from * to last st, K1.
2nd row: K1, * P1, K1 rep from * to end.
Work in rib for 2¾in, ending with a 1st row.
Next row: Rib 1, (inc into next st, rib 2) 31[33:35] times, inc into next st, rib to end. (129[137:145] sts.)
Change to size 6 needles and work from chart.
Work the extra st at end of K rows and beg of P rows until work meas approx 14in from beg, ending with 8th row of chart.

Shape armholes
Keeping patt correct, bind off 6[7:8] sts at beg of next 2 rows.
Dec 1 st at each end of every row until 95[101:107] sts rem, then at each end of every alt row until 85[89:93] sts rem. * Work even on these sts until armhole meas 7[7¾:8]in from beg of shaping, ending with WS row.
Shape shoulders
Bind off 8[9:9] sts at beg of next 4 rows.
Bind off 9[8:9] sts at beg of foll 2 rows.
Leave rem 35[37:39] sts on a spare needle.

2 Front
Work as for back to *.
Work even until armhole meas 5¼[5½:6]in from beg of armhole shaping, ending with a WS row.
Shape neck
Next row: Patt 32[33:34] sts, turn and work on these sts.
Dec 1 st at neck edge on next and every row until 25[26:27] sts rem.
Work a few rows even until front meas same as back to shoulder edge.
Shape shoulder
Bind off 8[9:9] sts at beg of next and foll alt row. Work 1 row. Bind off rem 9[8:9] sts.
Shape second side of neck
With RS facing sl next 21[23:25] sts onto a stitch holder, rejoin yarn and patt to end of row.
Now work as for first side of neck reversing all the shapings.

3 Sleeves
Using size 3 needles, cast on 47[49:51] sts. Work in rib as for back for 4in, ending with a 1st row.
Next row: Rib 11[9:11] sts, inc into each of the next 26[32:30] sts, rib to end. (73[81:81] sts.)
Change to size 6 needles and work from chart. Inc 1 st at each end every 6th[8th:6th] row, 5[6:5] times, then 1 st at each end of every 8th[10th:8th] row until there are 95[99:103] sts, taking inc sts into patt.
Work even on these sts until sleeve

meas approx 17in from beg, ending with same color triangle as on back and fronts before start of shaping, ending with a WS row.

Shape cap

Keeping patt correct, bind off 6[7:8] sts at beg of next 2 rows then dec 1 st at each end of every 4th row until 61 sts rem.

Bind off 5 sts at beg of next 6 rows. (31 sts.)

Next row: K1, (K2 tog) to end.

Bind off rem 15 sts.

4 Neckband

Join right shoulder seam.

Using size 3 needles and m.c., pick up and K24 sts down left side of neck, K across sts on front dec 3 sts evenly across, pick up and K24 sts up right side, K across sts on back dec 2 sts evenly. (99[103:107] sts.) Starting with a 2nd row work 8 rows in rib as on back.

Next row: K1, * K twice into next st, P1, rep from * to end.

Next row: * K1, P2, rep from * to last st, K1.

Next row: K3, * P1, K2, rep from * to last st, K1. Rep the last 2 rows, once more. Bind off loosely in rib.

5 To finish

Press on the WS with a warm iron and damp cloth. Join left shoulder and border. Join side and sleeve seams. Sew in sleeves easing extra fullness at crown. Press seams.

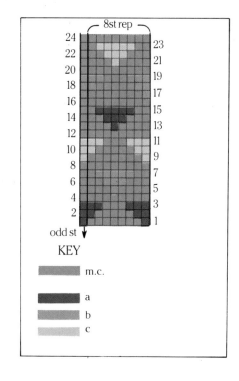

8st rep

odd st

KEY

m.c.

a

b

c

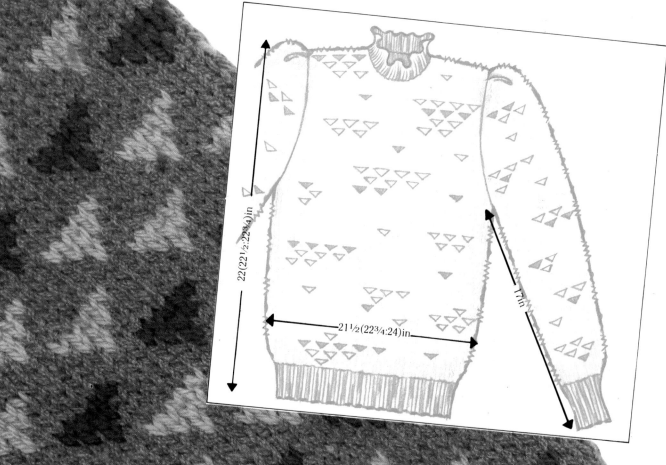

22(22½:22¾)in

21½(22¾:24)in

17in

Lacy Summer Top

Make this delicate lacy summer top in a fine white cotton. It has two different lace patterns separated by a cable panel.

BEFORE YOU BEGIN

As the garment has several different patterns, all sections have been drawn on graph paper to make it easier to follow. Every twist of the cable pattern is marked. The first few rows have been written out in full to set the pattern.

Sizes

Bust	34[36:38]in
Length	21½in
Sleeve seam	4¾in

Note: Instructions for larger sizes are in brackets [ ]; where one set of figures is given it applies to all sizes.

Gauge

36 sts and 50 rows to 4in over St st on size 0 needles.

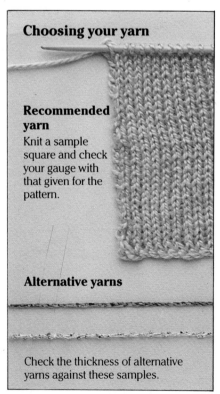

Choosing your yarn

Recommended yarn

Knit a sample square and check your gauge with that given for the pattern.

Alternative yarns

Check the thickness of alternative yarns against these samples.

Materials

☐ 11[11:13]oz of Pingouin 'Fil d'Ecosse Fin' cotton
☐ 1 pair size 0 needles

INSTRUCTIONS

Daisy patt

One daisy pattern is made up of 8 sts and 10 rows and is shown as a rectangle on the chart.
1st row: K2, K2 tog, (yo) twice, sl 1, K1, psso, K2.
2nd row: P working (K1, P1) into every double yo.
3rd row: * K2 tog, (yo) twice, sl 1, K1, psso, rep from * once.
4th row: Work as 2nd row.
5th row: Work as 1st row.
6th row: Work as 2nd row.
7th row: Work as 3rd row.
8th row: Work as 2nd row.
9th row: Work as 1st row.
10th row: Work as 2nd row.

Cable patt

1st row: P2, K8, P2.
2nd row: K2, P8, K2.
3rd row: Work as 1st row.
4th row: Work as 2nd row.
5th row: Work as 1st row.
6th row: Work as 2nd row.
7th row: P2, C8B sl next 4 sts onto a cable needle and hold at back of work, K4 then K4 from cable needle),

P2, or C4F (sl next 4 sts onto a cable needle and hold at front of work, K4 then K4 from cable needle).
8th row: Work as 2nd row.

Mesh patt

1st row: K1, (yo, K2 tog) 21 times, K1.
2nd row: P44.

1 Back

Using size 0 needles, cast on 174[182:190] sts.
1st row: K2, * P2, K2, rep from * to end.
2nd row: P2, * K2, P2, rep from * to end.
Rep last 2 rows for 4in, ending with a 2nd row.
Next row: * K28, inc 1, rep from * to last 0[8:16] sts, K0[8:16] sts. (180[188: 196] sts.)
Next row: P. **
With RS facing, work from chart as folls:
1st row: K.
2nd row: P.
3rd row: K21[25:29], * K2, K2 tog, (yo) twice, sl 1, K1, psso, K2 – (1st row daisy patt), * K23, rep from * to * K26, rep from * to *, K to end.
4th row: P, working (K1, P1) into every double yo.
5th row: K21[25:29], * K2 tog, (yo) twice, sl 1, K1, psso *, rep from * twice (3rd row daisy patt), K23, rep from * to * twice, K62, rep from * to * twice. K to end.
6th row: Work as 4th row.
Cont in patt, working from chart, until rows 1-226 inclusive have been worked. Bind off.

2 Front

Work exactly as back until **.
Cont as folls, working from chart:
1st row: K56[60:64], * P2, K8, P2 – (1st row cable patt), * K1, (yo, K2 tog) 21 times, K1 – (mesh patt), rep from * to * once, K to end.
2nd row: P56[60:64], * K2, P8, K2 – (2nd row cable patt), P44, rep from *

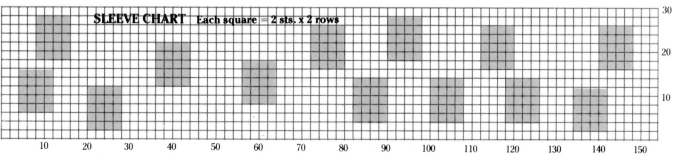

SLEEVE CHART Each square = 2 sts. x 2 rows

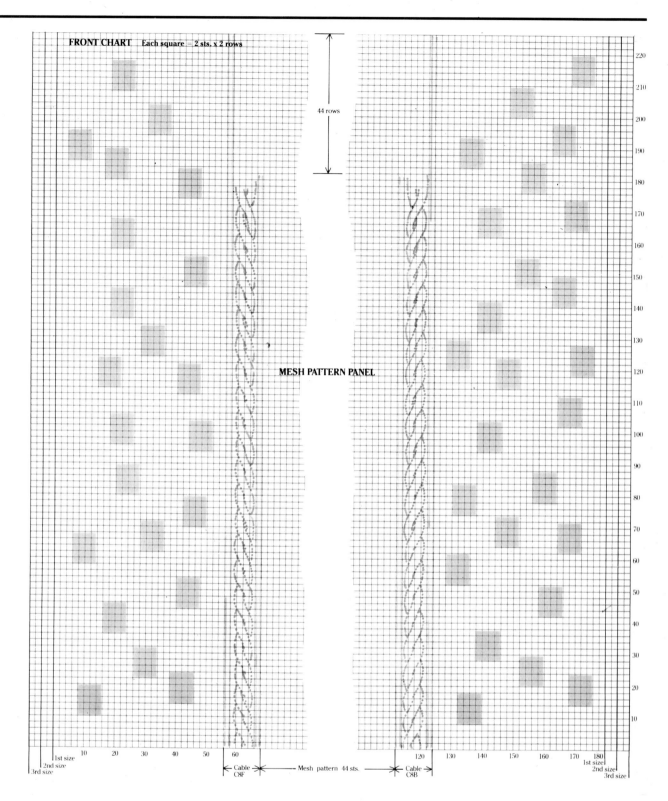

FRONT CHART Each square = 2 sts. x 2 rows

44 rows

MESH PATTERN PANEL

1st size
2nd size
3rd size

10 20 30 40 50 60

←Cable→
C8F

— Mesh pattern 44 sts. —

120 130 140 150 160 170 180

←Cable→
C8B

1st size
2nd size
3rd size

220
210
200
190
180
170
160
150
140
130
120
110
100
90
80
70
60
50
40
30
20
10

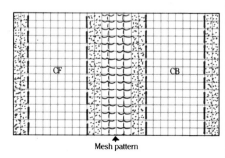

CF CB

Mesh pattern

to * P, to end.
3rd row: As 1st row.
4th row: As 2nd row.
5th row: As 1st row.
6th row: As 2nd row.
7th row: As 1st row.
8th row: As 2nd row.
9th row: K39 [43:47], K2, K2 tog, (yo) twice, sl 1, K1, psso, K2 – (1st row of daisy patt), K9, P2, C8B, P2 – (7th row cable patt), K1, (yo, K2 tog) 21 times, K1 – (mesh patt), P2, C4F, P2 –

(7th row cable patt), K to end.
10th row: P56[60:64],* K2, P8, K2* – (8th row cable patt), P44, rep from * to * once, P to end working K1, P1, into every double yo. Cont in patt, working from chart until row 182 has been completed.
Shape neck
Next row: Patt 66[70:74] sts, turn. Working in 1st set of sts only, work from chart dec 1 st at neck edge on every row until 58[62:66] sts are on

36

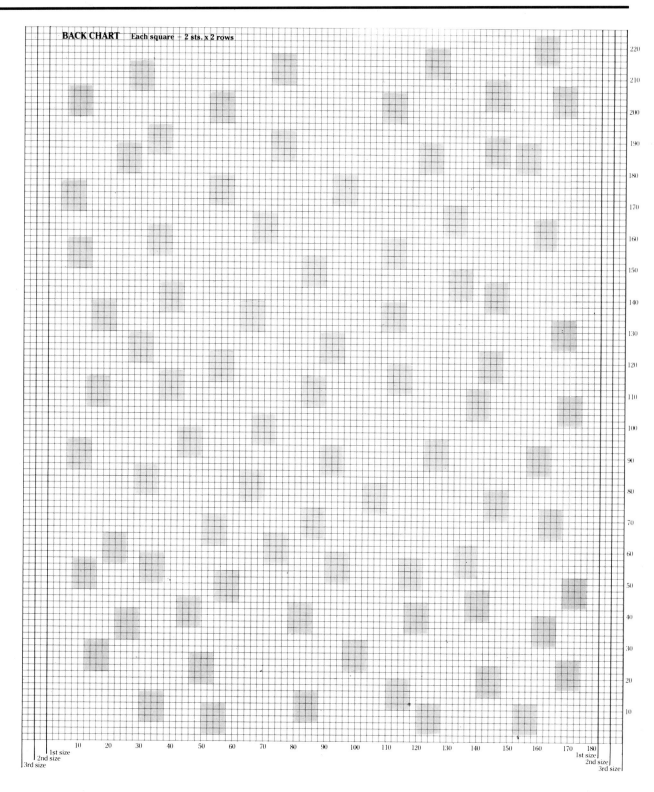

BACK CHART Each square = 2 sts. x 2 rows

the needle. Cont from chart, without further dec, until 226th row is completed. Bind off.

Shape second side of neck
With RS facing rejoin yarn and bind off 48 sts, patt to end of row. Complete to match first side of neck reversing shapings. Bind off.

3 Sleeves
Using size 0 needles, cast on 110 sts.
1st row: K2, * P2, K2, rep from * to end.
2nd row: P2, * K2, P2, rep from * to end.
Rep these 2 rows until meas 2¼in.
Next row: K11, * K1, inc 1, rep from * to last 11 sts, K11. (154 sts.)
Next row: P.
With RS facing, work from chart until 30th row is completed. Bind off.

4 Collar
Using size 0 needles, cast on 206 sts.

Next row: K2, * P2, K2, rep from * to end.
Next row: P2, * K2, P2, rep from * to end.
Work until meas 19in. Bind off.

5 To finish
Press all pieces as instructed on ball band. Join shoulder seams. Set in sleeve, matching center of sleeve cap to shoulder seam. Join side and sleeve seams. Sew on collar. Darn in ends.

37

Angora Sampler Sweater

Each body section is knitted in one piece. The six samples are all very simple to work and are planned as part of the whole design.

BEFORE YOU BEGIN

The width and depth of each sample remain the same throughout all the garment. It is necessary to write down the rows and keep a careful check on all four patterns throughout the row.

Sizes

Bust	34[36:38]in
Length	24¼[25¼:27½]in
Sleeve seam	19½[20¼:20¼]in

Note: Instructions for the larger sizes are in brackets [ ]; where there is one set of figures it applies to all sizes.

Gauge

28 sts and 36 rows to 4in over St st on size 3 needles.

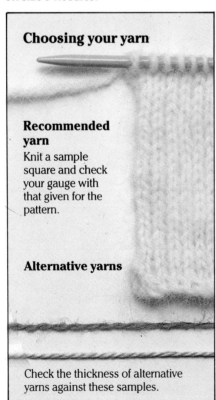

Choosing your yarn

Recommended yarn

Knit a sample square and check your gauge with that given for the pattern.

Alternative yarns

Check the thickness of alternative yarns against these samples.

Materials
☐ Approx 10[11:12]oz of medium weight angora type yarn
☐ 1 pair each sizes 2 and 3 needles

INSTRUCTIONS

Note: Work all the foll patts over 40[42:46] rows.

Sample A—Reverse stockinette stitch
1st row: (RS) P.
2nd row: K.
These 2 rows form the patt.

Sample B—Bobble pattern
1st row: (RS) * K2, MB (make bobble) by K1, P1 3 times into the next st, then pass the 5th, 4th, 3rd, 2nd and 1st st over the 6th st), P3; rep from * to last 2[4:0] sts, K2[2:0], MB 0[1:0] time, P0[1:0].
2nd row: K0[1:0], P2[3:0], * K3, P3, rep from * to end.
3rd row: P1, * K2, MB, P3, rep from * to last 1[3:5] sts, K1[2:2], MB 0[1:1] time, P0[0:2].
4th row: K0(0:2], P1[3:3], * K3, P3, rep from * to last st, K1.
5th row: P2, * K2, MB, P3, rep from * to last 0[2:4] sts, K0[2:2], (MB, P1) 0[0:1] time.
Cont moving bobble 1 st to the left on every RS row.

Sample C—Stockinette stitch
1st row: (RS) K.

2nd row: P.
These 2 rows form the patt.

Sample D—Waffle Stitch
1st row: (RS) P1[1:2], * K2, P1, rep from * to last 1[0:1] st, P1[0:1].
2nd row: K all K sts and P all P sts from previous row.
3rd row: Work as 1st row.
4th row: K.
These 4 rows form the patt.

Sample E—Eyelet pattern
1st row: (RS) K.
2nd row: P.
3rd row: K.
4th row: P.
5th row: K2[3:4], * yo, sl 1, K2 tog, psso, yo, K5, rep from * to last 6[7:0] sts, (yo, sl 1, K2 tog, psso, yo) 1[1:0] time, K3[4:0].
6th row: P.
7th row: K3[4:5], * yo, sl 1, K1, psso, K6, rep from * to last 5[6:7] sts, yo, sl 1, K1, psso, K3[4:5].
8th row: P.
9th row: K.
10th row: P.
11th row: K6[7:8], * yo, sl 1, K2 tog, psso, yo, K5, rep from * to last 2[3:4] sts, K to end.
12th row: P.
13th row: K7[8:9], * yo, sl 1, K1, psso, K6, rep from * to last 1[2:3] sts, K to end.
14th row: P.
Rep 3rd-14th rows twice more.
3rd size only
Work 3rd to 8th rows again.
All sizes
Next row: K.
Next row: P.
Rep the last 2 rows 0[1:0] times more.

Sample F—Diagonals
1st row: (RS), * K3, P3, rep from * to last 2[4:0] sts, K2[3:0], P0[1:0].
2nd and foll alt rows: K all K sts, P all P sts from previous row.
3rd row: K2, * P3, K3, rep from * to

last 0[2:4] sts, P0[2:3], K0[0:1].
5th row: K1, * P3, K3, rep from * to
last 1[3:5] sts, P1[3:3], K0[0:2].
Cont moving the diagonal by 1 st to
the right on every RS row.

1 Back
Using size 2 needles, cast on
117[125:133] sts. Work in rib as folls:
1st row: (RS) K1, * P1, K1, rep from
* to end.
2nd row: P1, * K1, P1, rep from * to
end.
Rep the last 2 rows for 2¼in.
Inc row: Rib 8[8:6], (M1 by picking
up the horizontal loop lying before the
next st and working into the back of
it, rib 10[11:12]) 10 times, M1, rib to
end. (128[136:144] sts.)
Change to size 3 needles and work in
patt as folls:
1st row: (RS) Patt 32[34:36] sts as 1st
row sample A, patt next 32[34:36] sts
as 1st row sample b, patt next
32[34:36] sts as 1st row sample C, patt
next 32[34:36] sts as 1st row sample D.
2nd row: Patt 32[34:36] sts as 2nd
row sample D, patt next 32[34:36] sts
as 2nd row sample C, patt next
32[34:36] sts as 2nd row sample B,
patt next 32[34:36] sts as 2nd row
sample A.
These two rows establish the patt for
the 1st line of samples.
Cont working even in patt until
40[42:46] rows have been worked.
Next row: Patt 32[34:36] sts as 1st
row sample C, patt next 32[34:36] sts
as 1st row sample E, patt next
32[34:36] sts as 1st row sample A, patt
next 32[34:36] sts as 1st row sample F.
These 2 rows establish the patt for the
2nd line of samples.
Cont in patt as set until 40[42:46] rows
have been completed.
3rd line of sample: Work samples
B, A, D and C.
4th line of samples: Work samples
D, C, A and B.
5th line of samples: Work samples
E, D, F and C.
Shape shoulders
Working in St st, bind off 34[35:36] sts
at beg of next 2 rows. Leave rem
60[66:72] sts on a spare needle.

2 Front
Work as for back until front meas 2¼in
less than on back to shoulder, ending
with a RS facing for next row.
Shape neck
Keeping patt correct, patt 52[53:54] sts,
turn and leave rem sts on a spare
needle. Keeping side edge even,

bind off 3 sts at beg of next and every
foll alt row 5 times in all, then dec 1
st at neck edge on next and every foll
alt row until 34[35:36] sts rem. Work
even until front matches back to
shoulder ending with a WS row. Bind
off loosely in patt.
Shape second side of neck
With RS facing rejoin yarn to rem sts,
bind off the center 24[30:36] sts loosely
and complete as for 1st side of neck,
reversing all the shapings.

3 Sleeves
Using size 2 needles, cast on
53[57:63] sts and work in rib as for
back for 2in, ending with 1st row.
Inc row: Rib 2[4:4], (M1, rib 5[5:7])
10[10:8] times, M1, rib to end.
(64[68:72] sts.)
Change to size 3 needles and work in
patt as folls:
1st row: (RS) Patt 32[34:36] sts as 1st
row sample B, patt 32[34:36] sts as 1st
row sample D. Cont in samples B and
D as set, at the same time shape side
by inc 1 st at each end of the 6th and
every foll 4th row until there are
82[88:86] sts, taking inc sts in to
sample A.
These 40[42:46] rows complete 1st
line of samples.
Next row: K1[0:2], (P1, K2) 2[3:1]
times, P2[1:2] (sts sample D), patt
next 32[34:36] sts sample C, patt next
32[34:36] sts sample E, patt to end in
sample F.
Cont in patts as set, shaping sides as
before until there are 96[108:108] sts,
taking inc sts into patt.

1st sizes only
Now cont shaping sides by inc 1 st at
each end of every foll 6th row from
previous inc until there are 100 sts,
taking inc sts into patt.
All sizes
These 40[42:46] rows complete 2nd
line of samples.
Next row: P0[2:0], (K3, P3) 3 times
(sts sample F), Patt next 32[34:36] sts
sample A, patt next 32[34:36] sts
sample B, patt to end in sample E.
Cont in patts as set shaping sides as
before and taking inc sts into patt
until 40[42:46] rows have been
worked. (114[130:132] sts.)
Next row: Patt 25[31:30] sts sample
E, patt 32[34:36] sts sample D, patt
32[34:36] sts sample C, patt to end in
sample F as set.
Cont in patt as before until there are
122[134:144] sts, taking inc sts into
patt. Work even in patt until 4th
line of samples are complete. Bind off.

4 Neckband
Join right shoulder seam. Using size 2
needles and RS facing, pick up and
K68[72:78] sts around front neck evenly,
K across sts from back neck inc 1 st.
(129[139:151] sts.) Work in K1, P1 rib
for 2¾in. Bind off loosely in rib.

5 To finish
Join left shoulder. Fold neckband in
half to WS and sew in position. Place
center bound-off edge sleeve to shoulder
and sew in position to front and
back. Join side and sleeve seams.
Press lightly.

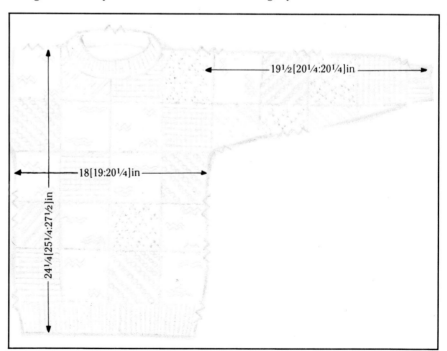

19½[20¼:20¼]in

18[19:20¼]in

24¼[25¼:27½]in

Sweater With Motifs

Combine Fair Isle and lace patterns to make this unusual sweater. Gather the sleeves to form a puff and make a separate collar.

BEFORE YOU BEGIN
When working in the contrast colors, carry the yarn not in use loosely up the side of the work. To work the Fair Isle pattern, strand yarn at the back of the fabric over not more than five stitches at a time, to keep the fabric elastic.

Sizes
Bust	32[34:36:38]in
Length	22¾[23¼:23½:24]in
Sleeve seam	17½in

Note: Instructions for the larger sizes are in brackets [ ]; where there is only one set of figures, it applies to all sizes.

Gauge
22 sts and 30 rows to 4in over St st on size 6 needles.

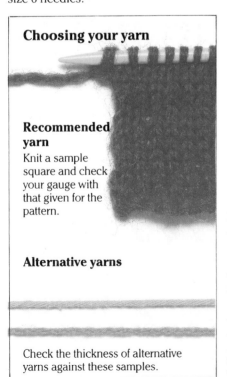

Choosing your yarn

Recommended yarn
Knit a sample square and check your gauge with that given for the pattern.

Alternative yarns

Check the thickness of alternative yarns against these samples.

Materials
☐ Approx 10[12:13]oz of knitting worsted weight yarn in main color (m.c.)
☐ Approx 2[3:3:4]oz in 1st contrast (a)
☐ Approx 2[3:3:4]oz in 2nd contrast (b)
☐ 1 pair each sizes 3 and 6 needles

INSTRUCTIONS
1 Back
Using size 3 needles and m.c., cast on 88[94:100:106] sts.
Work in K1, P1 rib for 2¼in.
Next row: Rib 8, M1 (make a stitch by picking up the horizontal loop lying before next stitch and working into back of it), (rib 12[13:14:15], M1) 6 times, rib 8. (95[101:107:113] sts.)
Change to size 6 needles, join in contrast yarn when required and patt as folls:
1st row: (RS) Using m.c., K.
2nd row: Using m.c., P.
3rd row: K3[6:5:4] m.c., K1 a, * K7 m.c., K1 a, rep from * to last 3[6:5:4] sts, K to end with m.c.
4th row: P2[4:4:3] m.c., P3 a, * P5 m.c., P3 a, rep from * to last 2[5:4:3] sts, P to end with m.c.
5th row: K2[5:4:3] m.c., K3 a, * K5 m.c., K3 a, rep from * to last 2[5:4:3] sts, K to end with m.c.
6th row: Work as 4th row.
7th, 9th and 11th rows: K3[6:5:4] m.c., K1 b, * K7 m.c., K1 b, rep from * to last 3[6:5:4] sts, K to end using m.c.
8th, 10th and 12th rows: P3[6:5:4] m.c., P1 b, * P7 m.c., P1 b, rep from * to last 3[6:5:4] sts, P to end using m.c.
13th row: Using m.c., K2[5:4:3], yarn to front of work (yf), sl 1 K-wise, yarn to back of work over top of right-hand needle (ybk) and K2 tog, psso, yo, * K5, yf, sl 1 K-wise, ybk and K2 tog, psso, yo, rep from * to last 2[5:4:3] sts, K to end.
14th, 16th and 18th rows: Using m.c., P.
15th row: Using m.c., K3[6:5:4], yf, sl 1 K-wise, ybk and K1, psso, * K6, yf, sl 1 K-wise, ybk and K1, rep from * to last 2[5:4:3] sts, K to end.
17th row: Using m.c., K.
19th row: K7[10:9:8] m.c., * K1 a, K7 m.c., rep from * to last 0 [3:2:1] sts, K0[3:2:1] m.c.
20th row: P6[9:8:7] m.c., * P3 a, P5 m.c., rep from * to last 1[4:3:2] sts, P to end, using m.c.
21st row: K6[9:8:7] m.c., * K3 a, K5 m.c., rep from * to last 1[4:3:2] sts, K to end, using m.c.
22nd row: Work as 20th row.
23rd, 25th and 27th rows: K7[10:9:8] m.c., * K1 b, K7 m.c., rep from * to last 0[3:2:1] sts, K0[3:2:1] m.c.
24th, 26th and 28th rows: P7[10:9:8], * P1 b, P7 m.c., rep from * to last 0[3:2:1] sts, P0[3:2:1] m.c.
29th row: Using m.c., K6[9:8:7], * yf, sl 1 K-wise, ybk and K2 tog, psso, yo, K5, rep from * to last 1[4:3:2] sts, K to end.
30th row: Using m.c., P.
31st row: Using m.c., K7[10:9:8], * yf, sl 1 K-wise, ybk and K1, psso, K6, rep from * to last 0[3:2:1] sts, K to end.
32nd row: Using m.c., P.
These 32 rows form the patt.
Cont in patt until back meas approx 15in, ending with 32nd row of patt.

Shape armholes

Keeping patt correct, bind off 5
sts at beg of next 2 rows.
Dec 1 st at each end of next 3[3:5:5]
rows, then every foll alt row until
71[73:75:77] sts rem.
Work even until armholes meas
8[8¼:8½:9]in from beg of shaping
ending with a WS row.

Shape shoulders

Bind off 7 sts at beg of next 4 rows
then 6[7:7:7] sts at beg of foll 2 rows.
Bind off rem 31[31:33:35] sts.

2 Front

Work as given for back until front is
19 rows shorter than back to start of
shoulder shaping, ending with RS row.

Shape neck

Next row: Keeping patt correct,
work 27[28:28:28] sts, turn. Work on
these sts only.
Dec 1 st at neck edge on the next 3
rows, then foll 4 alt rows.
(20[21:21:21]) sts. Work even until
front meas same as back to start of
shoulder shaping, ending with a RS
row.

Shape shoulder

Bind off 7 sts at beg of next and foll alt
row. Work 1 row.
Bind off rem 6[7:7:7] sts.

Shape second side of neck

Rejoin yarn to rem sts, bind off the next
17[18:19:21] sts, patt 27[28:28:28] sts.
Now work to match first side of neck
reversing all the shapings.

3 Sleeves

Using size 3 needles and m.c., cast on

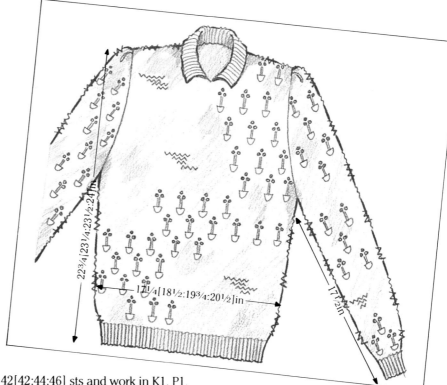

42[42:44:46] sts and work in K1, P1,
rib for 2¼in.
Next row: Rib 5[5:4:5], M1, (rib
8[8:9:9], M1) 4 times, rib 5[5:4:5].
(47[47:49:51] sts.)
Change to size 6 needles, starting with
a 15th row, work 8[6:6:6] rows of patt
as given for 1st[1st:4th:3rd] sizes of
back. Keeping patt correct, inc 1
st at each end of next and every foll
10th[9th:8th:8th] row until there are
67[69:73:75] sts. Work even until
sleeve seam meas approx 17½in,
ending with the same row of patt as
on back before start of armhole

shaping, ending with a WS row.

Shape cap

Bind off 5 sts at beg of next 2 rows.
Dec 1 st at each end of next and
every foll 4th row until 51[51:57:57]
sts rem.
Work 3 rows even.
Now dec 1 st at each end of next and
every alt row until 17 sts rem, ending
with a WS row.
Bind off.

4 Collar

Using size 3 needles and m.c., cast on
97[97:101:105] sts.
1st row: K1, * P1, K1, rep from * to
end.
2nd row: P1, * K1, P1, rep from * to
end.
Rep these 2 rows until collar meas
1½in ending with a WS row.
Now work as folls:
Next row: Rib to last 9 sts, turn.
Next row: Rib to last 9 sts, turn.
Next row: Rib to last 18 sts, turn.
Next row: Rib to last 18 sts, turn.
Cont in this way until the row rib to
last 45 sts turn has been worked out.
Now rib across all sts until collar meas
3¼in at center back neck.
Bind off evenly in rib.

5 To finish

Do not press. Join shoulder seams.
Join side and sleeve seams. Insert
sleeves. Sew cast-on edge of collar to
the neck, starting and finishing at the
center front.

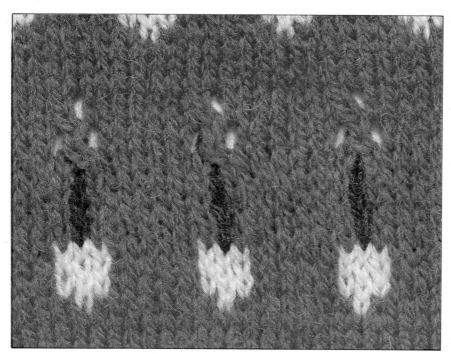

Sweater With Triangles

Knit triangles into the fabric and sew on colored glass beads to add to the decoration. Work in a range of pastel colors.

BEFORE YOU BEGIN
Leave sufficient yarn on each triangle to sew in the glass beads, and darn in all the loose ends afterwards. It is advisable to wash by hand only, so as not to break or damage the beads and spoil the look of the garment.

Sizes
Bust   32[34:36:38]in
Length   23¼[23½:24:24½]in
Sleeve seam   17[17:17¼:17¼]in

Note: Instructions for larger sizes are in brackets [ ]; where there is only one set of figures it applies to all sizes.

Gauge
22 sts and 30 rows to 4in over St st on size 6 needles.

Choosing your yarn

Recommended yarn

Knit a sample square and check your gauge with that given for the pattern.

Alternative yarns

Check the thickness of alternative yarns against these samples.

Materials
☐ Approx 9[9:10:11]oz of knitting worsted weight yarn in main color (m.c.)
☐ Approx 2[2:3:3]oz in 1st contrast (a)
☐ Approx 3[3:4:4]oz in 2nd contrast (b)
☐ Approx 2[2:3:3]oz in 3rd contrast (c)
☐ 1 pair each sizes 3 and 6 needles
☐ Approx 100 small beads in pink and brown

INSTRUCTIONS
1 Back
* Using size 3 needles and m.c., cast on 94[100:104:112] sts.
Work in K1, P1 rib for 2in.
Next row: Inc 1 st at end of last row. (95[101:105:113] sts.)
Change to size 6 needles and K1 row. Using a, P1 row.
1st row: (RS) Using m.c., K.
2nd row: P7[5:7:6] m.c., * 1b, 9 m.c., rep from * to last 8[6:8:7] sts, 1b, 7[5:7:6] m.c.
3rd row: K6[4:6:5] m.c., * 3b, 7 m.c., rep from * to last 9[7:8:7] sts, 3b, 6[4:5:4] m.c.
4th row: P5[3:5:4] m.c., * 2b, 1 m.c., 2b, 5 m.c., rep from * to last 0[8:0:9]

sts, 0[2:0:2] a, 0[1:0:1] m.c., 0[2:0:2] a, 0[3:0:4] m.c.
5th row: K1[0:1:0] b, 3[2:3:3] m.c., * 2b, 1 m.c., MB using a, by (K1, yo, K1, yo, K1, then sl the 1st, 2nd, 3rd and 4th sts, over the last st), 1 m.c., 2b, 1 m.c., MB using c, 1 m.c., rep from * to last 1[9:1:0] sts, 1[0:1:0] m.c., 0[2:0:0] b, 0[1:0:0] m.c., MB using a, 0[1:0:0] time, P0[1:0:0] m.c., 0[2:0:0] b, 0[2:0:0] m.c.
6th row: P2[0:2:2] b; * 1 m.c., 2b, 5 m.c., 2b, rep from * to last 3[1:3:2] sts, 1 m.c., 2[0:2:1] b.
7th row: K1[0:1:0] m.c., 3[2:3:3] b, *7 m.c., 3b, rep from * to last 1[9:1:0] sts, 1[7:1:0] m.c., 0[2:0:0] b.
8th row: P2[0:2:1] m.c., * 1b, 9 m.c., rep from * to last 3[1:3:2] sts, 1b, 2[0:2:1] m.c.
9th row: K2[0:2:1] m.c., * 1b, 9 m.c., rep from * to last 3[1:3:2] sts, 1b, 2[0:2:1] m.c.
10th row: P in m.c.
11th row: K in a.
Starting with a P row, work in St st until row 22 has been completed using m.c.
23rd row: K4[2:4:3] m.c., * K7 c, turn. Make triangle by working on the 7c sts as folls:
Using c, P7, turn, sl 1, K1, psso, K3, K2 tog, turn, P5, turn, sl 1, K1, psso, K1, K2 tog, turn, P3, turn, sl 1, K2, tog, psso, fasten off, leaving a long loose end for bead.
With RS facing, using the left-hand needle, pick up each of the 7 loops of a, lying flat against the contrast sts of the triangle, working from RS of work towards WS when picking up each loop. K10 m.c., (across the 7 picked-up sts, plus 3), then rep triangle using b, as before from *. Rep until 9[10:10:11] triangles in all have been worked, alternating the colors, K to end.
24th row: P in a.
These 24 rows form the patt, rep them 3 times more.
Shape armholes
Keeping patt correct, bind off 4[5:5:6]

23¼[23½:24:24½]in

17[17:17¼:17¼]in

17[18:19¼:20½]in

sts at beg of next 2 rows.
Dec 1 st at each end of every row
until 80[85:88:93] sts rem.
Dec 1 st at each end of every alt row
until 74[79:78:81] sts rem.
* Cont even until 2 complete patt
reps have been worked from beg of
armhole shaping. Work a further
8[10:14:18] rows patt.

Shape shoulders
Bind off 8 sts at beg of next 4 rows
and 7[9:9:9] sts at beg of next 2 rows,
leave rem sts on a holder.

2 Front
Work as given for back from * to *
Cont even until 1[1:2:2]
complete patt reps have been
worked, but for 1st and 2nd sizes
only, work a further 20 rows of
patt.

Shape neck
Patt 27[29:29:30], turn, leave rem sts
on a spare needle.
Work on first set of sts as folls. ** Dec
1 st at neck edge on every row until
23[25:25:25] sts rem. Cont even
until work meas same as back
to beg of shoulder shaping, ending
at side edge.
Bind off 8 sts at beg of next and foll alt
row.
Work 1 row.
Bind off rem sts.

Shape second side of neck
Return to sts on spare needle, slip
the first 20[21:20:21] sts onto a
holder. Complete to match first side of
neck reversing all the shapings.

3 Sleeves
Using size 3 needles and m.c.,
cast on 64[64:70:70] sts, work
2¼[2¼:2¾:2¾]in K1, P1 rib.
Next row: Inc 1 st at end of last row.
(65[65:71:71] sts.)
Change to size 6 needles and K1 row.
Using a, P1 row.
1st row: (RS) Using m.c., K.
2nd row: P7[7:5:5] m.c., * 1b, 9 m.c.,
rep from * to last 8[8:6:6] sts, 1b,
7[7:5:5] m.c.
3rd row: K6[6:4:4] m.c., * 3b, 7 m.c.,
rep from * to last 9[9:7:7] sts, 3b,
6[6:4:4] m.c.
4th row: P5[5:3:3] m.c., * 2b, 1m.c.,
2b, 5m.c., rep from * to last 0[0:8:8]
sts, 0[0:2:2] b, 1m.c., 2b, 0[0:3:3]
m.c.
5th row: K4[4:2:2] m.c., * 2b, 1m.c., MB
using a, 1m.c., 2b, 1 m.c., MB using c,
1 m.c., rep from * to last 1[1:9:9] sts,
1[1:0:0] m.c., 0[0:2:2] b, 0[0:1:1] m.c.,
(MB using a) 0[0:1:1] time, 0[0:1:1] m.c.,
0[0:2:2] b, 0[0:2:2] m.c.
6th row: 3[3:1:1] m.c., * 2b, 5m.c.,
2b, 1m.c., rep from * to last 2[2:0:0]
sts, 2[2:0:0] b.
7th row: 0[0:2:2] b, 1[1:7:7] m.c., *
3b, 7m.c., rep from * to last 4[4:2:2]
sts, 3[3:2:2] b, 1[1:0:0] m.c.
8th row: 0[0:1:1] b, 1[1:9:9] m.c., *
1b, 9m.c., rep from * to last 3[3:1:1]
sts, 1b, 2[2:0:0] m.c.
9th row: As 8th row but read K for P.
10th row: P in m.c.

11th row: K in a.
Starting with a P row work in St st
until row 22 has been completed.
23rd row: K3[3:2:2] m.c., * K7c, turn,
make triangle by working on the 7c
sts as folls: K7, turn, P7, turn, sl 1,
K1, psso, K3, K2 tog, turn, P5, turn, sl
1, K1, psso, K1, K2 tog, turn, P3, turn,
sl 1, K2, tog, psso, fasten off leaving a
long thread for bead.
With RS facing, using the left hand
needle, pick up each of the 7 loops of
a lying flat against the contrast sts of
the triangle, working from RS of work
towards WS when picking up each loop.
K10a (across the 7 picked up sts,
plus 3), then rep triangle using b as
before from *, rep until 6[6:7:7] triangles
in all have been worked.
K to end in m.c.
24th row: P in a.
These 24 rows form the patt, rep 3
more times.

Shape cap
Keeping patt correct, bind off
4[5:5:6] sts at beg of next 2 rows, dec 1 st
at each end of next row. Work 3 rows
even.
Rep these 4 rows until 34[30:37:33] sts
rem.
Dec 1 st at each end of every row
until 12[12:13:13] sts rem.
Bind off.

4 Neckband
Join right shoulder seam. Using m.c.,
and size 3 needle with RS facing,
pick up and K15[15:16:15] sts down
left side of neck, K across the
20[21:20:21] sts from front neck
holder, pick up and K15[15:16:15] sts
up right side of neck, K across the
28[29:28:31] sts from back neck holder.
(78[80:80:82] sts.) Work 2¾in in K1, P1
rib.
Bind off loosely in rib.

5 To finish
Attach a bead to each point of every
triangle as folls: thread a loop of
cotton through bead hole and place
yarn at point of triangle in the loop
and pull through.
Push bead up to point of triangle,
sew end to back of fabric very securely.
Do not pull the bead up too tightly
or the work may pucker.
Join left shoulder and neckband. Join
side and sleeve seams, set in sleeves.
Fold neckband in half on to the WS
and sew in place.

Floral Sweater

This sweater is ideal to wear on a spring or summer's day. Embroider French knots in soft colors on the front piece to form flowers. Finish off with a crochet neckline and hem.

BEFORE YOU BEGIN

When making a bobble, knit the first and last stitch of the bobble tightly on every row. On the last row pass the made stitches over the first stitch and pull, making sure the bobble is taut. On the following row, purl into the bobble stitches tightly.

Size

One size only
Bust 34in
Length 20in
Sleeve seam 16½in

Gauge

17 sts and 24 rows to 4in over patt on size 8 needles.

Choosing your yarn

Recommended yarn

Knit a sample square and check your gauge with that given for the pattern.

Alternative yarns

Check the thickness of alternative yarns against these samples.

Materials

☐ Approx 25oz of bulky weight cotton yarn in main color (m.c.)
☐ Small amounts of colors a, b and c
☐ 1 pair each sizes 6 and 8 needles
☐ 1 cable needle
☐ Size G/6 crochet hook
☐ 6 buttons

INSTRUCTIONS

1 Back

Using size 8 needles and m.c., cast on 70 sts. Work patt as folls:
1st row: P.
2nd row: K3, * MB (make bobble by working K1, P1, K1, P1 all into the next st, turn, P4, pass the 2nd, 3rd and 4th st over the 1st st, turn, K1), K8, rep from * to last 4 sts, MB, K3.

3rd row: P.
4th row: K.
Rep rows 1 to 4 inclusive until work meas 11in from the beg, ending with a WS row.

Armhole shaping

Keeping patt correct, bind off 5 sts at the beg of next 2 rows and 2 sts at the beg of foll 2 rows. Dec 1 st at the beg of next 2 rows. (54 sts.)
Cont even until work meas 18½in from the cast on edge, ending with a WS row.

Shape shoulders

Bind off 15 sts at the beg of the next 2 rows. (24 sts.) Work 4 rows even in patt. Bind off.

2 Front

Using size 8 needles and m.c., cast on 70 sts. Work patt as folls:
1st row: P.
2nd row: K3, * MB, K2, sl 1b (sl next st onto a cable needle and hold at the back of the work, K1, then K the st from cable needle), sl 1f (sl next st onto a cable needle and hold at the front of the work, K1 then K the st from cable needle), K2, MB, K8, rep from * to last 13 sts, MB, K2, sl 1b, sl 1f, K2, MB, K3.
3rd row: P.
4th row: K5. * sl 1b, K2, sl 1f, K12, rep from * to last 11 sts, sl 1b, K2, sl 1f, K5.
5th row: P.
6th row: K3, * MB, K8, rep from * to last 4 sts, MB, K3.
7th row: P.
8th row: K.
9th row: P.
10th row: K3, * MB, K8, MB, K2, sl 1b, sl 1f, K2, rep from * to last 13 sts, MB, K8, MB, K3.
11th row: P.
12th row: K14, * sl 1b, K2, sl 1f, K12, rep from * to last 2 sts, K2.
13th row: P.
14th row: K3, * MB, K8, rep from * to last 4 sts, MB, K3.
15th row: P.
16th row: K.

Rows 1 to 16 form the patt, rep these rows until front meas same as back to armhole shaping, ending with a WS row.

Shape armhole
Keeping patt correct, bind off 5 sts at the beg of the next 2 rows and 2 sts at beg of the foll 2 rows.
Dec 1 st at the beg of next 2 rows, (54 sts) Cont on these sts until work meas 16¼in from beg, ending with a WS row.

Shape neck
Next row: Patt 21 sts, bind off the next 12 sts, patt to end.
Next row: Patt to end.
* **Next row:** Bind off 2 sts, patt to end.
Next row: Patt to end.
Next row: Dec 1 st at neck edge on next and foll 4 alt rows. (14 sts.)
Cont even until work matches back to shoulder shaping, ending at armhole edge.
Bind off *.

Shape second side of neck
With WS facing, rejoin yarn to rem sts. Work as for first side of neck from * to * reversing all the shapings.

3 Sleeves
Using size 6 needles and m.c., cast on 29 sts.
1st row: K1, * P1, K1, rep from * to end.

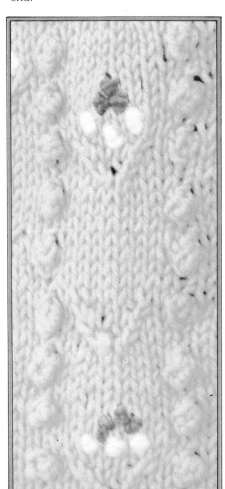

2nd row: P1, * K1, P1, rep from * to end.
Rep these 2 rows until work meas 2in, ending with a WS row.
Inc row: Rib 1, M1, rib 1, * M1, rib 2, rep from * 13 times, M1, rib 1. (44 sts.)
Change to size 8 needles and work in patt as folls:
1st row: (RS) K8, * MB, K8, rep from * to end.
2nd row: P.
3rd row: K.
4th row: P.
Work in patt at the same time inc 1 st at each end of every 8th row until there are 56 sts on the needles.
Cont even until sleeve meas 16½in from beg, ending with a WS row.

Shape sleeve cap
Keeping patt correct, bind off 5 sts at the beg of the next 2 rows. Dec 1 st at each end of next and foll 4th rows until 30 sts rem.
Dec 1 st at each end of every row until 20 sts rem.
Bind off.

4 Front embroidery
Using darning needle, work 3 French knots in color a to form a V; these are the leaves. Work 2 French knots in b above the leaves to form the petals and 1 French knot in c to form the flower head.

5 Crochet neckline
Front
Using G/6 crochet hook and m.c., starting at top left shoulder, make 2 ch to start, then work a row hdc around front neck to right shoulder. Fasten off.
Back
Starting at top bound off edge and right shoulder make 2 ch to start, then work a row of hdc across back neck. Fasten off.

6 Shoulder openings
Back and front alike
With RS facing of left shoulder, 3 ch, work 11 dc along top of shoulder, 3 ch and turn.
Next row: 1dc into each dc to end, fasten off.
Rep for right shoulder

7 To finish
Press pieces lightly on the WS with a cool iron. Join side and sleeve seams. Join shoulder by overlapping the 2 rows of dc on front with corresponding dc on back. Set in the sleeves, gathering the sleeve head to form a puff. Sew on 3 buttons to each shoulder, using the spaces between dc on front as buttonholes.

8 Bottom edge
Starting at left side seam, work 2 ch, 76 hdc around bottom edge. Join with a slip stitch to first hdc.

Flowers And Bows For Spring

K nit this lightweight spring sweater using a fine bouclé yarn. All four pieces are worked following one chart. Decorate the center of the flowers with French knots.

BEFORE YOU BEGIN
Read the instructions carefully and mark off the row which begins the garment piece on the chart. Block out in pencil any part of the chart which is not required; this can be erased for the remaining sections.

Sizes
Bust   32[34:36:38]in
Length   22[22½:23¾:22¾]in
Sleeve seam   17[17¼:17¼:17¾]in

Note: Instructions for larger sizes are in brackets [ ]; where there is only one set of figures, it applies to all sizes.

Gauge
32 sts and 40 rows to 4in over St st on size 2 needles.

Choosing your yarn

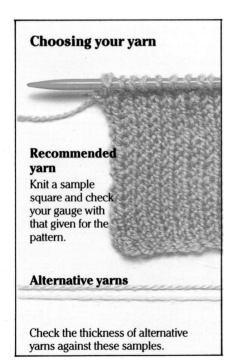

Recommended yarn
Knit a sample square and check your gauge with that given for the pattern.

Alternative yarns

Check the thickness of alternative yarns against these samples.

17¾[18½:19¾:20½]in

17[17¼:17¼:17¾]in

22[22½:22¾:23¾]in

Materials
☐ Approx 9[11:11:11]oz of fingering weight yarn in main color (m.c.)
☐ Approx 2oz each in contrast colors (a, b and c)
☐ 1 pair each sizes 1 and 2 needles
☐ Set of four size 1 double-pointed needles

INSTRUCTIONS
1 Back
Using size 1 needles and c, cast on 108[112:116:120] sts.
1st row: K1, * K2, P2, rep from * to last 3 sts, K3.
2nd row: K1, * P2, K2, rep from * to last 3 sts, P2, K1.
Change to m.c., rep rows 1 and 2, 11 times more.
Next row: Rib 4[4:7:7], * rib 1, M1 (by picking up the loop that lies in front of the next st on the left hand needle), rib 9[8:6:5], rep from * to last 5[4:7:8] sts, rib to end. (120[126:134:142] sts.)
Change to size 2 needles. Now foll from chart, commencing with the chart row 39[35:35:31], read all K rows from left to right and all P rows from right to left.
Use separate balls of contrast colors

for all the motifs, twisting the yarns either side to avoid a hole. At the same time inc 1 st at each end of the 11th and every foll 10th row as indicated, until there are 140[148:156:165] sts.
Work even until chart row 154 has been completed.
Shape raglan armholes
*** Cont reading from chart, at the same time shape as folls:
Bind off 8 sts at beg of next 2 rows.
Next row: K1, sl 1, K1, psso, work to last 3 sts, K2 tog, K1.
Next row: K1, work to last st, K1.
Cont to dec in this way.
Work until chart row 214[216:218:220] is completed. (66[72:78:84] sts.)
** Cont in m.c. only, rep the dec rows until 44[54:64:74] sts rem, ending with a WS row.
1st size only
Hold rem 44 sts on a spare needle.
2nd, 3rd and 4th sizes only
Next row: K1, sl 1, K1, psso, work to last 3 sts, K2 tog, K1.
Next row: K1, P2 tog, P to last 3 sts, P2 tog tbl, K1.
Rep these 2 rows until [46:48:50] sts rem, ending with a WS row.
*** Hold these sts on a spare needle.

2 Front
Work as back to **.
Cont in m.c. throughout.
Shape neck
1st row: K1, sl 1, psso, K16[18:20:22] turn.
2nd row: P2 tog, P to last st, K1.
3rd row: K1, sl 1, K1, psso, K to last 2 sts, K2 tog.
Rep 2nd and 3rd rows 2[3:3:3] times more. (9[8:10:12] sts.)
10th row: K1, P to last st, K1.
1st, 2nd and 3rd sizes only
11th row: K1, sl 1, K1, psso, K to end.
12th row: K1, P to last st, K1.
1st size only
Rep rows 11 and 12 until 3 sts rem, ending with the 12th row.
Next row: K1, sl 1, K1, psso, break

off yarn. Fasten off.
2nd and 3rd sizes only
Rep rows 11 and 12 until [4:8] sts rem, ending with the 12th row.
3rd and 4th sizes only
Next row: K1, sl 1, K1, psso, K to end.
Next row: K1, P to last 3 sts, P2 tog tbl, K1.

Rep these 2 rows until 4 sts rem, ending with a WS row.
2nd, 3rd and 4th sizes only
Next row: K1, sl 1, K1, psso, K1.
Next row: P2 tog, K1.
Next row: K2 tog, break off yarn and fasten off.
Shape second side of neck
With RS of work facing, sl 28[30:32:34]

sts at center onto a spare needle, rejoin m.c. at right of rem sts and complete to match first side, reversing all the shapings. Work the armhole edge K2 tog, K1 on RS rows and K1, P2 tog on WS rows, the neck edge is worked sl 1, K1, psso on RS rows and P2 tog tbl on WS rows.
Fasten off securely.

KEY

a
b
c
m.c.

90
100
110
120
130
140
150
160
170
180
190
200
210
220

Chart for all 4 main pieces

1st size – All pieces
2nd size – All pieces
3rd size – All pieces
4th size – All pieces

3 Sleeves

Using size 1 needles and c, cast on
56[60:60:64] sts.
Work 2 rows rib as for back.
Change to m.c., work a further 22
rows in rib.
Change to size 2 needles.

1st size only
Inc row: K twice into every st.
Next row: P, inc 1 st at each end.

2nd size only
Inc row: K twice into every st.
Next row: K twice into the next st, P
to last st, K twice into last st.

3rd and 4th sizes only
Inc row: K twice into every st.
Next row: K1, P1, * P[12:13] sts, P
twice into next st, rep from * to last
14 sts, P13, K1.

All sizes (114[120:128:136] sts.) Cont
working in St st, commencing
9th[5th:5th:1st] row of chart.
At the same time, inc 1st at each end
of the 11th and every foll 10th row as
indicated, until there are
140[148:156:164] sts.
Work even until row 154 has been
completed.

Shape raglan sleeve
Work raglan shapings as for back from
*** to **.

4 Neckband

Join raglan seams.
With RS of work facing, using set of 4
double-pointed needles size 1
and c, pick up and K44[46:48:50] sts
from back of neck, K2 tog across all the
44[46:48:50] sts at top of sleeve,
(22[23:24:25] sts), pick up and
K12[11:12:11] sts from left front neck
shaping, pick up and K28[30:32:34] sts
from center front, pick up and
K12[11:12:11] sts from right front neck
edge, K2 tog across the 44[46:48:50]
sts at top of sleeve. (140[144:152:156]
sts.)

1st round: * K2, P2, rep from * to
end.
Work 1 more round.
Change to m.c., and work a further 22
rounds.
Bind off in rib loosely.

5 To finish

Join side and sleeve seams. Fold
neckband in half on to the wrong side
and slipstitch down neatly.
Press all the pieces lightly with a cool
iron and dry cloth.
Using contrast color c, embroider 4
or 5 French knots at center of each
flower.

Shawl And Sweater Set

This pretty lacy sweater and shawl are worked in different lace patterns, with an added ruffle on the edge of the shawl. Mix and match with your wardrobe.

BEFORE YOU BEGIN
To make the shawl, use either a pair of extra long needles, or a circular needle. If a circular needle is used, work on it as though working on a pair of needles. Slide the stitches once worked to the next point and continue working.

Sizes
Bust   32[34:36:38]in
Length   22[22½:22¾:23¼]in
Sleeve seam   17¼in

Note: Instructions for larger sizes are in brackets [ ]; where there is only one set of figures it applies to all sizes.

Gauge
26 sts and 37 rows to 4in over St st on size 3 needles.

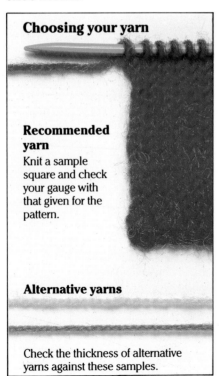

Choosing your yarn

Recommended yarn
Knit a sample square and check your gauge with that given for the pattern.

Alternative yarns

Check the thickness of alternative yarns against these samples.

Materials
☐ Approx 9[9:10:10]oz of sport weight yarn in blue for the sweater
☐ Approx 5oz in white for the shawl
☐ 1 pair each sizes 2 and 3 needles
☐ Extra long size 3 needles

Instructions for sweater
1 Back
Using size 2 needles, cast on 112[118:124:132] sts, work in K1, P1 rib for 2in.
Change to size 3 needles and work in patt as folls:
1st row: (RS) K.
2nd row: P.
3rd row: K2[5:2:2], K2[2:0:2] tog, yo2, sl 1, K1, psso) 1[1:0:1] time, * (K2 tog, yo2, sl 1, K1, psso, K4) twice, K2 tog, yo2, sl 1, K1, psso, rep from * to last 6[9:2:6] sts, K2[2:0:2] tog, (yo2, sl 1, K1, psso) 1[1:0:1] time, K2[5:2:2].
4th row: P, working P1, K1, into all the yo2 of previous row.
5th, 9th, 13th, 17th, 21st, 25th, 29th, 33rd and 37th rows: K.
6th, 10th, 14th, 18th, 22nd, 26th, 30th, 34th and 38th rows: P.
7th row: K0[1:0:0], (yo, sl 1, K1, psso) 0[1:0:0] time, K4[4:0:4], K2 tog, yo2, * sl 1, K1, psso, K4 (K2 tog, yo2, sl 1, K1, psso) twice, K4, K2 tog, yo2, rep from * to last 6[9:2:6] sts, sl 1, K1, psso, K4[4:0:4], (K2 tog, yo, K1) 0[1:0:0] time.
8th, 12th, 16th, 20th, 24th, 28th, 32nd and 36th rows: As 4th row.
11th row: (K1, K2 tog, yo2, sl 1, K1, psso) 0[1:0:0] time, K6[4:2:6], * K4, (K2 tog, yo2, sl 1, K1, psso) 3 times, K4, rep from * to last 6[9:2:6] sts, K6[4:2:6], (K2 tog, yo2, sl 1, K1, psso, K1) 0[1:0:0] time.
15th row: K2[1:0:2], (yo, sl 1, K1, psso, K2 tog) 0[1:0:0] time (yo) 1[1:0:1] time, (yo) 0[1:0:0] time, (sl 1, K1, psso) 1[1:0:1] time, K2, * K2, (K2 tog, yo2, sl 1, K1, psso) 4 times, K2, rep from * to last 6[9:2:6] sts, K2, K2 tog, yo) 1[1:0:1] time, (yo, sl 1, K1, psso, K2 tog, yo) 0[1:0:0] time, K2[1:0:2].
19th row: As 11th row.
23rd row: As 7th row.
27th row: As 3rd row.
31st row: K2[3:0:2]. K0[2:0:0] tog, (yo, 1[1:0:1] time, (yo) 0[1:0:0] time, (sl, 1, K1, psso) 1[1:0:1] time, K2 tog, yo2, * sl 1, K1, psso, K2 tog, yo2, sl 1, K1, psso, K8, K2 tog, yo2, sl 1, K1, psso, K2 tog, yo2, rep from * to last 6[9:2:6] sts, sl 1, K1, psso, (K2 tog, yo) 1[1:0:1] time, (yo, K2 tog) 0[1:0:0] time, K2[3:0:2].
35th row: K2[1:2:2], (K2 tog, yo2, sl 1, K1, psso) 1[2:0:1] time, * (K2 tog, yo2, sl 1, K1, psso) twice, K4, (K2 tog, yo2, sl 1, K1, psso) twice, rep from * to last 6[9:2:6] sts, (K2 tog, yo2, sl 1, K1, psso) 1[2:0:1] time, K2[1:2:2].
39th row: As 31st row.
40th row: As 4th row.
These 40 rows form the patt, work even in patt until back meas 14¼in ending with a 36th row of patt.
Shape armholes
Keeping patt correct, bind off 6 sts at beg of next 2 rows. Dec 1 st at each end of every row 3[5:5:7] times. Dec 1 st at each end of every alt row until

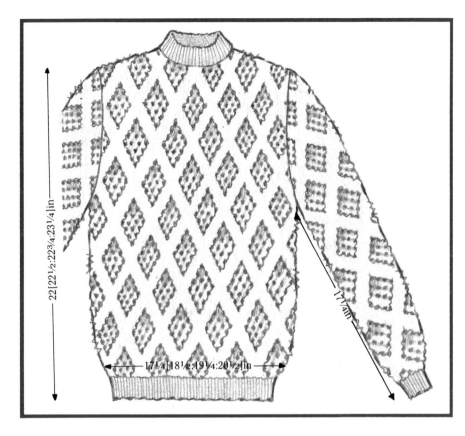

22[22½:22¾:23¼]in

17¼in

17¼[18½:19¼:20½]in

86[88:92:94] sts rem. Work even in patt until armhole meas 7[7½:8:8½]in ending with a WS row.

Shape shoulders
Bind off 7 sts at beg of next 2 rows.
Bind off 6 sts at beg of next 6 rows.
Leave rem 36[38:42:44] sts on a spare needle.

2 Front
Work as for back until front meas 2¼in less than back to beg of shoulder shaping, ending with a WS row.

Shape neck
Next row: Patt 34[35:37:38], turn and leave rem sts on a spare needle.
Keeping armhole edge straight dec 1 st at neck edge on every row 6[6:8:8] times then 1 st on every alt row until 25 sts rem. Work a few rows even in patt until front matches back to shoulder ending with a WS row.

Shape shoulder
Bind off 7 sts at beg of next row.
Work 1 row.
Bind off 6 sts at beg of next and 2 foll alt rows.

Shape second side of neck
With RS of work facing rejoin yarn to rem sts, bind off center 18 sts loosely and complete to match first side reversing all the shapings.

3 Sleeves
Using size 2 needles, cast on

49[53:55:59] sts.
1st row: K1, * P1, K1, rep from * to end.
2nd row: P1, * K1, P1, rep from * to end.
Rep these 2 rows 8 times.
Inc row: Rib 8[6:10:6], (M1, rib 16[10:18:12]) times, M1, rib to end. (52[58:58:64] sts.)
Change to size 3 needles and starting with 29th row of patt, work in patt as for 1st[2nd:2nd:3rd] size on back. At the same time shape sides by inc 1 st at each end of every 10th[10th:11th:12th] row until there are 76[78:80:84] sts taking inc sts into patt. Work even in patt until sleeve meas approx 17¼in, ending with same patt row as on back.

Shape cap
Bind off 6 sts at beg of next 2 rows.
Dec 1 st at each end of next and every foll 4th row 6[7:8:7] times more. (50[50:50:56] sts.)
Dec 1 st at each end of every alt row until 30 sts rem.
Dec 1 st at each end of every row until 20 sts rem.
Bind off.

4 Neckband
Join shoulder seam. Using size 2 needles and RS facing, pick up and K74 sts evenly around front neck to right shoulder, K across back neck sts as

folls: K4[5:5:4], (M1, K7[7:8:9] 4 times, M1, K to end inc 1 st at end of row (116[118:122:124] sts). Work in K1, P1 rib for 2¾in.
Bind off loosely in rib.

5 To finish
Join left shoulder and neckband. Fold neckband in half onto the WS and sew loosely in position.
Join side and sleeve seams.
Insert sleeves.

Instructions for shawl
1 Main piece
Using size 3 needles, cast on 2 sts.
Next row: K2.
Next row: Inc into each st (by knitting into the front and back of st) (4sts).
Next row: K4.
Next row: P, inc into 1st and last st (6 sts).
Next row: K1, K2 tog, yo2, sl 1, K1, psso, K1.
Next row: P, inc 1 st at each end of row, working P1, K1, into all the yo2 of previous row.
Next row: K.
Next row: P, inc into 1st and last st (10 sts).
Work in patt as folls:
1st row: (RS) K1, K2 tog, yo2, sl 1, K1, psso) twice, K1.
2nd row: P, inc 1 st at each end of row working P1, K1, into yo2 of previous row.
3rd row: K.
4th row: P, inc into 1st and last st (14 sts).
Cont working in patt as set, on every subsequent 1st row the instruction in brackets will be repeated one more time, the next time 3 times, the foll 4 times. Work in this way until the shawl meas 21¾in from the point, ending with a P row.
Bind off loosely.

2 Ruffle
Using size 3 needles, cast on 454 sts loosely work in patt as folls:
1st row: K3, * yo, K2, sl 1, K1, psso, K2 tog, K2, yo, K1, rep from * to last st, K1.
2nd row: P.
3rd row: K2, * yo, K2, sl 1, K1, psso, K2 tog, K2, yo, K1, rep from * to last 2 sts, K2.
4th row: P.
Rep last 4 rows twice more.
Next row: (K1, K2 tog) to last st K1.
Bind off loosely.
Join ruffle to edge of shawl.

Jigsaw Sweater

Knit yourself a jigsaw design using three bright contrast colors. The sleeves of the sweater are worked in the main color. Wear with jeans or casual trousers for a fun look.

BEFORE YOU BEGIN
Wind the three contrast colors into smaller balls, and use a small ball for each jigsaw piece. Twist the yarns together at the back of the work after each block of color to avoid a hole.

Sizes
Bust   34[36:38:40]in
Length   25[24¼:26:26½]in
Sleeve seam 19½[19½:20:20]in

Note: Instructions for larger sizes are given in brackets [ ]; where one

Choosing your yarn

Recommended yarn
Knit a sample square and check your gauge with that given for the pattern.

Alternative yarns

Check the thickness of alternative yarns against these samples.

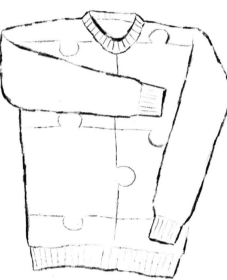

set of figures is given it applies to all sizes.

Gauge
22 sts and 30 rows to 4in over St st on size 5 needles.

Materials
☐ 20[21:23:25]oz of Pingouin Laine et Mohair in main color (m.c.)
☐ 4[4:6:6]oz of Pingouin Laine et Mohair in contrast color (a)
☐ 4[4:6:6]oz of Pingouin Laine et Mohair in contrast color (b)
☐ 1 pair each sizes 2 and 5 needles

INSTRUCTIONS
1 Front
Using size 2 needles and m.c., cast on 98[106:110:114] sts. Work in rib as folls:
1st row: K2, * P2, K2, rep from * to end.
2nd row: P2, * K2, P2, rep from * to end.
Rep these 2 rows for 2¾in, ending with a 2nd row. Inc 1 st at each end of 1st and 4th size only. (100[106:110:116] sts.)

Change to size 5 needles.
Next row: K50[53:55:58] a, K50[53:55:58] m.c.
Next row: P50[53:55:58] m.c., P50[55:58] a.
Rep last 2 rows 4[5:6:7] times more.
Cont in patt as folls:
1st row: K22[24:25:26] a, K6 m.c., K22[23:24:26] a, K22[23:24:26] m.c. K6b, K22[24:25:26] m.c.
2nd row: P21[23:24:25] m.c., P8 b, P21[22:23:25] m.c., P21[22:23:25] a, P8 m.c., P21[23:24:25] a.
3rd row: K20[22:23:24] a, K10 m.c., K20[21:22:24] a, K20[21:22:24] m.c., K10 b, K20[22:23:24] m.c.
4th row: P19[21:22:23] m.c., P12 b, P19[20:21:23] m.c., P19[20:21:23] a, P12 m.c., P12[21:22:23] a.
5th row: K19[21:22:23] a, K12 m.c., K19[20:21:23] a, K19[20:21:23] m.c., K12 b, K19[21:22:23] m.c.
Rep last 2 rows once more.
8th row: P19[21:22:23] m.c., P12 b, P19[20:21:23] m.c., P19[20:21:23] a, P12 m.c., P19[21:22:23] a.
9th row: K20[22:23:24] a, K10 m.c., K20[21:22:24] a, K20[21:22:24] m.c., K10 b, K20[22:23:24] m.c.
10th row: P21[23:24:25] m.c., P8 b, P21[22:23:25] m.c., P21[22:23:25] a, P8 m.c., P21[23:24:25] a.
11th row: K50[53:55:58] m.c., K50[53:55:58] b.
12th row: P50[53:55:58] b, P50[53:55:58] m.c.
Rep last 2 rows 12 times more.
37th row: K50[53:55:58] m.c., K50[53:55:58] b.
38th row: P50[53:55:58] b, P1 m.c., P4 b, P45[48:50:53] m.c.
39th row: K44[47:49:52] m.c., K56[59:61:64] b.
40th row: P57[60:62:65] b, P43[46:48:51] m.c.
41st row: K42[45:47:50] m.c., K58[61:63:66] b.
42nd row: P58[61:63:66] b, P42[45:47:50] m.c.
Rep last 2 rows once more.
45th row: K42[45:47:50] m.c., K58[61:63:66] b.

46th row: P57[60:62:65] b, P43[46:48:51] m.c.

47th row: K44[47:49:52] m.c., K56[59:61:64] b.

48th row: P50[53:55:58] b, P1 m.c., P4 b, P45[48:50:53] m.c.

49th row: K50[53:55:58] m.c., K50[53:55:58] b.

50th row: P50[53:55:58] b, P50[53:55:58] m.c.

Rep last 2 rows 7 times more.

65th row: K50[53:55:57] m.c., K50[53:55:58] b.

66th row: P50[53:55:58] b, P22[23:24:26] m.c., P6 b, P22[24:26:26] m.c.

67th row: K21[23:24:25] m.c., K8 b, K21[22:23:25] m.c., K50[53:55:58] b.

68th row: P50[53:55:58] b, P20[21:22:24] m.c., P10 b, P20[22:23:24] m.c.

69th row: K19[21:22:23] m.c., K12 b, K19[20:21:23] m.c., K50[53:55:58] b.

70th row: P50[53:55:58] b, P19[20:21:23] m.c., P12 b, P19[21:22:23] m.c.

Rep last w rows once more.

73rd row: K19[21:22:23] m.c., K12 b, K19[20:21:23] m.c., K50[53:55:58] b.

74th row: P50[53:55:58] b, P20[21:22:24] m.c., P10 b, P20[22:23:24] m.c.

75th row: K21[23:24:25] m.c., K8 b, K21[22:23:25] m.c., K50[53:55:58] b.

76th row: P21[23:24:25] a, P8 b, P21[22:23:25] a, P50[53:55:58] b.

77th row: K50[53:55:58] b, K20[21:22:24] m.c., K10 b, K20[22:23:24] a.

78th row: P19[21:22:23] a, P12 b, P19[20:21:23] a. P50[53:55:58] b.

79th tow: K50[53:55:58] b, K19[20:21:23] a, K12 b, K19[21:22:23] a.

Rep last 2 rows once more.

82nd row: P19[21:22:23] a, P12 b, P19[20:21:23] a, P50[53:55:58] b.

83rd row: K50[53:55:58] b, K20[21:22:24] a, K10b, K20[22:23:24] a.

84th row: P21[23:24:25] a, P8 b, P21[22:23:25] a, P50[53:55:58] b.

85th row: K50[53:55:58] b, K22[23:24:26] a, K6 b, K22[24:25:26] a.

86th row: P50[53:55:58] a, P50[53:55:58] b.

87th row: K50[53:55:58] b, K50[53:55:58] a.

Rep last 2 rows 7 times more.

102nd row: P50[53:55:58] a, P50[53:55:58] b.

103rd row: K1 b, K4 m.c. K45[48:50:53] b, K1 a, K4 b, K45[48:50:53] a.

104th row: P44[47:49:52] a, P50[53:55:58] b, P6 m.c.

105th row: K7 m.c., K50[53:55:58] b,

K43[46:58:51] a.

106th row: P42[45:47:50] a, P50[53:55:58] b, P8 m.c.

107th row: K8 m.c., K50[53:55:58] b, K42[45:47:50] a.

Rep last 2 rows once more.

110th row: P42[45:47:50] a, P50[53:55:58] b, P8 m.c.

111th row: K7 m.c., K50[53:55:58] b, K43[46:48:51] a.

112th row: P44[47:49:52] a, P50[53:55:58] b, P6 m.c.

113th row: K1b, K4 m.c., K45[48:50:53] b, K1 a, K4 b, K45[48:50:53] a.

114th row: P50[53:55:58] a, P50[53:55:58] b.

115th row: K50[53:55:58] b, K50 [53:55:58] a.

Rep last 2 rows 7 times more.

130th row: P50[53:55:58] a, P50[53:55:58] b.

131st row: K50[53:55:58] b, K22[23:24:26] a, K6 m.c., K22[24:25:26] a.

132nd row: P21[23:24:25] a, P8 m.c., P21[22:23:25] a, P50[53:55:58] b. **

Neck shaping

K across 45[48:50:53] sts in b, turn, P2 tog, P to end. Working in b, dec 1 st at neck edge on every row until 41[44:46:49] sts rem.

Next row: P to end in b.

Next row: K to last 2 sts in b, K2 tog.

Rep last 2 rows once more.

Next row: P to end in b.

Next row: K21[23:24:25] a, K8 b, K9[10:11:13] a, K2 tog.

Next row: P9[10:11:13] a, P10 b, P20[22:23:24] a.

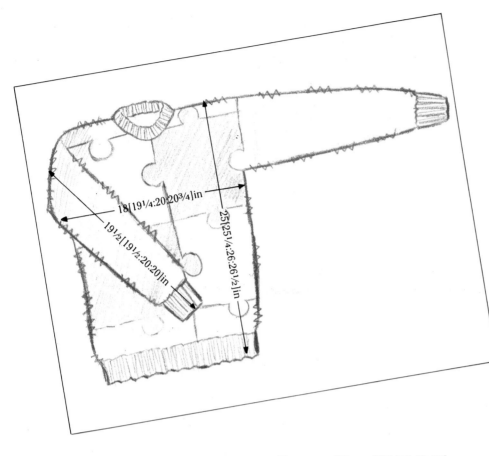

18[19¼:20:20¾]in

19½[19½:20:20]in

25[25¼:26:26½]in

Next row: K19[21:22:23] a, K12 b, K6[7:8:10] a, K2 tog.
Next row: P7[8:8:11] a, P12 b, P19[21:22:23] a.
Next row: K19[21:22:23] a, K12 b, K5[6:7:9] a, K2 tog.
Next row: P6[7:8:10] a, P12 b, P19[21:22:23] a.
Next row: K19[21:22:23] a, K12 b, K4[5:6:8] a, K2 tog.
Next row: P6[7:8:10] a, P10 b, P20[22:23:24] a.
Next row: K21[23:24:25] a, K8 b, K5[6:7:9] a, K2 tog.
Next row: P7[8:9:10] a, P6 b, P22[24:25:26] a.
Next row: K to last 2 sts in a, K2 tog.
Next row: P to end in a.
Rep last 2 rows 2[3:4:5] times more.
Work 2 rows in St st using a.
Bind off rem 32[34:35:37] sts.
Shape second side of neck
Next row: Sl next 10 sts onto spare needle for center, K15[16:17:19] a, K10 m.c., K20[22:23:24] a.
Next row: P19[21:22:23] a, P12 m.c., P12[13:14:16] a, P2 tog.

Next row: K2 tog, K11[12:13:15] a, K12 m.c., K19[21:22:23] a,
Next row: P19[21:22:23] a, P12 m.c., P10[11:12:14] a, P2 tog.
Next row: K2 tog, K9[10:11:13] a, K12 m.c., K19[21:22:23] a.
Next row: P19[21:22:23] a, P12 m.c., P10[11:12:14] a.
Next row: K2 tog, K9[10:11:13] a, K10 m.c., K20[22:23:24] a.
Next row: P21[23:24:25] a, P8 m.c., P11[12:13:15] a.
Next row: K2 tog, K to end using m.c.
Next row: P to end using m.c.
Rep the last 2 rows 7[8:9:10] times more. Work 2 rows in St st using m.c.
Bind off rem 32[34:35:37] sts.

2 Back
Work as for front until **.
Next row: K50[53:55:58] b, K20[21:22:24] a, K10 m.c., K20[22:23:24] a.
Next row: P19[21:22:23] a, P12 m.c., P19[20:21:23] a, P50[53:55:58] b.
Next row: K50[53:55:58] b, K19[20:21:23] a, K12 m.c., K19[21:22:23] a.
Rep last 2 rows once more.
Next row: P19[21:22:23] a, P12 m.c., P19[20:21:23] a, P50[53:55:58] b.
Next row: P50[53:55:58] b, K20[21:22:24] a, K10 m.c., K20[22:23:24] a.
Next row: P21[23:24:25] a, P8 m.c., P21[22:23:25] a. P50[53:55:58] b.
Next row: K21[23:24:25] a, K8 b, K21[22:23:25] a, K50[53:55:58] m.c.
Next row: P50[53:55:58] m.c., P20[21:22:24] a, P10 b, P20[22:23:24] a.
Next row: K19[21:22:23] a, K12 b, K19[20:21:23] a, K50[53:55:58] m.c.
Next row: P50[53:55:58] m.c., P19[20:21:23] a, P12 b, P19[21:22:23] a.
Rep last 2 rows once more.
Next row: K19[21:22:23] b, K12 b, K19[20:21:23] a, K50[53:55:58] m.c.
Next row: P50[53:55:58] m.c., P20[21:22:24] a, P10 b, P20[22:23:24] a.
Next row: K21[23:24:25] a, K8 b, K21[22:23:25] a, K50[53:55:58] m.c.
Next row: P50[53:55:58] m.c. P22[23:24:26] a, P6 b, P22[24:25:26] a.
Next row: K50[53:55:58] a, K50[53:55:58] m.c.
Next row: P50[53:55:58] m.c., P50[53:55:58] a.
Rep last 2 rows 3[4:5:6] times more.
Bind off 32[34:35:37] sts.
K36[38:40:42] sts at center on spare needle and leave rem 32[34:35:37] sts.
Bind off.

3 Sleeves
Using size 2 needles and m.c., cast on 50[52:54:56] sts. Work 2¾in in K2, P2 rib. Change to size 5 needles working in St st, inc 1 st at both ends of every 6th row until 88[90:92:94] sts are on the needles and work meas 19½[19½:20:20]in from cast-on edge. Bind off.

4 Neckband
Join right shoulder seam. Using size 2 needles and m.c., pick up and K27[29:31:33] sts down left side front. K across 10 sts at center front, pick up and K26[29:31:33] sts up right side of neck. K across 36[38:40:42] sts on center back neck. (100[106:112:118] sts.) Work in K2, P2 rib for 1in. Bind off in rib.

5 To finish
Using backstitch and m.c., stitch sleeves to body. Join side seams of body and sleeves. Join neckband.

Cable Sweater And Pullover

This pullover and sweater has been worked in one of the easiest cable patterns. It has been designed with or without sleeves, following the same set of instructions.

BEFORE YOU BEGIN

Work the stitch immediately in front and after the cable panels tightly. If it is worked loosely, it produces a long uneven stitch which will spoil the look of the fabric. Keep a careful count of all the rows.

Sizes

Chest/bust   30[32:34:36]in
Length   20[21:21¾:22½]in
Sleeve seam   15¾[16:16½:17]in

Note: Instructions for the larger sizes are in brackets [ ]; where one set of figures is given it applies to all sizes.

Gauge

30sts and 32 rows to 4in over patt on size 5 needles.

Choosing your yarn

Recommended yarn

Knit a sample square and check your gauge with that given for the pattern.

Alternative yarns

Check the thickness of alternative yarns against these samples.

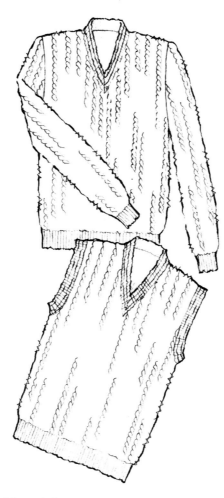

Materials

For the sweater
☐ 14[14:16:16]oz of Pingouin Pingofrance in main color (m.c.)
☐ 2oz of Pingofrance in contrast color (a)
For the pullover
☐ 9[9:11:11]oz of Pingouin Pingofrance in main color (m.c.)
☐ 2oz of Pingofrance in contrast color (a)
☐ 1 pair each sizes 2 and 5 needles
☐ Cable needle

Instructions for sweater

1 Back

* Using size 2 needles and m.c., cast on 93[99:105:111] sts.

1st row: K1, * P1, K1, rep from * to end.
2nd row: P1, * K1, P1, rep from * to end.
Rep the last 2 rows for 2in, ending with 1st row.
Inc row: (Rib 3, M1) 9[9:10:11] times, (rib 4, M1) 9[11:11:11] times, (rib 3, M1) 9[9:10:11] times, rib to end. (120[128:136:144] sts.)
Change to size 5 needles and work patt as folls:
1st row: P6[2:6:2], * K4, P4, rep from * to last 2[6:2:6] sts, K0[4:0:4], P2.
2nd row: K6[2:6:2], * P4, K4, rep from * to last 2[6:2:6] sts, P0[4:0:4].
3rd row: Work as 1st row.
4th row: Work as 2nd row.
5th row: P6[2:6:2], C4F (slip the next 2 sts onto a cable needle and hold at the front of the work, K2, then K2 from cable needle), P4, rep from * to last 2[6:2:6] sts, C4F 0[1:0:1] time, P2.
6th row: Work as 2nd row.
These 6 rows form the patt.
Cont in patt until work meas 12½[13:13½:13¾]in, ending with a WS row.
Shape armholes
Bind off 7[6:6:7] sts at the beg of next 2 rows. *
Dec 1 st at each end of next and every foll row 5[7:7:9] times in all.
Dec 1 st at each end of every alt row until 92[96:100:102] sts rem.
Work even on these sts until back meas 6¾[7:7½:7¾]in from beg of armhole shaping, ending with a WS row.
Shape shoulders
Bind off 9[8:9:9] sts at the beg of next 2 rows. Bind off 8[9:9:9] sts at beg of next 4 rows. Leave rem 42[44:46:48] sts on a spare needle.

2 Front

Work as for back from * to *.
Shape neck
Next row: K2 tog, patt 50[54:58:61], K2 tog, turn, leave rem sts on a spare needle. Cont on these 52[56:60:63] sts for first side.
Next row: Patt to last 2 sts, P2 tog.
Dec 1 st at neck on next and every

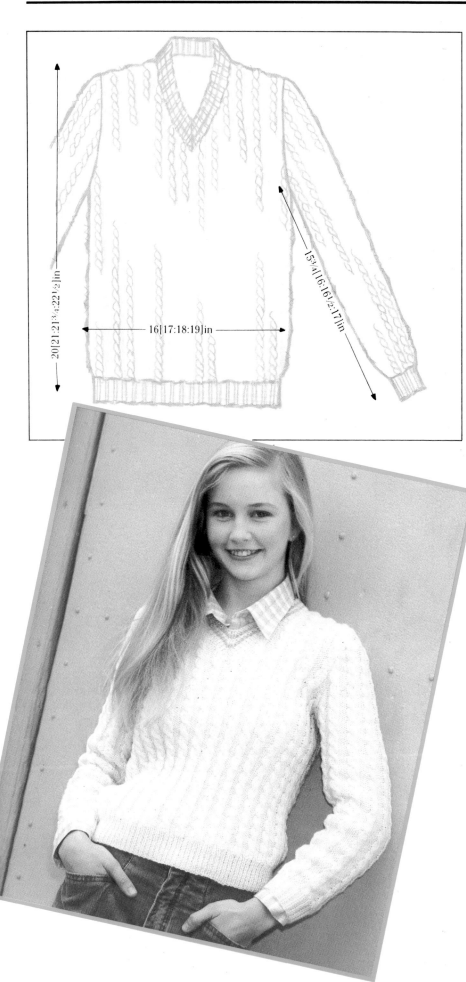

foll alt row, at the same time dec 1 st at armhole edge on every row 5[7:7:9] times in all, then 1 st on every alt row until 40[41:41:41] sts rem. Keeping armhole edge even dec 1 st at front slope on every alt row as before until 25[26:27:27] sts rem.

Work a few rows even until front matches back to shoulder shaping ending with a WS row.

Shape shoulder
Bind off 9[8:9:9] sts at beg of next row.
Work 1 row.
Bind off 8[9:9:9] sts at beg of next and foll alt row.

Shape second side of neck
With RS facing rejoin yarn to rem sts, sl next st on to safety pin for the center, K2 tog and complete to match first side reversing all the shapings.

3 Sleeves
Using size 2 needles and m.c., cast on 35[37:39:41] sts, work in rib as for back.
Inc row: Rib 1, (rib 1, M1) 7[6:7:6] times, (rib 2, M1) 9[11:11:13] times (rib 1, M1) 7[6:7:6] times, rib to end. (58[60:64:66] sts.)
Change to size 5 needles and work patt as folls:
1st row: (RS) P3[4:2:3], * K4, P4, rep from * to last 7[0:6:7] sts, K4[0:4:4], P3[0:2:3].
2nd row: K3[4:2:3], * P4, K4, rep from * to last 7[0:6:7] sts. P4[0:4:4], K3[0:2:3].
3rd row: Work as 1st row.
4th row: Work as 2nd row.
5th row: P3[3:2:3], C4F, P4, rep from * to last 7[0:6:1] sts, C4F 1[0:1:1] time, P3[0:2:2].
6th row: Work as 2nd row.
These 6 rows form the patt.
Cont in patt at the same time inc 1 st at each end of every 8th[7th:8th:8th] row until there are 80[88:88:92] sts on the needles.
Work even in patt until sleeve meas approx 15¾[16:16½:17]in ending with a WS row.

Shape cap
Bind off 6[6:6:7] sts at beg of next 2 rows.

1st and 4th sizes only
Dec 1 st at each end of next and foll 4th row 1[2] times, ending with a WS row.

All sizes
Dec 1 st at each end of next and every foll alt row until 36[40:36:40] sts rem.
Dec 1 st at each end of every row until 18 sts rem.
Bind off.

4 Neckband

Join right shoulder. With RS facing and size 2 needles pick up and K42[44:46:50] sts down left side of neck, K center st, mark this stitch with a colored thread, pick up and K42[44:46:50] sts up right side of neck, K across back neck sts as folls: (K2, K2 tog) 4[4:3:2] times, (K3, K2 tog) 2[3:4:6] times, (K2, K2 tog) 4[3:3:2] times, K0[1:2:2]. (117[123:129:139] sts.)

1st row: (WS) Rib to within 2 sts of the marked st, P2 tog, P1, P2 tog tbl, rib to end.

2nd row: Rib to within 2 sts of the marked thread st, P2 tog tbl, K1, P2 tog, K1 rib to end.

3rd row: Work as 1st row.

4th row: Using a, K to within 2 sts of the marked st, K2 tog tbl, K1, K2 tog, K to end.

5th row: Using a, work as 1st row.

6th row: Using m.c, work as 4th row.

7th row: Using m.c, work as 1st row.

8th row: Using a, work as 4th row.

9th row: Using a, work as 1st row.

10th row: Using m.c, work as 4th row.

11th row: Using m.c, work as 1st row.

12th row: Using m.c, bind off evenly in rib, dec 1 st each side of marked st as before.

5 To finish

Do not press.
Join left shoulder and neckband seam.
Join side seam and sleeve seams.
Insert sleeves.

Instructions for pullover

1 Front and back

Work as for sweater, using the same neckband.

2 Armbands

Join remaining shoulder and neckband seam.
With RS facing, using size 2 needles and m.c, pick up and K81[87:91:97] sts around edge of armhole.
Work 3 rows in K1, P1 rib.

Next row: Change to a, K to end.

Next row: Using a, rib to end.

Next row: Using m.c, K to end.

Next row: Using m.c, rib to end.

Next row: Using a, K to end.

Next row: Using a, rib to end.

Next row: Using m.c, K to end.

Next row: Using m.c, rib to end.

3 To finish

Do not press. Join side and armband seams.

Classic Country Cardigan

Make this super-soft and cuddly country cardigan with high-fashion ruffles that combines style with comfort. It is really easy to make – a deceptively simple design – because you make the ruffles separately and just sew them into the sleeve seam. Wear it by day or by night – a few accessories are all you need to transform your look.

BEFORE YOU BEGIN
It is preferable to use a yarn with some wool content when making a style with ruffles, as the finished knitting has more bounce; when you press the ruffle it will retain its shape.

Sizes
Bust   32[34:36:38]in
Length   22[22½:22¾:23½]in
Sleeve seam   15¼[16:16½:17]in

Choosing your yarn

Recommended yarn
Knit a sample square and check your gauge with that given for the pattern.

Alternative yarns

Check the thickness of alternative yarns against these samples.

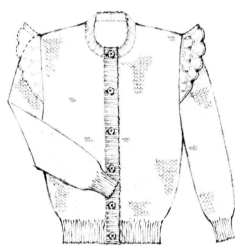

Note: Instructions for larger sizes are in brackets [ ]; where one set of figures is given, it applies to all sizes.

Gauge
22 sts and 28 rows to 4in over St st on size 6 needles.

Materials
☐ 13[13:14:14]oz of knitting worsted weight yarn for style without ruffle
☐ 13[13:14:14]oz of knitting worsted weight yarn for style with ruffle
☐ 1 pair each sizes 3 and 6 needles
☐ 6 buttons

INSTRUCTIONS
1 Back
Using size 3 needles, cast on 78[82:84:88] sts and work 2¾in in K1, P1 rib.
Inc row: Rib 1[3:3:1], * inc into next st, rib 4[4:3:3]; rep from * to last 2[4:5:3] sts, inc into next st, rib 1[3:4:2]. (94[98:104:110] sts.)
Change to size 6 needles and cont working even in St st until work meas 14½in from beg.
Shape armhole
Bind off 4[5:6:7] sts at beg of next 2 rows. Dec 1 st at each end of next and 4 foll rows. Dec 1 st at each end of next and foll alt rows until there are

72[74:78:80] sts. Work even until work meas 21[21½:22:22½]in from beg.
Shape shoulders
Bind off 5 sts at the beg of the next 2 rows. Bind off 5[5:6:6] sts at beg of the next 2 rows. Bind off 6 sts at beg of the next 4 rows. Leave rem 28[30:32:34] sts on a stitch holder.

2 Left front
Using size 3 needles, cast on 37[38:39:42] sts and work 2¾in in K1, P1 rib.
Inc row: Rib 2[1:3:2], * inc into next st, rib 4[4:3:3]; rep from * to last 5[2:4:4] sts, inc into next st, rib 4[1:3:3]. (44[46:48:52] sts.)
Change to size 6 needles and cont working even in St st until work meas 14½in from beg.
Shape armhole
Bind off 4[5:6:7] sts at beg of next row. Work 1 row. Dec 1 st at armhole edge on next and foll alt rows until 33[34:36:37] sts rem.
Cont working even in St st until work meas 19[19¼:20:20½]in from beg, ending with a K row.
Shape neck
Bind off 3[4:4:5] sts at beg of next row. Work 1 row. Bind off 3 sts at beg of next row. Then dec 1 st at neck edge on next and every alt row until there are 22[22:23:23] sts. Cont on these sts until work meas same as back to shoulder shaping.
Shape shoulders
With RS of work facing, bind off 5 sts at beg of next row. Work 1 row. Bind off 5[5:6:6] sts at beg of next row, bind off 6 sts at beg of the 2 foll alt rows.

3 Right front
Work as for the left front but reversing all shapings.

4 Sleeves
Using size 3 needles, cast on 42[42:44:46] sts and work 3¼in in K1, P1 rib.
Inc row: Rib 2[2:3:4], * inc into the next st, rib 3, rep from * to last 4[4:5:6] sts, inc into next st, rib

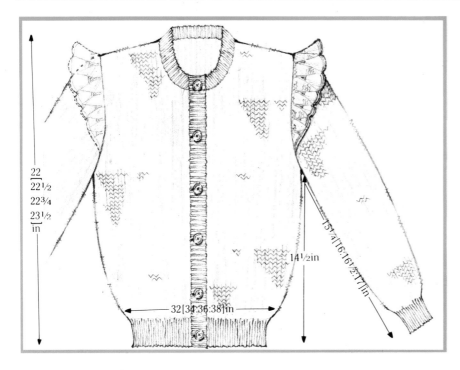

22
22½
22¾
23½
in

32[34:36:38]in

14½in

15¾[16:16½:17]in

4th row: * P4, K1; rep from * to last 5 sts, turn.

5th row: * K4, P1; rep from * to last 5 sts, turn.

6th row: * P4, 3 from 1 (pick up and K the bar before the next st. K1, pick up and K the bar before the next st thus making 3 st from 1); rep from * to last 10 sts, turn.

7th row: * K4, P3; rep from * to last 12 sts, turn.

8th row: * P4, inc into next st, K1 inc into next st; rep from * to last 17 sts, turn.

9th row: * K4, P5; rep from * to last 21 sts, turn.

10th row: * P4, inc into next st, K3, inc into next st; rep from * to last 26 sts, turn.

11th row: * K4, P7; rep from * to last 32 sts, turn.

12th row: * P4, inc into next st, K5, inc into next st; rep from * to last 37 sts, turn.

13th row: * K4, P9; rep from * to last 45 sts, turn.

14th row: * P4, inc into next st, K7, inc into next st; rep from * to last 50 sts *then* K all K sts and P all P sts to end.

15th row: K.

16th row: K. Bind off.

9 To finish

Press with a warm iron over a damp cloth. Sew side seams and sleeve seams. Pin ruffle around the armhole edge and sew into the armhole along with the sleeve. Sew on buttons.

3[3:4:5]. (52[52:54:56] sts.) Change to size 6 needles and work 8 rows in St st. Inc 1 st at each end of the next and every foll 7th[7th:6th:6th] row until 72[74:78:80] sts. Cont even in St st until work meas 15¼[16:16½:17]in from beg.

Shape cap

Bind off 4[5:6:7] sts at the beg of next 2 rows. Dec 1 st at each end of the next and every foll alt row 7[9:11:13] times. Dec 1 st at each end of next and every foll row until there are 14[14:16:16] sts. Bind off.

5 Neckband

Join shoulder seams. With RS of work facing using size 3 needles, pick up and K28 sts evenly from the right front neck edge, K across the 28[30:32:34] sts from the stitch holder and pick up and K 28 sts from left front edge. (84[86:88:90] sts.) Work 1¼in in K1, P1 rib. Bind off.

6 Left front band

With size 3 needles and RS of left front facing, pick up and K 121[123:126:128] sts evenly from along front edge. Work 13 rows in K1, P1 rib. Bind off.

7 Right front band

Work as for left band but working buttonholes on rows 7 and 8 of rib as folls:

7th row: Rib 5[6:5:6], * bind off 2 sts, rib 20[20:21:21]; rep from * ending last rep rib 4[5:4:5].

8th row: Rib 4[5:4:5], * cast on 2 sts,

rib 20[20:21:21]; rep from * ending 1st rep rib 5[6:5:6].

8 Ruffle

For ruffle, cast on 79 sts for all sizes using size 6 needles.

1st and 3rd rows: K.

2nd row: P.

Make sure you always count the number of stitches, every time when turning, to make the ruffle.

Checked Evening Jacket

Work this jacket in mohair – white and black with a gold thread – for a stunning evening look. For country wear choose tan and gold, and red and white for a summery feel.

BEFORE YOU BEGIN

To work this looped pattern, a stitch is slipped over four rows; take care not to twist the loops. Carry the contrast color loosely up the side of the work when knitting the pattern.

Sizes

Bust 32[34:36:38]in
Length 23¼[23½:24:24½]in
Sleeve seam 17¼in

Note: Instructions for the larger sizes are in brackets [ ]; where one set of figures is given it applies to all sizes.

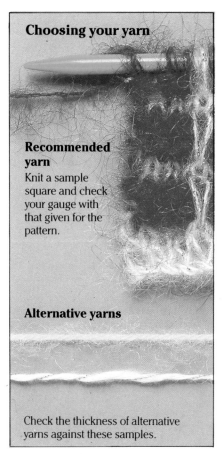

Choosing your yarn

Recommended yarn

Knit a sample square and check your gauge with that given for the pattern.

Alternative yarns

Check the thickness of alternative yarns against these samples.

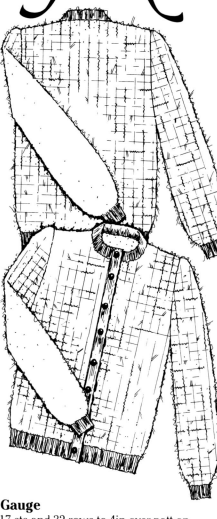

Gauge

17 sts and 32 rows to 4in over patt on size 9 needles.

Materials

☐ Approx 10[11:12:13]oz of medium weight mohair yarn in main color (m.c.)
☐ Approx 5[6:6:7]oz in contrast color (a)
☐ 1 pair each sizes 7 and 9 needles
☐ 8 buttons

INSTRUCTIONS

1 Back

Using size 7 needles and m.c., cast on 65[69:73:77] sts.
1st row: K1, * P1, K1, rep from * to end.

2nd row: P1, * K1, P1, rep from * to end.
Rep the last 2 rows for 2¼in, ending with WS.
Inc row: Rib 5[3:4:2], M1 (rib 6[7:7:8], M1) 9 times, rib 6[3:5:3]. (75[79:83:87] sts.)
Change to size 9 needles and work in patt as folls:
1st row: With a, K.
2nd row: With a, P.
3rd row: With m.c., K3, * sl 1 purlwise [sl 1 pw], K3, rep from * to end.
4th row: With m.c., K3, * yarn to front of work (yf), sl 1 purlwise (sl 1 pw), yarn to back of work (ybk) and K3, rep from * to end.
5th row: As 3rd row.
6th row: As 4th row.
Cont in patt as set until back meas approx 15in, ending with 6th row of patt (RS facing for next row).

Shape armholes

Bind off 3 sts at beg of next 2 rows.
Dec 1 st at each end of every row 5 times. Dec 1 st at each end of every alt row until 53[55:57:59] sts rem.
Work even in patt until armhole meas 8¼[8½:9:9½]in, ending with a WS row.

Shape shoulders

Bind off 5 sts at beg of next 4 rows, then 5[6:6:6] sts at beg of foll 2 rows.
Leave rem 23[23:25:27] sts on a spare needle.

2 Left front

**Using size 7 needles and m.c. cast on 33[35:37:39] sts, work in rib as back.
Inc row: Rib 4, M1, (rib 8[9:9:10] M1) 3 times, rib to end. (37[39:41:43] sts.)
Change to size 9 needles and work in patt as folls:
1st row: With c, K.
2nd row: With c, P.**
3rd row: With m.c., * K3, sl 1 pw, rep from * to last 1[3:1:3] sts, K to end.
4th row: With m.c., K1[3:1:3], yf, sl 1 pw, ybk and K3, rep from * to end.
5th row: As 3rd row.
6th row: As 4th row.
Cont in patt until front matches back

69

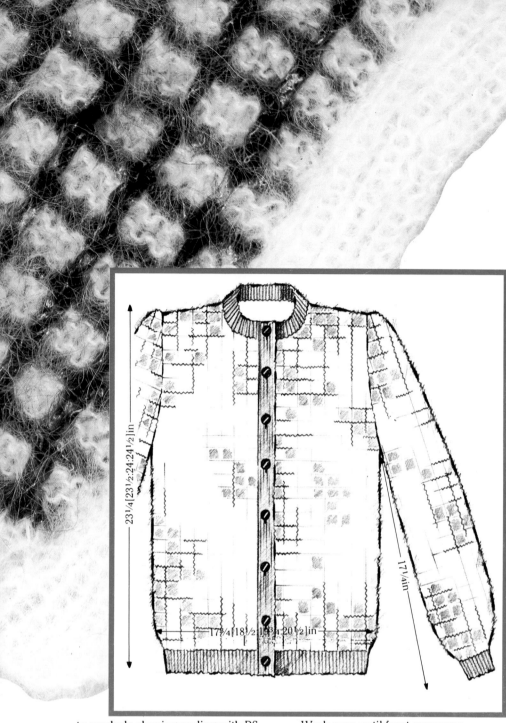

to armhole shaping ending with RS facing for next row.
Shape armhole
Bind off 3 sts at beg of next row.
Work 1 row.
Dec 1 st at armhole edge on every row 5 times.
Dec 1 st at armhole edge on every foll alt row until 26[27:28:29] sts rem.
Work even in patt until 20 rows less than back have been worked to start of shoulder shaping.
Shape neck
Next row: Patt 20[21:21:21], work 2 tog, turn and leave rem 4[4:5:6] sts on a safety pin.
Dec 1 st at neck edge on next 2 rows then 1 st on every foll alt row until 15[16:16:16] sts rem.

Work even until front measures same as back to start of shoulder shaping, ending with a WS row.
Shape shoulder
Bind off 5 sts at beg of next and foll alt row.
Work 1 row.
Bind off rem sts.

3 Right front
Work as for left front from ** to **.
3rd row: With m.c., K1[3:1:3] sts, * sl 1 pw, K3, rep from * to end.
4th row: * K3, wyif, sl 1 pw, wyib, rep from * to last 1[3:1:3] sts, K to end.
5th row: As 3rd row.
6th row: As 4th row.
Complete to match left front reversing shapings.

4 Sleeves
Using size 7 needles and m.c. cast on 29[29:31:33] sts and work in rib as for back for 2¼in.
Inc row: (Rib 1, M1) 9[12:13:11] times, (rib 2, M1) 4[2:2:4] times, (rib 1, M1) 9[12:13:11] times, rib to end. (51[55:59:59] sts.)
Change to size 9 needles and work in patt as for back until sleeve meas approx 17¼in, ending with same patt row as on back (RS facing for next row).
Shape cap
Bind off 3 sts at beg of next 2 rows.
Dec 1 st at each end of next and every foll 4th row until 19[21:27:23] sts rem. Work 3 rows in patt.
2nd, 3rd and 4th sizes
Dec 1 st at each end of next and foll 0[3:1] alt rows. Work 1 row.
All sizes
Bind off.

5 Neckband
Join shoulders using size 7 needles and m.c., RS facing, K4[4:5:6] sts from right front, pick up and K18 sts up right side of neck, K across 23[23:25:27] sts across back neck, pick up and K18 sts down left side of neck, K4[4:5:6] sts from left front. Work in P1, K1 rib for 1¼in. Bind off evenly in rib.

6 Buttonband
Using size 7 needles and m.c., cast on 9 sts and work as folls:
1st row: K2, (P1,K1) to last st, K1.
2nd row: P2, (K1, P1) to last st, P1.
Rep these 2 rows until band when slightly stretched fits up left front to top of neck band.
Sew in position and bind off in rib.

7 Buttonhole band
Using size 7 needles and m.c. cast on 9 sts, work as folls:
1st row: K2, (P1, K1) to last st, K1.
2nd row: P2 (K1, P1) to last st, P1.
Buttonhole row: Rib 3, bind off 3 sts, rib to end.
Next row: Rib, casting on 3 sts over the bound off sts, rib to end. Cont as for buttonband working a further 8 buttonholes, the last being placed at the center of neckband and the others evenly spaced in between.

8 To finish
Join side and sleeve seams. Sew in sleeves gathering fullness into top. Sew on buttons to correspond with buttonholes.

Aran Cardigan

Wear this Aran cardigan and wrap up warmly for winter. For milder spring days it can be worn as a jacket, teamed with casual wear.

BEFORE YOU BEGIN
The instructions are written in pattern panels. Write down the number of rows for every pattern panel and cross it off once completed. Return to the first row of the panel on the following row.

Sizes
Bust	34-36[36-38]in
Length	23½[24¾]in
Sleeve seam	14½[15¾]in

Note: Instructions for the larger sizes are in brackets [ ]; where there is one set of figures it applies to both sizes.

Gauge
18 sts and 24 rows to 4in over St st on size 7 needles.

Choosing your yarn

Recommended yarn
Knit a sample square and check your gauge with that given for the pattern.

Alternative yarns
Check the thickness of alternative yarns against these samples.

Materials
- Approx 29[32]oz of Aran weight yarn
- 1 pair each sizes 5 and 7 needles
- Cable needle
- 8[9] buttons

Panel patt A
1st and every alt rows: (WS) (K2, yarn to front of work between 2 needles – called yf, sl 1, yarn to back of work between 2 needles – called ybk) twice, K2.
2nd row: P2, K1, yo, K2 tog tbl, K1, P2.
4th row: P2, K1, K2 tog, yo, K1, P2.
6th row: As 2nd row.
8th row: As 4th row.
10th row: As 2nd row.
12th row: P2, K4, P2.
14th row: P2, sl next 3 sts onto a cable needle and leave at back of work, K1, sl 2nd and 3rd sts from cable needle to left-hand needle and K2, K1 from cable needle, P2.
16th row: P2, K1, K2 tog, yo, K1, P2.
18th row: P2, K1, yo, K2 tog tbl, K1, P2.
20th row: As 16th row.
22nd row: As 18th row.
24th row: As 16th row.
26th row: As 12th row.
28th row: P2, sl next 3 sts onto a cable needle and leave at the front of work, K1, then sl 2nd and 3rd sts from

cable needle back to left-hand needle and K2, K1 from cable needle, P2. These 28 rows form the patt.

Panel patt B
1st row: (WS) P5, sl 1, P4, sl 1, P2.
2nd row: K2, sl 1f (sl next st onto a cable needle and leave at front of work, K1, K st from cable needle) K2, sl 1b (sl next st onto a cable needle and leave at back of work, K1, K st from cable needle), K5.
3rd row: P6, sl 1, P2, sl 1, P3.
4th row: K3, sl 1f, sl 1b, K6.
5th row: P7, sl 2, P4.
6th row: K4, sl 1f, K4, MB (make bobble, by K1, yo twice into next st, K1, turn, K5, turn, P5, turn, K1, sl 1, K2 tog, psso, K1, turn, P3 tog) K2.
7th row: P2, sl 1, P4, sl 1, P5.
8th row: K5, sl 1f, K2, sl 1b, K2.
9th row: P3, sl 1, P2, sl 1, P6.
10th row: K6, sl 1f, sl 1b, K3.
11th row: P4, sl 2, P7.
12th row: K2, MB, K4, sl 1b, K4.
These 12 rows form the patt.

Panel patt C
1st row: (WS) K1, (yf, sl 1, ybk, K3) 4 times, yf, sl 1, ybk, K1.
2nd row: P4, BPC (back purl cross, sl next st onto a cable needle and hold at back of work, K next stitch, P st from cable needle), P3, K1, P3, FPC (front purl cross, slip next st on to a cable needle and hold at front, P next st, K st from cable needle), P4.
3rd row: (K4, yf, sl 1, ybk) 3 times, K4.
4th row: P3, BPC, P2, BPC, K1, FPC, P2, FPC, P3.
5th row: (K3, yf, sl 1, ybk) twice, K1, yf, sl 1, ybk, K1 (yf, sl 1, ybk, K3) twice.
6th row: (P2, BPC) twice, P1, K1, P1, (FPC, P2) twice.
7th row: K2, yf, sl 1, ybk, K3, (yf, sl 1, ybk, K2) twice, yf, sl 1, ybk, K3, yf, sl 1, ybk, K2.
8th row: P1, (BPC, P2) twice, K1, (P2, FPC) twice, P1.
These 8 rows form patt.

INSTRUCTIONS
1 Back
Using size 5 needles, cast on 92[104] sts. Work in K1, P1 rib for 2¾in.

1st size: (Rib 4, M1) twice, (rib 6, M1) 12 times, (rib 4, M1) twice, rib 4.

2nd row: (Rib 5, M1) 20 times, rib 4. (108[124] sts.) Change to size 7 needles, place patt as folls:

1st row: (WS) Work patt A 1st row, once [twice], patt B 1st row, (patt A 1st row, P1, patt C 1st row, P1) twice, patt A 1st row, patt B 1st row, (patt A as 1st row) once [twice].

2nd row: Patt A 2nd row, once (twice), patt B 2nd row, (patt A 2nd row, K1B – knit one below by knitting into the st below the next st on the

left-hand needle – patt C 2nd row, K1B) twice, patt A as 2nd row, patt B 2nd row, (patt A 2nd row) once (twice). Cont in patt as set until meas 14¼in, ending with a WS row.

Shape armholes
Bind off 4 sts at beg of next 2 rows. Dec 1 st at each end of every foll row until 84[96] sts rem, then at each end

72

of every alt row until 68[80] sts rem.
Work even until back meas
23½[24¾]in, ending with a WS row.
Shape shoulders
Bind off 7 sts at beg of next 4 rows,
then bind off 6[10] sts at beg foll 2
rows. Leave rem 28[32] sts on a spare
needle.

2 Left front
Using size 5 needles, cast on 38[46]
sts. Work in K1, P1, rib for 2¾in.
Next row: Rib 1[5], M1, (rib 3, M1) 12
times, rib to end, 51[59] sts. Change to
size 7 needles, place patt as folls:
1st row: (WS) K1, P1, patt C 1st
row, P1, patt A 1st row, patt B 1st row,
(patt A 1st row) once [twice].
2nd row: (panel patt A 2nd row)
once [twice], patt B 2nd row, patt A
2nd row, K1B, patt C 2nd row, K1B,
P1. Cont in patt as set until front
matches back to armhole shapings,
ending with a WS row.
Shape armhole
Bind off 4 sts at beg of next row. Work
1 row. Dec 1 st at armhole edge
on every foll row until 39[45] sts rem,
then at armhole edge of every alt row
until 31[37] sts rem. Work even until
12[14] rows less than back have been
worked to start of shoulder shaping,
ending with a WS row.
Shape neck
Next row: Patt to last 2 sts, K2 tog.
Keeping armhole edge even, dec
1st at neck edge on every foll alt row
until 20[24] sts rem, ending with a WS
row.
Shape shoulder
Bind off 7 sts at beg of next and foll alt
row. Work 1 row.
Bind off rem 6[10] sts.

3 Right front
Work as for left front reversing
shapings and placing the pattern
panels in reverse order to left front.

4 Sleeves
Using size 5 needles, cast on 44[48]
sts, work in K1, P1 rib for 2¼in.
Next row: Rib 3[1], M1, rib 3[2], M1,
(rib 2[3], M1) 16 [14] times, rib 3[2], M1,
rib to end (63[65] sts). Change to
size 7 needles, place patt as folls:
1st row: (WS) K0[1], patt B 1st [7th]
row, patt A 17th [11th] row, P1, patt C
5th [7th] row, P1, patt A 17th [11th]
row, patt B 1st [7th] row, K0[1].
2nd row: P0[1], patt B 2nd [8th] row,
patt A 18th [12th] row, K1B, patt C
6th [8th] row, K1B, patt A 18th [11th]
row, patt B 2nd [8th] row, P0[1].

Cont in patt as set at the same time
shape sides by inc 1 st at each end of
the 8th and every foll 10th [11th] row,
until there are 70[95] sts, taking inc
sts into P then patt A as appropriate.
Work even in patt until sleeve meas
approx 17[18]in, ending with same
panel patt rows as on back to start of
armhole shaping, ending with a WS
row.
Shape cap
Bind off 4 sts at beg of next 2 rows.
Dec 1 st at each end of every foll alt
row until 55[71] sts rem. Then at each
end of every row until 11 sts rem.
Bind off.

5 Buttonband
Using size 5 needles, cast on 9 sts
work as folls:
1st row: (RS) K2, (P1, K1) 3 times, K1.
2nd row: (K1, P1) 4 times, K1.
Rep these 2 rows until strip when
slightly stretched fits up left front to
start of neck shaping, ending with a
2nd row.
Leave sts on a safety pin and sew
border in position.

6 Buttonhole band
Using size 5 needles, cast on 9 sts
work as folls:
1st row: (RS) K2, (P1, K1) 3 times, K1.

2nd row: (K1, P1) 4 times, K1.
Rep these 2 rows once.
Buttonhole row: Rib 3, bind off 3, rib
to end.
Next row: Rib casting on 3 sts over
the bound off sts, rib to end. Cont as
button band and work a further 7[8]
buttonholes, allowing for the last being
placed at the center of neck band; leave
sts on a safety pin.

7 Neckband
Join shoulder seams with RS facing
and using size 5 needles, rib 9 sts
across front band, pick up and K22[25]
sts up right side of neck, K across 28[32]
sts back neck, dec 1 st at center, pick up
and K22[25] sts down left side of neck,
rib across front band 89[99] sts. Work
3[4] rows in rib, make a buttonhole as
before over the next row, work 7[11]
rows in rib. Work a buttonhole over
the next row, work 4[5] rows. Bind off
loosely in rib.

8 To finish
Do not press. Join side and sleeve
seam, set in sleeves. Join on button
band. Fold neckband in half onto
wrong side and sew hem loosely in
position all around. Oversew loosely
around buttonhole. Sew on buttons to
correspond with buttonholes.

Fringed Jacket

Mix and match this attractive bobbled jacket with your wardrobe. It will go well with casual sporty wear, or brighten up your more classic everyday wear.

BEFORE YOU BEGIN
When working in the bobble pattern, carry the contrast yarns very loosely across the back of the work. Fasten off colors securely at each end of the row.

Sizes
Bust   32[34:36:38]in
Length   25½[26:26¼:26¾]in
Sleeve seam 17¼in

Note: Instructions for larger sizes are given in square brackets [ ], where there is one only set of figures, it applies to all sizes.

Gauge
22 sts and 30 rows to 4in over St st on size 6 needles.

Choosing your yarn

Recommended yarn
Knit a sample square and check your gauge with that given for the pattern.

Alternative yarns
Check the thickness of alternative yarns against these samples.

Materials
☐ Approx 18[20:21:23]oz of knitting worsted weight yarn in main color (m.c.)
☐ Approx 1oz in 1st contrast (a)
☐ Approx 1oz in 2nd contrast (b)
☐ Approx 1oz in 3rd contrast (c)
☐ 1 pair each sizes 3 and 6 needles
☐ 9 buttons
☐ 2 shoulder pads
☐ Medium-sized crochet hook

INSTRUCTIONS
1 Back
Using size 3 needles and m.c., cast on 91[97:101:107] sts and work in rib as folls:

1st row: (RS) K1, * P1, K1, rep from * to end.
2nd row: P1, * K1, P1, rep from * to end.
Rep last 2 rows for 2¼in, ending with a 1st row.
Inc row: Rib 8, (M1, rib 15[16:14:13]) 5[5:6:7] times, M1, rib to end. (97[103:108:115] sts.)
Change to size 6 needles, starting with a K row work even in St st until back meas 17in, ending with a P row.

Shape armholes
Bind off 5 sts at the beg of next 2 rows. Dec 1 st at each end of next and every foll row 3[5:5:7] times in all. Work 1 row.
Dec 1 st at each end of the next and every foll alt row until 77[77:82:87] sts rem. Work 1 row, ending with a WS row.

Yoke
1st row: K2, * P1, K1, P1, K2, rep from * to end.
2nd row: P2, * K1, P1, K1, P2, rep from * to end.
3rd row: K2, * P1, using a, MB (K1, P1, K1, P1, K1 into next st making 5 sts from 1, with the point of the left-hand needle, pass the 2nd, 3rd, 4th and 5th sts over 1st st), P1, K2, rep from * to end.
4th row: Work as 2nd row.
These 4 rows form patt rep, work in the foll color sequence: b, c, now rep a, b and c until armholes meas 8[8¼:8¾:9]in ending, with a WS row.

Shape back neck
Next row: Keeping patt correct, patt 34[33:37:39] sts, turn, leaving rem sts on a spare needle.
Next row: Bind off 4[4:5:5] sts, patt to end.
Next row: Patt to end.
Rep the last 2 rows once more then the first row again.
Bind off rem 22[21:22:24] sts.

Shape second side of back neck
With RS of work facing, rejoin yarn to rem sts, bind off the center 9[11:8:9] sts and work as for first side reversing all the shapings.

2 Pocket linings (make 2)
Using size 6 needles and m.c., cast on 23 sts, starting with a K row, work in St st for 4¾in, ending with a P row. Leave sts on a spare needle.

3 Left front
** Using size 3 needles and m.c., cast on 45[[47:51:53] sts, work in rib as for back.
Inc row: Rib 7, (M1, rib 15[11:18:13]) 2[3:2:3] times, M1, rib to end. (48[51:54:47] sts.)
Change to size 6 needles and patt**.

1st row: (RS) K12 [14:15:16], P1, K1, P1, (K2, P1, K1, P1) 4 times, K13 [14:16:18].
2nd row: K all K sts, P all P sts across the row.
3rd row: K12[14:15:16], P1, MB in a, P1, (K2, P1, MB in a, P1) 4 times, K13[14:16:18].
4th row: Work as 2nd row.
Cont in St st and patt as set, changing colors as on back until front meas approx 7in, ending with 4th row.
Place pocket
Next row: K12[14:15:16], sl next 23 sts on to a stitch holder, K across sts from first pocket linings, K to end. (48[51:54:57] sts.)
Cont in St st only until front matches back to start of armhole shaping, ending with a WS row.
Shape armhole
Bind off 5 sts at beg of next row.
Work 1 row.
Keeping front edge even dec 1 st at armhole edge on next and every foll row 3[5:5:7] times, then 1 st on every foll alt row until 38[38:41:43] sts rem.
Work 1 row, so ending with a WS row.
Yoke
1st row: * K2, P1, K1, P1, rep from * to last 3[3:1:3] sts, K2[2:1:2], P1[1:0:1].
2nd row: K all K sts and P all P sts across the row.
3rd row: * K2, P1, MB in a, P1, rep from * to last 3[3:1:3] sts, K2[2:1:2], P1[1:0:1].
4th row: Work as for 2nd row.
Cont in patt as set, changing colors until armhole meas 6[6¼:6¾:7]in, ending with a RS row.
Shape neck
Bind off 4[5:7:7] sts at the beg of next row.
Keeping armhole edge even dec 1 st at neck edge on the next and every foll row 10 times in all, then dec 1 st on every foll alt row until 22[21:22:24] sts rem.
Work a few rows even until front meas the same to shoulder as on back. Bind off.

4 Right front

Work as for left front ** to **.
1st row: (RS) K13[14:16:18], P1, K1, P1, (K2, P1, K1, P1) 4 times, K12[14:15:16].
Cont patt as set until front meas approx 7in, ending with a 4th row.
Place pocket
Next row: K13[14:16:18], sl next 23 sts on to a stitch holder, K across sts from second pocket lining, K to end. (48[51:54:57] sts.)

Cont as for left front reversing shapings until 38[38:41:43] sts rem.
Work 1 row, so ending with a WS row.
Yoke
1st row: P1[1:0:1], K2[2:1:2], * P1, K1, P1, K2, rep from * to end.
Cont in yoke patt as set, complete as for left front reversing all shapings.

5 Sleeves

Using size 3 needles and m.c., cast on 45[47:49:51] sts. Work in rib as for back until meas 2in, ending with a 1st row.
Inc row: Rib 5 (M1, rib 11[12:13:14]) 3 times, M1, rib to end. (49[51:53:55] sts.)
Change to size 6 needles. Starting with a K row work in St st, at the same time shape sides by inc 1 st at each end of every 7th row 8 times, then 1 st at each end of every foll 9th row until there are 73[74:77:79] sts. Work a few rows even until sleeve meas 17¼in, ending with a P row.
Shape cap
Bind off 5 sts at the beg of next 2 rows.
Dec 1 st at each end of next and every foll 6th row until 47[47:47:49] sts rem.
Work 3[1:2:0] rows straight.
Dec 1 st at each end of next and every foll row until 39 sts rem.
Bind off.

6 Pocket tops

Using size 3 needles and m.c., with RS of work facing, K across sts from pocket top as folls:
K4, (M1, K5) 3 times, M1, K4. (27 sts.)
1st row: P2, * K1, P1, rep from * to last st, P1.
2nd row: K2, * P1, K1, rep from * to last st, K1.
Rep last 2 rows until pocket top meas 1in, ending with a 1st row.
Bind off evenly in rib.

7 Buttonband

Using size 3 needles and m.c., cast on 13 sts. Work in rib as for pocket top, starting with a 2nd row. Work until band fits up right front when slightly stretched, ending with a 1st row.
Leave sts on a safety pin. Sew in position.

8 Buttonhole band

Work 4 rows of rib as for buttonband.
Next row: Rib 5, bind off 2 sts, rib to end.
Next row: Rib casting on 2 sts over those bound off.

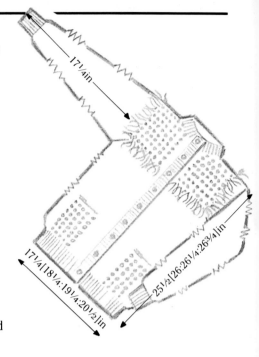

Work a further 8 buttonholes with approx 2¾[2¾:2½:2]in rib between each buttonhole. Sew in position.

9 Neckband

Using size 3 needles and m.c., and with RS of work facing, rib across sts from buttonhole band as folls:
K2, [P1, K1] 4 times, P1, K2 tog, K up 17[18:18:20] sts up right side of neck, 37[39:41:43] sts from back neck, K up 17[18:19:20] sts down left side of neck, rib across sts from button band as folls: K2 tog, (P1, K1) to last st, K1. (95[99:103:107] sts.)
Next row: P2, * K1, P1, rep from * to last st, P1.
Rib 2 rows.
Buttonhole row: Rib 5, bind off 2 sts, rib to end.
Next row: Cast on 2 sts over those bound off.
Work 16 rows in rib then rep buttonhole rows.
Work 2 rows in rib.
Bind off evenly in rib.

10 To finish

Fold neckband in half on to the WS and sew in position. Catch together at buttonhole. Join side and sleeve seams. Make pleat in top of sleeve. Sew in sleeves, placing pleat to top of shoulder. Sew in shoulder pads. Sew on buttons to match buttonholes. To make a fringe, cut 4in lengths of all three contrast colors. Using the crochet hook, make a fringe across the front and back yoke and over the shoulder seam. Trim to neaten.

Embroidered Twin Set

Wear this delicate twin-set with matching sweater and cardigan in a soft pastel yarn. Decorate the lace panels with embroidery.

BEFORE YOU BEGIN

Knit a small sample of the lace panel and practice the embroidery before working on the garments. Work French knots in cream between the two rows of eyelet holes. Using green, work three chain stitches into the first hole. Work three more chain stitches in maroon above the green stem.

Sizes

Sweater

Bust	32[34:36:38]in
Length	22in
Sleeve seam	5½in

Cardigan

Bust	32[34:36:38]in
Length	22¾in
Sleeve seam	16in

Choosing your yarn

Recommended yarn

Knit a sample square and check your gauge with that given for the pattern.

Alternative yarns

Check the thickness of alternative yarns against these samples.

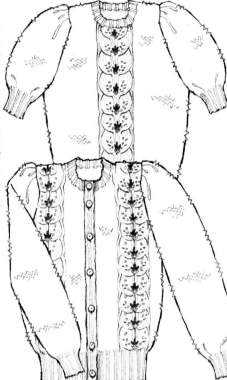

Note: Instructions for larger sizes are in brackets [ ]; where there is only one set of figures it applies to all sizes.

Gauge

22 sts and 30 rows to 4in over St st on size 6 needles.

Materials

☐ Approx 13[13:14:14] of knitting worsted weight yarn for sweater
☐ Approx 16[16:18:18]oz for cardigan
☐ Small amounts of green, maroon and cream for embroidery
☐ 1 pair each size 3 and 6 needles
☐ 6 buttons

Instructions for sweater

1 Back

* Using size 3 needles, cast on 86 [90:94:98] sts.

1st row: * K2, P2, rep from * to last 2 sts, K2.

2nd row: * P2, K2, rep from * to last 2 sts, P2.

Rep last 2 rows for 4in, ending with a 1st row.

Inc row: Rib 3[5:7:4], [M1, rib 8[8:8:9] 10 times, M1, rib to end. (97[101:105:109] sts.) *

Change to size 6 needles, starting with 1 K row work in St st until work meas 14½in from beg, ending with a P row.

Shape armholes

Bind off 10 sts at beg of next 2 rows. Bind off 3 sts at beg of next 2 rows. Bind off 2 sts at beg of next 2 rows. Dec 1 st at each end of 2nd and every foll 4th row until there are 57[61:65:69] sts on the needles. ** Cont in St st until work meas 20½in, ending with a WS row.

Shape shoulders

Bind off 5 sts at beg of next 2[4:6:4] rows. Bind off 4[4:0:6] sts at beg of next 2 rows.

Leave rem 31[33:35:37] sts on spare needle.

2 Front

Work as for back from * to *.
Change to size 6 needles, work in patt as folls:

1st row: K35[37:39:41], P2, K8, K2 tog, yo, K1, P1, K1, yo, ssk, K8, P2, K35[37:39:41].

2nd row: P35[37:39:41], K2, P7, P2 tog tbl, P2, yo, K1, yo, P2, P2 tog, P7, K2, P35[37:39:41].

3rd row: K35[37:39:41], P2, K6, K2 tog, K1, yo, K2, P1, K2, yo, K1, ssk, K6, P2, K35[37:39:41].

4th row: P35[37:39:41], K2, P5, P2 tog tbl, P3, yo, P1, K1, P1, yo, P3, P2 tog, P5, K2, P35[37:39:41].

5th row: K35[37:39:41], P2, K4, K2 tog, K2, yo, K3, P1, K3, yo, K2, ssk, K4, P2, K35[37:39:41].

6th row: P35[37:39:41], K2, P3, P2 tog tbl, P4, yo, P2, K1, P2, yo, P4, P2 tog, P3, K2, P35[37:39:41].

7th row: K35[37:39:41], P2, K2, K2 tog, K3, yo, K4, P1, K4, yo, K3, ssk, K2, P2, K35[37:39:41].

8th row: P35[37:39:41], K2, P1, P2 tog, tbl, P5, yo, P3, K1, P3, yo, P5,

P2 tog, P1, K2 P35[37:39:41].
9th row: K35[37:39:41] P2, K2 tog, K4, yo, K5, P1, K5, yo, K4, ssk, P2, K35[37:39:41].
10th row: P35[37:39:41], K2, P11, K1, P11, K2, P35[37:39:41].
11th row: K35[37:39:41], P2, K11, P1, K11, P2, K35[37:39:41].
12th row: As 10th row.
Rep rows 1–12 inclusive until work meas 14½in from beg, ending with a WS row. Keeping patt correct, foll armhole shaping as for back until **. Cont even, keeping patt correct until work meas 18½in from the beg, ending with a WS row.

Shape neck
Patt 22 sts and turn leaving rem sts on a square needle.

Next row: Work 2 tog, work to end of row. Cont to dec 1 st at neck edge 3 times more then dec 1 st on every alt row until 16 sts rem. Work even until front meas the same as back to shoulder shaping, ending with a WS row.

Shape shoulder
Bind off 4 sts at beg of next and foll alt rows.

Shape second side of neck
With RS facing sl the center 13[17:21:25] sts onto a stitch holder. Rejoin yarn to rem sts and complete work to match first side reversing all the shapings.

3 Sleeves
Using size 3 needles cast on 60 sts.

Work in K2, P2 rib for 2½in ending with a WS row.
Change to size 6 needles.

Next row: K3, *M1, K3, rep from * to last 3 sts, K3. (78 sts.)
Beg with a P row, cont in St st until work meas 4¼in from beg, ending with a P row.

Shape cap
Bind off 10 sts at beg of next 2 rows.
Bind off 2 sts at beg of next 2 rows. (54 sts.)
Cont in St st until work meas 10½in from beg ending with a WS row.
Bind off 5 sts at beg of next 4 rows. (34 sts.)

Next row: K2 tog to end.
Bind off.

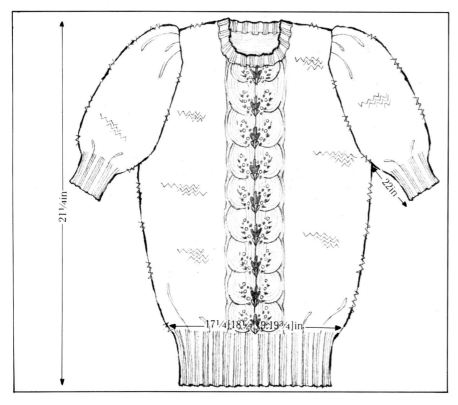

Bind off 2 sts at beg of next 4 rows. Dec 1 st at each end of next and every foll 4th row until 66[74:82:90] sts are on the needles. Cont in St st until work meas 22½in from beg, ending with a WS row.

Shape shoulders

Bind off 6[7:8:9] sts at beg of next 4 rows. Bind off 5[6:7:8] sts at beg of next 2 rows. Bind off rem 32[34:36:38] sts.

2 Right front

** Using size 3 needles, cast on 42[46:50:54] sts.

1st row: * K2, P2, rep from * to last 2 sts, K2.

2nd row: * P2, K2, rep from * to last 2 sts, P2.

Rep these 2 rows until work meas 4in, ending with a 2nd row. Change to size 6 needles.

Next row: K2[6:10:14], * M1, K7, rep from * to end, (47[51:55:59] sts).

Next row: P. **

Work patt as folls:

1st row: (RS) K12[14:16:18], P2, K8, K2 tog, yo, K1, P1, K1, yo, ssk, K8, P2, K8[10:12:14].

2nd row: P8[10:12:14], K2, P7, P2 tog tbl, P2, yo, K1, yo, P2, P2 tog, P7, K2, P12[14:16:18].

3rd row: K12[14:16:18] P2, K6, K2 tog, K1, yo, K2, P1, K2, yo, K1, ssk, K6, P2, K8[10:12:14].

4th row: P8[10:12:14] K2, P5, P2 tog tbl, P3, yo, P1, K1, P1, yo, P3, P2

---

4 Neckband

Join shoulder seams.

Using size 3 needles, pick up and K20 sts down left side of neck, K across the center 13[17:21:25] sts, inc 2[0:2:0] sts across these sts. K up the 20 sts down right side of neck. K across 31[33:35:37] sts on back neck, inc 4 sts. (90[94:102:106] sts.)

Work in K2, P2 rib for 1in. Bind off loosely in rib.

5 To finish

Work embroidery before sewing up. Join side sleeve seams, sew in sleeves, gathering slightly at top.

Instructions for cardigan
1 Back

Using size 3 needles, cast on 90[94:98:102] sts.

1st row: * K2, P2, rep from * to last 2 sts, K2.

2nd row: * P2, K2, rep from * to last 2 sts, P2.

Rep these 2 rows until meas 4in, ending with a 2nd row.

Change to size 6 needles and work inc row as folls:

1st size only

K4, * M1, K15, rep from * to last 11 sts, M1, K11.

2nd size only

* K9, M1, rep from * to last 4 sts, K4.

3rd size only

K3, M1, * K7, M1, rep from * to last 4 sts, K4.

4th size only

K7, * K5, M1, rep from * to last 13, K13.

All sizes

Beg with a P row, cont on these 96[104:112:120] sts in St st until meas 15¼in from beg, ending with a P row.

Shape armholes

Bind off 10 sts at beg of next 2 rows.

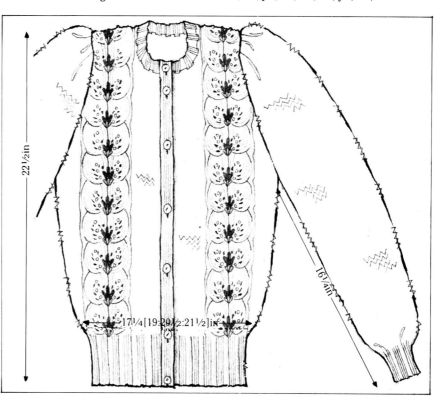

tog, P5, K2, P12[14:16:18].
5th row: K12[14:16:18], P2, K4, K2 tog, K2, yo, K3, P1, K3, yo, K2, ssk, K4, P2, K8[10:12:14].
6th row: P8[10:12:14], K2, P3, P2 tog tbl, P4, yo, P2, K1, P2, yo, P4, P2 tog, P3, K2, P12[14:16:18].
7th row: K12[14:16:18], P2, K2, K2 tog, K3, yo, K4, P1, K4, yo, K3, ssk K2, P2, K12[10:14:16].
8th row: P8[10:12:14], K2, P1, P2 tog tbl, P5, yo, P3, K1, P3, yo, P5, P2 tog, P1, K2, P12[14:16:18].
9th row: K12[14:16:18], P2, K2 tog, K4, yo, K5, P1, K5, yo, K4, ssk, P2, K8[10:12:14].
10th row: P8[10:12:14], K2, P11, K1, P11, K2, P12[14:16:18].
11th row: K12[14:16:18], P2, K11, P1, K11, P2, K8[10:12:14].
12th row: P8[10:12:14], K2, P11, K1, P11, K2, P12[14:16:18].
Rep rows 1–12 inclusive until work meas 15¼in from beg, ending with a RS row.
Shape armhole
Keeping patt correct, bind off 10 sts at beg of next row.
Work 1 row.
Bind off 2 sts at beg of next and foll alt row.
Work a further 4 rows in patt.
Cont in patt, dec 1 st at beg of side edge of next and every foll 4th row until 31[35:39:43] sts are on needle.
Work even on these sts until work meas 19¼in from beg, ending with a WS row.
Shape neck
Bind off 10 sts at beg of row, work to end.
Keeping armhole edge even dec 1st at neck edge on every row until 17[20:23:26] sts rem.
Cont even until work meas 22½in from beg, ending with a RS row.
Shape shoulders
Bind off 6[7:8:9] sts at beg of next foll alt row.
Work 1 row.
Bind off rem sts.

3 Left front
Work exactly as right front to **. Cont in patt as folls:
1st row: K8[10:12:14], P2, K8, K2 tog, yo, K1, P1, K1, yo, ssk, K8, P2, K12[14:16:18].
2nd row: P12[14:16:18], K2, P7, P2 tog tbl, P2, yo, K1, yo, P2, P2 tog, P7, K2, P8[10:12:14].
These rows set the patt, work as for right front reversing all the shapings.

4 Sleeves
Using size 3 needles, cast on 46 sts, work in K2, P2 rib as given for back for 4in, ending with a WS row.
Change to size 6 needles.
Next row: * K4, M1, rep from * to last 6 sts, K6 (56 sts.)
Next row: P.
Cont to inc as folls:
1st row: K2, M1, K to last 2 sts, M1, K2.
Work 5 rows in St st.
Cont inc on every 6th row until there are 86 sts on the needles.
Cont in St st until work meas 16in from beg, ending with a WS row.
Shape sleeve cap
Bind off 8 sts at beg of next 2 rows.
Bind off 2 sts at beg of next 4 rows. (62 sts).
Cont in St st without further dec, until work meas 22¾in, ending with a WS row.
Bind off 4 sts at beg of next 4 rows (46 sts.)
Next row: K2 tog all along row.
Bind off.

5 Right front band
Using size 3 needles, cast on 10 sts.
Work 3 rows in K2, P2 rib, as given for back. Make buttonhole.

1st row: Rib 4, bind off 2 sts, rib to end.
2nd row: Rib 4, cast on 2 sts, rib to end.
Cont in rib, making a buttonhole on every foll 22nd row until work meas 19¼in.
Slip these sts onto a holder.

6 Left front band
Using size 3 needles, cast on 10 sts.
Work 19¼in in K2, P2 rib, as given for back, ending with a WS row.
Slip these sts on to a holder.

7 Neckband
Join shoulder seams. Using size 3 needles pick up and K27[28:27:28] sts up right side of neck, K across the 36[38:40:42] sts at back neck and pick up and K27 [28:27:28] sts down left side of neck (110[114:114:118] sts.)
Work in K2, P2 rib for 1in, making buttonhole on 4th row.
Bind off loosely in rib.

8 To finish
Work embroidery before sewing up.
Join side and sleeve seams.
Set in sleeves gathering slightly at top.
Sew on buttons to correspond with buttonholes.

Woven Look Jacket

K nit this jacket in a textured stitch. Slipping the stitches alternately produces the woven pattern. Work in a mohair-type yarn.

BEFORE YOU BEGIN

When working in pattern take care not to twist the slipped stitches. Slip all stitches on the right side rows with the yarn at the back of work (wyib), and all stitches on wrong side rows with the yarn at the front of the work (wyif).

Sizes

Bust   32[34:36:38]in
Length   24½[24¾:25¼:25½]in
Sleeve seam 17¼in

Note: Instructions for the larger sizes are in brackets [ ]; where there is one set of figures, it applies to all sizes.

Gauge

18 st and 24 rows to 4in over patt on size 10½ needles.

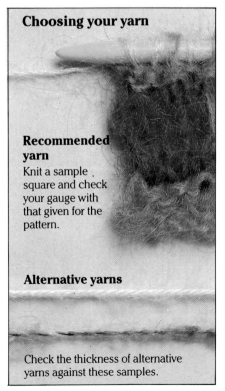

Choosing your yarn

Recommended yarn

Knit a sample square and check your gauge with that given for the pattern.

Alternative yarns

Check the thickness of alternative yarns against these samples.

Materials

□ Approx 11[12:13:13]oz of medium weight mohair yarn in main color (m.c.)
□ Approx 2[3:3:3]oz each in 3 contrast colors (a, b and c)
□ 1 pair each sizes 9 and 10½ needles
□ 2 pairs size 7 needles
□ 5 buttons

INSTRUCTIONS

1 Pocket linings (make 2)

Using size 9 needles and m.c., cast on 20 sts, starting with a K row work in St st for 4in, ending with a P row. Inc 1 st at center of last row. (21 sts.) Leave these sts on a spare needle.

2 Left front

* Using size 7 needles and m.c., cast on 37[39:41:43] sts, work rib as folls:
1st row: (RS) K1, * P1, K1, rep from * to end.
2nd row: P1, *K1, P1, rep from * to end.
Rep the last 2 rows for 2¾in.
Inc row: Rib 6, (M1, rib 8[9:10:10]) 3 times, M1, rib to end. (41[43:45:47] sts.) Change to size 10½ needles and work in patt as folls.*
1st row: (RS) With m.c., K.
2nd row: With m.c., P.
3rd row: With a, K2[1:2:1], sl 1[0:1:1], * K3, (sl 1, K1) twice, sl 1, rep from * to last 6[2:2:5] sts, K3[2:2:3], sl

1[0:0:1], K2[0:0:1].
4th row: With a, K2[0:0:1], sl 1[0:0:1], P3[2:2:3], * (sl 1, K1) twice, sl 1, P3, rep from * to last 3[1:3:2] sts, sl 1 [0:1:1], K2[1:2:1].
5th row: With m.c., K3[1:3:2], * sl 3, K5, rep from * to last 6[2:2:5] sts, sl 3 [1:1:3], K3[1:1:2].
6th row: With m.c., slipping sts wyif, K3[1:1:2], sl 3[1:1:3], * K5, sl 3, rep from * to last 3[1:3:2] sts, K to end.
7th row: With a, work as 3rd row.
8th row: Work a, work as 4th row.
9th row: With m.c., work as 1st row.
10th row: With m.c., work as 2nd row.
11th row: With b, K2[2:2:1], (sl 1, K1) 2[1:2:2] times, sl 1, * K3, (sl 1, K1) twice, sl 1, rep from * to last 2[6:6:1] sts, K2[3:3:1], sl 0[1:1:0], K0[2:2:0].
12th row: With b, P2[0:0:1], K0[2:2:0], (sl 1[0:0:1], K1[0:0:1]) 2[0:0:2] times, sl 1, * P3, (sl 1, K1) twice, sl 1, rep from * to last 2[8:2:1] sts, P2[3:2:1], (sl 1, K1) 0[2:0:0] times, K0[1:0:0].
13th row: With m.c., K1[0:1:1], sl 1[0:1:0], * K5, sl 3, rep from * to last 7[3:3:6] sts, K5[3:3:6], sl 1[0:0:0], K1[0:0:0].
14th row: With m.c., sl sts wyif, K1[3:3:1], sl 1[3:3:0], * K5, sl 3; rep from * to last 7[5:7:6] sts, K5[5:5:6], sl 1[0:1:0], K1[0:1:0].
15th row: With b, work as 11th row.
16th row: With b, work as 12th row.
Cont in patt changing to c then a, b, c, until front meas approx 6¾in ending with 8th row of patt.

Place pocket lining

Next row: K10[11:12:13], sl next 21 sts onto a length of yarn, K across sts from first pocket lining, K to end (41[43:45:47] sts.)
Work even in patt until front meas 15¼in, ending with a 12th row of patt and RS facing.

Shape front

Next row: Patt to last 2 sts, K2 tog.
Next row: Patt to end.
Rep 1st and 2nd row 2[2:3:3] times more, (38[40:41:43] sts.)
Now dec 1 st at same edge on every foll 4th row until 35[37:39:41] sts rem, ending with a 14th row of patt.

Shape armhole

Bind off 5 sts, patt to end.

Next row: Patt to end.

Cont to dec 1 st at front edge on every 4th row at the same time dec 1 st at armhole edge on every row 5[5:5:7] times then 1 st on every alt row until 20[21:20:21] sts rem.

Keeping armhole edge even cont to dec 1 st at front edge on every 4th row until 16 sts rem.

Work even in patt until armhole meas 7½[8:8¼:8½]in ending with a WS row. Bind off.

3 Right front

Work as for left front from * to *.

1st row: (RS) with m.c., K.

2nd row: With m.c., P.

3rd row: With a, K2, (sl 1, K0[1:1:0]) 1[2:2:1] times, sl 0[1:1:0], * K3, (sl 1, K1) twice, sl 1, rep from * to last 6[4:6:4] sts, K3[4:3:4], sl 1[0:1:0], K2[0:2:0].

4th row: with a, K2[1:2:1], sl 1[0:1:0] * P3, (sl 1, K1) twice, sl 1, rep from * to last 6[2:2:6] sts, P3[2:2:3], sl 1 [0:0:1] K2[0:0:2].

5th row: With m.c., K3[1:1:3], sl 3[1:1:3], * K5, sl 3, rep from * to last 3[1:3:1] sts, K to end.

6th row: With m.c., K3[1:3:1], * sl 3, K5, rep from * to last 6[2:2:6] sts, sl 3[1:1:3], K3[1:1:3].

7th, 8th, 9th and 10th rows: Work as given for 3rd, 4th, 1st and 2nd rows.

11th row: With b, K2 (sl 1, K1) 2[0:0:2] times, sl 1, * K3 (sl 1, K1) twice, sl 1, rep from * to last 2[8:2:8] sts, K2[3:2:3], (sl 1, K1) 0[2:0:2] times, K0[1:0:1].

12th row: With b, P2[0:2:1], K0[2:0:1], (sl 1, K1) 2[1:2:1] times, sl 1, * P3 (sl 1, K1) twice, sl 1, rep from * to last 2[6:6:2] sts, P0[3:3:1], sl 0[1:1:0] K2[2:2:1].

13th row: With m.c., K1[3:3:6], sl 1 [3:3:3], * K5, sl 3, rep from * to last 7[5:7:5] sts, K5, (sl 1, K1) 1[0:1:0] times.

14th row: With m.c., K1[5:1:5], sl

3[3:1:3], * K5, sl 3, rep from * to last 7[3:3:7] sts, K5[3:3:7], (sl 1, K1) once.
15th and 16th rows: With b, work as 11th and 12th row.
Now complete to match left front reversing all shapings.

4 Back

Using size 7 needles and m.c., cast on 73[77:81:87] sts and work rib as front.
Inc row: Rib 5[7:5:9], (M1, rib 9[9:10:10]) 7 times, M1, rib to end. (81[85:89:95] sts.)
Change to size 10½ needles. Work in patt as folls:
1st row: (RS) With m.c., K.
2nd row: With m.c., P.
3rd row: With a, K2[1:2:1], sl 1[0:1:1], * K3, (sl 1, K1) twice, sl 1, rep from * to last 6[4:6:5] sts, K3[4:3:3], sl 1 [0:1:1], K2[0:2:1].
4th row: With a, K2[1:2:1], sl 1[0:1:1], * P3, (sl 1, K1) twice, sl 1, rep from * to last 6[4:6:5] sts, P3, sl 1[0:1:1], K2[1:2:1].
5th row: With m.c., K3[1:3:2], * sl 3, K5, rep from * to last 6[4:6:5] sts, sl 3, K3[1:3:2].
6th row: With m.c., work as before.
7th and 8th rows: With a, work as 3rd and 4th rows.
9th and 10th rows: With m.c., work as 1st and 2nd rows.
11th row: With b, K2[2:2:1], (sl 1, K1) 2[1:2:2] times, sl 1, * K3, (sl 1, K1) twice, sl 1, rep from * to last 2[8:2:1] sts, K2[3:2:1], (sl 1, K1) 0[2:0:0] times, K0[1:0:0].
12th row: With b, K0[2:0:0], (sl 1, K1, sl 1) 0[1:0:0] times, P2[3:2:1], * (sl 1,

K1) twice, sl 1, P3, rep from * to last 7[5:7:6] sts, (sl 1, K1) twice, sl 1[0:1:1], P2[0:2:1], K0[1:1:0].
13th row: With m.c., K1[0:1:1], sl 1 [0:1:0], * K5, sl 3, rep from * to last 7[5:7: 6] sts, K5[5:5:6], sl 1[0:1:0], K1[0:1:0].
14th row: With m.c., work as before.
15th and 16th rows: With b, work as 11th and 12th rows.
Cont in patt until back matches front to armhole shaping, ending with a 14th patt row and RS facing.
Shape armholes
Keeping patt correct, bind off 5 sts at the beg of next 2 rows. Dec 1 st at each end of every row 5[5:5:7] times.
Dec 1 st at each end of every alt row until 59[61:63:65] sts rem. Work even in patt until back matches front to shoulder. Bind off, marking center 27[29:31:33] sts for back neck.

5 Sleeves

Using size 7 needles and m.c., cast on 29[31:33:35] sts and K6 rows.
Inc row: K4[3:4:3], (M1, K3[5:5:6]) 7[5:5:5] times, M1, K to end. (37[37:39:41] sts.) Change to size 10½ needles.
Work in patt as for 2nd[2nd:4th:1st] size on back starting with row 11, at the same time shape sides as folls:
1st size
Inc 1 st at each end of every 7th row twice, then 1 st at each end of every 9th row until there are 59 sts.
2nd, 3rd and 4th sizes only
Inc 1 st at each end of every 8th row until there are [61:63:65] sts.
All sizes
Work even in patt until sleeve meas

approx 17¼in ending with same patt stripe and row as before on back.
Shape cap
Bind off 5 sts at beg of next 2 rows. Dec 1 st at each end of next and every foll 4th row 5[6:6:7] times in all. Dec 1 st at each end of every alt row 5[3:4:2] times. Dec 1 st at each end of every row until 15 sts rem. Bind off.

6 Pocket tops

With RS facing and using size 7 needles and m.c., K across sts from pocket, inc 2 sts (23 sts.) K1 row.
1st row: (RS) K2, * P1, K1, rep from * to last st, K1.
2nd row: P2, * K1, P1, rep from * to last st, P1.
Rep last 2 rows for 1¼in. Bind off.

7 Right collar and buttonhole border

Join shoulders, using size 7 needles and RS facing with m.c., starting at lower right front edge K up 79 sts to front edge shaping, 59[61:63:65] sts to right shoulder, 13[15:17:19] sts to center back neck (151[155:159:163] sts.) Use extra needles. K1 row.
Next row: K2, * P1, K1 rep from * to last st, P1.
Shape collar
Next row: Rib 40[44:48:50], turn.
Next row: Sl 1, rib to end.
Next row: Rib 43[47:51:53], turn.
Next row: Sl 1, rib to end.
Cont in rib working 3 further sts on every alt row until the row rib 70[74:78:80], turn has been worked.
Next row: Sl 1, rib to end.
Next row: Rib over all sts.
Next row: make buttonholes, rib 3 (bind off 2 sts, rib 16) 4 times, bind off 2 sts, rib to end.
Rib casting on 2 sts over bound off sts.
Rib 4 rows over all sts. Bind off.

8 Left collar and button border

With RS facing, size 7 needles and m.c., starting at center back neck pick up and K13[15:17:19] sts to left shoulder, 59[61:63:65] sts to end of front shaping, 79 sts to lower edge. (151[155:159:163] sts.) K1 row.
Next row: P1, * K1, P1, rep from * to last 2 sts, K2.
Next row: P2, * K1, P1, rep from * to last st, K1.
Shape collar as for right side omitting buttonholes.

9 To finish

Join collar, side and sleeve seams. Insert sleeves. Sew on buttons.

Long And Lean Vest

This vest is made in a reversible stitch, using a bulky tweed yarn. Wear it long and belted.

BEFORE YOU BEGIN

To make this pattern, a stitch is held at the back of the work for the purl rows and held at the front of the work on the knit rows. Always make sure the yarn is in the correct place when slipped.

Sizes

Bust 32[34:36:38]in
Length 31½[32:32¾:32¾]in

Note: Instructions for the larger sizes are in brackets [ ]; where there is one set of figures it applies to all sizes.

Gauge

18 sts and 24 rows to 4in over St st on size 9 needles.

Choosing your yarn

Recommended yarn

Knit a sample square and check your gauge with that given for the pattern.

Alternative yarns

Check the thickness of alternative yarns against these samples.

Materials

☐ Approx 35[37:37:37]oz of bulky weight yarn
☐ 1 pair each sizes 7 and 9 needles
☐ 6 buttons

INSTRUCTIONS

1 Back

Using size 7 needles, cast on 104[108:112:116] sts.
Work in K2, P2 rib for 4in ending with a RS row. Change to size 9 needles.
Next row: K, inc into last st. (105[109:113:117] sts.)
Work patt as folls:
1st row: (RS) P.
2nd row: K1, * P1, K1, rep from * to end.
3rd row: P1, * sl 1, yarn to back of work over top of right-hand needle and to front of work between 2 needles to make a yo, P1, rep from * to end.
4th row: K1, * yarn to front of work between 2 needles (yf), sl 1, drop yo from previous row, yarn to back of work between 2 needles (ybk), K1, rep from * to end.
5th row: P1, * ybk, sl 1, yf, P1, rep from * to end.
6th row: K1, * yf, sl 1, ybk, K1, rep from * to end.
The last 6 rows form the patt, rep until work meas 31½[32:32¾:32¾]in from the beg. Bind off.

2 Right front

Using size 7 needles, cast on 44[46:48:50] sts. Work in K2, P2 rib for 4in.
Next row: K, inc 1 st at the end of row. (45[47:49:51] sts.)
Work in patt as for back until work meas 20½[20¾:21¼:21¼]in, from beg, ending with a WS row. Mark with a colored thread. Cont until work meas 31½[32:32¾:32¾]in from the beg. Bind off.

3 Left front

Work as for the right front.

4 Armbands (make 2)

Using size 7 needles, cast on 10 sts. Work 20in in K2, P2 rib. Bind off.

5 Frontband and collar

Using size 7 needles, cast on 14 sts, work 20½[21:21¼:21¼]in in K2, P2 rib. Keeping rib patt correct, inc 1 st at the beg (neck edge) of the next and every alt row, until there are 34 sts on the needles.
Cont even until work meas 47½[48:48½:48½]in. Keeping rib patt correct, dec 1 st at neck edge on next and every alt row until there are 14 sts on the needle.
Make buttonhole
1st row: Rib 6 sts, bind off 2 sts, rib to end.
2nd row: Rib 6 sts, bind on 2 sts, rib to end.
Cont in rib, making a buttonhole every 2¼in until 6 buttonholes have been worked. Cont in rib until work meas 72[73:74:74]in. Bind off.

6 To finish

Using a back stitch, join shoulder seams, with a flat stitch sew on front band, collar and armbands stretched slightly.
With a flat stitch join side seams and armbands. Sew on buttons. Darn in all loose ends and press lightly.

Tyrolean Cardigan

Simple bobbles, lazy daisy and chain stitch embroidery combine to create this beautiful Tyrolean cardigan. Knit it in a neutral color, or in black for evening wear.

BEFORE YOU BEGIN

As large and small bobbles are used to create this design, read through the pattern before working and circle each large bobble in one color and each small bobble in another. This will make the pattern easier to read.

Sizes

Bust	32[34:36:38]in
Length	21¼[21¾:22:22½]in
Sleeve seam	16½[17:17:17¼]in

Note: Instructions for the larger sizes are in brackets [ ]; where one set of figures is given it applies to all sizes.

Gauge

24 sts and 30 rows to 4in over patt on size 6 needles.

Choosing your yarn

Recommended yarn
Knit a sample square and check your gauge with that given for the pattern.

Alternative yarns

Check the thickness of alternative yarns against these samples.

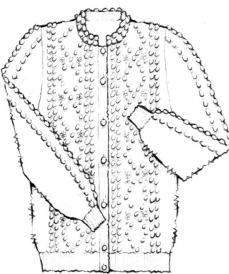

Materials

- ☐ Approx 25[25:27:27]oz of knitting worsted weight yarn in main color (m.c.)
- ☐ Small amounts of pink, claret, bottle green and gold for embroidery
- ☐ 1 pair each sizes 3 and 6 needles
- ☐ 8 buttons

INSTRUCTIONS

1 Back

Using size 3 needles, cast on 96[100:104:108] sts. Work in K1, P1 rib for 2½[2¾:3¼:3½]in, ending with a RS row.

Inc row: Rib 6, * M1 (by knitting into the loop before the next st), rib 12[8:6:5], rep from * 7[11:15:19] times, M1, rib to end. (104[112:120:128] sts.) Change to size 6 needles and work patt as folls:

1st row: (P1, K3), 4[5:6:7] times, P1, K2, MB – make bobble by (K1, P1, K1, P1, K1), into next st, turn, K5, turn, P5, turn, K5, turn, P5, sl 4th st over 5th st foll by 3rd, 2nd and 1st st) twice, K11, MSB – make small bobble by (K1, P1, K1, P1, K1) into same stitch, turn, K5, turn, P5, sl 4th st over 5th st foll by 3rd, 2nd and 1st st, K11, (MB, K2) 4 times, MB, K11, MSB, K11, (MB, K2) twice, (P1, K3) 4[5:6:7] times.

2nd and all alternate rows: P3, K1) 4[5:6:7] times, P71, K1, (P3, K1) 4[5:6:7] times.

3rd row: (P1, K3) 4[5:6:7] times, P1, K71, (P1, K3) 4[5:6:7] times.

5th row: (P1, K3) 4[5:6:7] times, P1, (K2, MB) twice, K8, MSB, K5, MSB, K8, (MB, K2) 4 times, MB, K8, MSB, K5, MSB, K8, (MB, K2) twice, (P1, K3) 4[5:6:7] times.

7th row: Work as 3rd row.

9th row: (P1, K3) 4[5:6:7] times P1, (K2, MB) twice, K6, MSB, K9, MSB, K6, (MB, K2) 4 times, MB, K6, MSB, K9, MSB, K6, (MB, K2) twice, (P1, K3) 4[5:6:7] times.

11th row: Work as 3rd row.

13th row: (P1, K3), 4[5:6:7] times, P1, (K2, MB) twice, K4, MSB, K13, MSB, K4, (MB, K2) 4 times, MB, K4, MSB, K13, MSB, K4, (MB, K2) twice, (P1, K3), 4[5:6:7] times.

15th row: Work as 3rd row.

17th row: Work as 9th row.

19th row: Work as 3rd row.

21st row: Work as 5th row.

23rd row: Work as 3rd row.

25th row: Work as 1st row.

26th row: Work as 2nd row.

Rep from row 3-26 inclusive throughout.

Cont even in patt until back meas 13¼[13¾:14:14½]in from the beg, ending with a WS row.

Shape armholes

With RS facing, bind off 5[7:9:11] sts at the beg of the next 2 rows. Dec 1 st at each end of next and every foll alt row until there are 78[82:86:90] sts. Cont even in patt on rem sts until back meas 21¼[21¾:22:22½]in, ending with a WS row.

Shape shoulders

Bind off 21[23:25:27] sts at the beg of next 2 rows.
Bind off rem 36 sts loosely.

2 Right front

Using size 3 needles, cast on 50[52:54:56] sts.
Work in single rib for 2½[2¾:3¼:3½]in, ending on a RS row.

Inc row. Rib 9[6:6:4], M1, (rib
16[10:7:6]), 2[4:6:8] times, M1, rib to
end. (53[57:61:65] sts.)
1st row: P1, K3, MB, K2, MB, K11,
MSB, K11, (MB, K2) twice, (P1, K3)
4[5:6:7] times.
2nd and all alternate rows: (P3,
K1) 4[5:6:7] times, P36, K1.
3rd row: P1, K36, (P1, K3) 4[5:6:7]
times.
5th row: P1, K3, MB, K2, MB, K8,
MSB, K5, MSB, K8, (MB, K2) twice,
(P1, K3) 4[5:6:7] times.
7th row: Work as 3rd row.
9th row: P1, K3, MB, K2, MB, K6,
MSB, K9, MSB, K6, (MB, K2) twice,
(P1, K3) 4[5:6:7] times.
11th row: Work as 3rd row.
13th row: P1, K3, MB, K2, MB, K4,
MSB, K13, MSB, K4, (MB, K2) twice,
(P1,K3) 4[5:6:7] times.
15th row: Work as 3rd row.
17th row: Work as 9th row.
19th row: Work as 3rd row.
21st row: Work as 5th row.
23rd row: Work as 3rd row.
25th row: Work as 1st row.
26th row: Work as 2nd row.
Cont in patt, rep rows 3 to 26 inclusive
throughout, until front meas 13½
[13¾:14:14½]in, ending on a RS row.
Shape armholes
With WS facing, bind off 5[7:9:11] sts at

beg of next row.
Dec 1 st at armhole edge on next and
every foll alt row until there are
40[42:44:46] sts.
Cont even on rem sts until front
meas 19[19¼:19¾:20]in, ending with a
WS row.
Shape neck
With RS facing, bind off 11 sts at beg
of next row, work to end.
Dec 1 st at neck edge on next and
every foll row 8 times until
21[23:25:27] sts rem.
Cont even on rem sts until front
matches back to shoulder shaping,
ending with a RS row.
Shape shoulder
With WS facing, bind off all sts.

3 Left front
Work exactly as for right front but
reverse all the shapings and start
working patt rows as folls:
1st row: (K3, P1) 4[5:6:7] times, K2,
MB, K2, MB, K11, MSB, K11, MB, K2,
MB, K3, P1.
2nd row: P37, (K1, P3) 4[5:6:7] times.
Cont on sts as set, foll instructions
given for right front.

4 Sleeves
Using size 3 needles, cast on 50
sts and work in single rib for 3¼in,
ending on a RS row.

Inc row: * Work twice into next st,
rep from * to end, (100 sts.)
Change to size 6 needles and work
patt as folls:
1st row: K2, (P1, K3) 10 times, MB,
K5, MB, K2, MB, K5, MB, (K3, P1) 10
times, K2.
2nd row: P2, (K1, P3) 10 times, P16,
(P3, K1) 10 times, P2.
3rd row: K2, (P1, K3) 10 times, K16,
(K3, P1) 10 times, K2.
4th row: Work as 2nd row.
Rep rows 1 to 4 until sleeve meas
16½[17:17:17¼]in, ending on a WS row.
Shape cap
Bind off 5[7:9:11] sts, at the beg of the
next 2 rows (90[86:82:78] sts.)
Dec 1st at each end of next and foll
alt rows until 74[70:66:62] sts, then
bind off 3 sts at beg of every row until
23[22:21:20] sts rem. Bind off.

5 Neckband
Join shoulder seams. Using size 3
needles and with RS facing, pick up and
K11 sts from right centre front, 16 sts
from right side of neck, 35 sts across
back neck, 16 sts from left side of neck
and 11 sts from left center front (89 sts)
K first row to form a ridge.
Work 2 rows in K1, P1 rib.
Next row: Rib 2, MB, * rib 3, MB, rep
from * to last 2 sts, rib to end.
Work 3 rows in K1, P1 rib.
Now work a further bobble row as
before.
Work 6 rows in K1, P1 rib.
Bind off loosely in rib.
Turn neckband inside and stitch down
loosely. The second bobble row
should be on top forming a ridge.

6 Right front band
Using size 3 needles, cast on 10
sts. Work 4 rows in K1, P1 rib.
Buttonhole row: Rib 4, yo, rib 2
tog, rib to end.
Cont in single rib, placing a
buttonhole at 18 row intervals,
making 8 buttonholes in all, placing
last one 2 rows from top of band.
Bind off.

7 Left front band
Work the same number of rows as for
right front band, omitting buttonholes.

8 To finish
Join side and sleeve seams. Insert
sleeves. Stitch on bands. Sew on
buttons. Embroider little lazy daisies
in pink and claret, stems and leaves
in bottle green and flower centers with
French knots in gold.

Glamorous Evening Knitwear
Ruffled Sweater

Knit this glamorous off-the-shoulder sweater. Add pearls for an elegant touch and wear it for the evening. The ruffle is made separately and sewn onto the neckband.

BEFORE YOU BEGIN

Buy lightweight pearls and use sparingly so the garment will not be too heavy. Sew on the pearls when completed, with a matching colored thread. Peardrop pearls have been used for the ruffle and small pearl beads for the body. Take care when washing; it is advisable to hand wash only.

 As this sweater is worn off the shoulder it will wear the ribbing. Thread shirring elastic loosely through each stitch in at least four rows of the neckband, especially the row before binding off as it will hold the rib in place.

Choosing your yarn

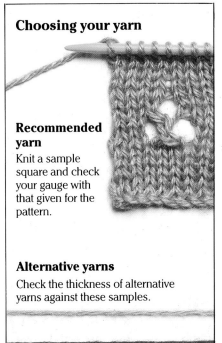

Recommended yarn

Knit a sample square and check your gauge with that given for the pattern.

Alternative yarns

Check the thickness of alternative yarns against these samples.

Sizes

Bust	32[34:36:38]in
Length	22½in
Sleeve seam	11½in

Note: Instructions for larger sizes are in brackets [ ]; where there is only one set of figures it applies to all sizes.

Gauge

30 sts and 34 rows to 4in over patt on size 2 needles.

Materials

- ☐ Approx 12[12:13:13]oz of wool/silk fingering yarn
- ☐ 1 pair each sizes 0, 2 and 6 needles
- ☐ Assorted pearl beads

INSTRUCTIONS
1 Back and front alike

Using size 0 needles, cast on 124 [138: 152:166] sts and work in K2, P2 rib for 5in. Change to size 2 needles.
Next row: K1 row inc 1 st at beg. (125 [139:153:167] sts.)
Next row: P.
Beg patt as folls:
1st row: (RS) K5, * yo, sl 1, K2 tog, psso, yo, K11, rep from * end last rep K5.
2nd and all alt rows: P.

3rd row: K6, * yo, ssk, K12, rep from * end last rep K5.
5th, 7th and 9th rows: K.
11th row: K12, * yo, sl 1, K2 tog, psso, yo, K11, rep from * end last rep K12.
13th row: K13, * yo, ssk, K12, rep from * to end.
15th, 17th and 19th rows: K.
Rep rows 1-20 inclusive 4 times more for all sizes.
Shape armholes
With RS facing and keeping patt correct, bind off 3 sts at beg of next 2 rows, then dec 1 st at each end of every foll alt row until there are 67 [81:95:109] sts on the needles. Dec 1 st at end of P row for 1st size only (66 sts) inc 1 st at end of P row for rem sizes ([82:96:110] sts.) Change to size 0 needles and work 1in in K2, P2 rib. Bind off.

2 Sleeves

Using size 0 needles, cast on 82 sts and work in K2, P2 rib for 2¼in.
Change to size 2 needles and K1 row, inc 1 st at beg of row. (83 sts.)
Next row: P.
Work in patt as given for back inc 1 st at each end of every foll 8th row until there are 99 sts on the needle. Cont in patt until 4 patt reps have been completed. (82 rows, excluding rib.)
Shape cap
With RS facing and keeping patt correct, bind off 3 sts at beg of next 2 rows then dec 1 st at each end of every foll 3rd row until 61 sts are on the needle. Work 4 rows more in patt. Dec 1 st at end of P row. (60 sts.)
Change to size 0 needles and work 1in in K2, P2 rib.
Bind off.

Ruffle (make 2)

Using size 6 needles, cast on 127[139:151:163] sts.
Next row: K.
Next row: P.
Next row: K1, * inc into every st except first st by working into front and back of same st. (253[277:301:

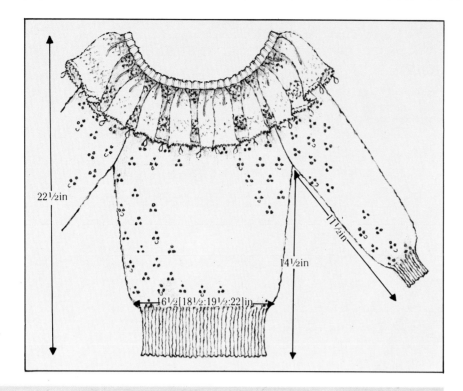

325] sts.) Cont in patt as folls:

1st row and all WS rows: P.

2nd row: K1, * K1, (K2 tog, yo) twice, K1, (yo, ssk) twice, K2, rep from * to end.

4th row: K1, * (K2 tog, yo) twice, K3, (yo, ssk) twice, K1, rep from * to end.

6th row: K2 tog, * yo, K2 tog, yo, K5, yo, ssk, yo, sl 1, K2 tog, psso, rep from * end last rep ssk.

8th row: K1 * (yo, ssk) twice, K3, (K2 tog, yo) twice, K1, rep from * to end.

10th row: K1, * K1, (yo, ssk) twice, K1, (K2 tog, yo) twice, K2, rep from * to end.

12th row: K1, * K2, yo, ssk, yo, sl 1, K2 tog, psso, yo, K2 tog, yo, K3, rep from * to end.

14th row: K6, * mb (make bobble: K1, yo, K1, yo, K1, all into next st, turn P5, turn K5, turn P5, turn K5, turn P2 tog, P1, P2 tog, turn and sl 1, K2 tog, psso), K11, rep from * end last rep K6.

14th – 19th rows: P.

20th row: K1, * yo, K2 tog, rep from * to end.

22nd row: As 20th row.

24th row: As 20th row.

26th row: As 20th row.

28th row: As 20th row.

30th row: As 20th row.

31st – 35th rows: P.

36th row: As 14th.

37th – 41st rows: P.

Bind off with picot edge as folls: Insert needle through the first st, *cast on 2 sts, knit and bind off 2 sts, knit the next st, there are now 2 sts on right-hand needle, knit and bind off 1, return st to left-hand needle, rep from * to end of row. Fasten off last st.

4 To finish

Join shoulder seam, set in sleeves, sew side and sleeve seams. Gather the ruffle and sew on to first row of neckband, and join side seam of ruffle. Sew on beads.

This off-the-shoulder sweater looks very pretty without the ruffle for casual wear. You will require approx 8[8:9:9]oz of wool/silk fingering yarn to make this version, and a small amount of beads. Pearl beads can still be sewn in for evening wear, but beads in a contrast color, or better still, multi-colored beads, will brighten it up for the day.

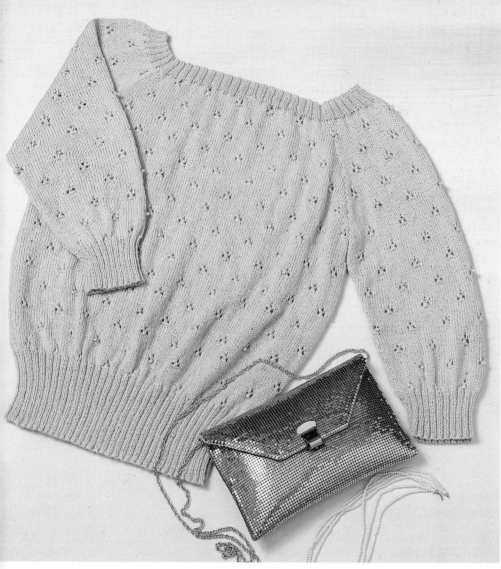

Silk Lace Top

This lovely lacy top is made in silk yarn. It has buttons which fasten down the center back and a pretty scalloped edge collar.

BEFORE YOU BEGIN

If you buy this yarn in hanks, you must wind it into balls before commencing knitting. Wind the silk very carefully and loosely, or it may stretch and break when knitted. If you do not have a hand winder, place the hank over the back of a chair.

Size

One size only
Bust   34in
Length   20in
Sleeve seam   16½in

Gauge

16 sts and 24 rows to 4in over St st on size 6 needles.

Choosing your yarn

Recommended yarn

Knit a sample square and check your gauge with that given for the pattern.

Alternative yarns

Check the thickness of alternative yarns against these samples.

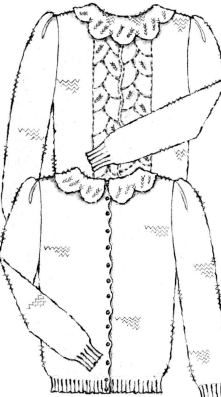

Materials

- ☐ Approx 22oz of bulky weight silk yarn
- ☐ 14 small buttons
- ☐ 1 pair each sizes 3 and 6 needles
- ☐ Size G/6 crochet hook

INSTRUCTIONS

1 Right side of back

Using size 3 needles, cast on 34 sts and work in K1, P1 rib for 1½in, ending with a RS row.
Next row: Rib 7, (inc into next st, rib 8) 3 times. (37 sts.)
Change to size 6 needles and starting with a K row work in St st. Cont until work meas 11¾in from beg, ending with a P row.
Shape armhole
*__Next row:__ Bind off 3 sts at beg of row K to end.
Next row: P.
Next row: Bind off 2 sts at beg of row,

K to end.
Next row: P.
Dec 1st at beg of next and foll alt row until 30 sts rem.
Work even until work meas 19¾in from beg, ending with a P row.
Shape shoulder
Next row: Bind off 15 sts at beg of row, K to end.
Next row: P.
Next row: Bind off rem 15 sts.*

2 Left side of back

Work as for right side of back until work meas 11¾in from beg, ending with a K row.
Shaping armhole
Work from * to * reversing shapings.

3 Front

Using size 3 needles, cast on 64 sts, and work in K1, P1 rib for 1½in, ending with a RS row.
Next row: Rib 9, (inc in next st, rib 10) 5 times. (69 sts.)
Change to size 6 needles and patt as folls:
1st row: K19, * yo, K1, sl 1, K1, psso, P1, K2 tog, K1, yo, P1, sl 1, K1, psso, P1, K2 tog, yo, K1, yo, K1, rep from * once, K20.
2nd row: P20, * P4, K1, P1, K1, P3, K1, P4, rep from * once, P19.
3rd row: K19, * yo, K1, sl 1, K1, psso, P1, K2 tog, K1, P1, sl 1, K2 tog, psso, yo, K3, yo, K1, rep from * once, K20.
4th row: P20, * P6, K1, P2, K1, P4, rep from * once, P19.
5th row: K19, * yo, K1, yo, sl 1, K1, psso, P1, K2 tog, K2 tog, yo, K5, yo, K1, rep from * once, K20.
6th row: P20, * P7, K1, P1, K1, P5, rep from * once, P19.
7th row: K19, * yo, K3, yo, sl 1, K2 tog, psso, P1, yo, K1, sl 1, K1, psso, P1, K2 tog, K1, yo, K1, rep from * once, K20.
8th row: P20, * P3, K1, P3, K1, P7, rep from * once, P19.
9th row: K19, * yo, K5, yo, sl 1, K1, psso, K1, sl 1, K1, psso, P1, K2 tog, K1, yo, K1, rep from * once, K20.

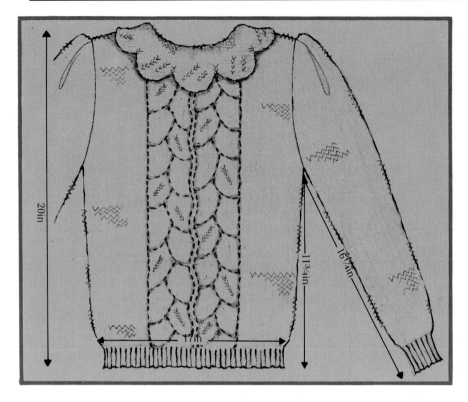

5th row: K4, P2, K3, yo, K1, yo, K4.
6th row: P10, inc into next st, K5.
7th row: K4, P3, K4, yo, K1, yo, K5.
8th row: P12, inc into next st, K6.
9th row: K4, P4, sl 1, K1, psso, K7, K2 tog, K1.
10th row: P10, inc into next st, K7.
11th row: K4, P5, sl 1, K1, psso, K5, K2 tog, K1.
12th row: P8, inc into next st, K2, P1, K5.
13th row: K4, P1, K1, P4, sl 1, K1, psso, K3, K2 tog, K1.
14th row: P6, inc into next st, K3, P1, K5.
15th row: K4, P1, K1, P5, sl 1, K1, psso, K1, K2 tog, K1.
16th row: P4, inc into next st, K4, P1, K5.
17th row: K4, P1, K1, P6, sl 1, K2 tog, psso, K1.
18th row: P2 tog, bind off next 5 sts using P2 tog st to bind off first st, P3, K4. Rep rows 1-18 inclusive eight times. Bind off.

6 To finish

Join shoulder seams. With WS of body facing and RS of collar join seam along neck edge. Join side and sleeve seams. Set in sleeves, gather top to form puff.

7 Buttonhole edge

Using crochet hook and left-hand side of back, start at bottom of rib and work along outside edge as folls. Ss into the same place as join, * into next row end work (1hdc, 1hdc, 2dc), (miss next row end, ss into row end) 4 times, miss next 2 row ends, rep from * to end. Fasten off. Sew on buttons to corresponding side.

10th row: P20, * P3, K1, P2, K1, P8, rep from * once, P19.
Rows 1–10 inclusive form the patt. Rep until work meas 11¾in, ending with WS.

Shape armholes

Keeping patt correct, bind off 3 sts at beg of next 2 rows, bind off 2 sts at beg of foll 2 rows. Dec 1 st at beg of next 4 rows (55 sts). Cont even until work meas 17¼in from cast on edge, ending with a WS row.

Shape neck

Next row: Patt 21, bind off next 13 sts, patt to end.
Next row: Patt to end.
Dec 1 st at neck edge on next and foll alt rows until there are 15 sts. Work on these sts, until front meas the same as back to shoulder shaping, ending with a WS row.

Shape shoulder

Bind off the 15 rem sts.

Shape second side of neck

With WS facings join in yarn to rem sts. Work as for the first side of neck reversing all the shapings.

4 Sleeves

Using size 3 needles, cast on 32 sts and work in K1, P1 rib for 2¾in. Change to size 6 needles, inc on next row as folls:
1st row: K1, * inc into next st, K3, rep from * to last 3 sts, inc into next st, K2. (40 sts.)
Now work in St st, beg with a P row, inc 1 st at each end of 5th and every foll 6th row until there are 64 sts. Cont on these sts until work meas 16¼in from beg

---

ending with a P row.

Shape sleeve cap

Bind off 3 sts at beg of next 2 rows, and 2 sts at beg of foll 2 rows. Now dec 1 st at each end of next and every alt row until 30 sts rem, work 5 rows on these sts. Bind off.

5 Collar

Using size 6 needles, cast on 8 sts.
1st row: (RS) K5, yo, K1, yo, K2.
2nd row: P6, inc into next st, K3.
3rd row: K4, P1, K2, yo, K1, yo, K3.
4th row: P8, inc into next st, K4.

Rugged Knitwear For Men

Cable And Rib Sweater

This man's sweater is worked in a pattern of double rib and simple cables. It has saddle shoulders with an opening on the left-hand side.

BEFORE YOU BEGIN
Keep a careful check of all the cabled rows. One simple error can spoil the look of the rope-like effect. Mark the rows on a piece of paper or alternatively use a row counter.

Sizes
Chest   38[40:42]in
Length   26¾[27¼:27½]in
Sleeve seam   19[19:19¾]in

Note: Instructions for the larger sizes are given in brackets [ ]; where one figure is given it applies to all sizes.

Gauge
30 sts and 30 rows to 4in over patt on size 6 needles.

Choosing your yarn

Recommended yarn
Knit a sample square and check your gauge with that given for the pattern.

Alternative yarns

Check the thickness of alternative yarns against these samples.

Materials
☐ Approx 19[19:20]oz of sport weight yarn
☐ 1 pair each sizes 3 and 6 needles
☐ Cable needle
☐ 4 buttons

INSTRUCTIONS
1 Back
* Using size 3 needles, cast on 111[117:123] sts and work in rib as folls:
1st row: (RS) K1, * P1, K1, rep from * to end.
2nd row: P1, * K1, P1, rep from * to end.
Rep last 2 rows for 2¾in, ending with a 1st row.
Inc row: (Rib 2, M1) 10 times, (rib 3, M1) 23 [25:27] times, (rib 2, M1) 10 times, rib 2. (154[162:170] sts.)
Change to size 6 needles and work in patt as folls:
1st row: (RS) P2, (K2, P2) 3[4:5] times, * K6, (P2, K2) 4 times, P2, rep from * 4 times more, K6, P2, (K2, P2) 3[4:5] times.
2nd row: K2, (P2, K2) 3[4:5] times, * P6, (K2, P2) 4 times, K2, rep from * 4 times more, P6, K2 (P2, K2) 3[4:5] times.
3rd row: P2, (K2, P2) 3[4:5] times, * sl 3f (sl next 3 sts onto a cable needle and hold at front of work, K3, then K3 sts from cable needle), (P2, K2) 4 times, P2, rep from * 4 times

more, K6, P2, (K2, P2) 3[4:5] times.
4th row: As 2nd row.
These 4 rows form the patt. Cont in rib and cable patt until back meas 16½in, ending with a WS row.
Shape armholes
Keep patt correct throughout shaping. Bind off 6[7:8] sts at beg of next 2 rows. Dec 1 st at each end of next and every foll row 7[9:11] times in all, then dec 1 st at each end of every foll alt row until 120[120:128] sts rem. * Work even in patt until armhole meas 9[9½:9¾]in, ending with a WS row.
Shape shoulder
Bind off 11 sts at beg of next 4 rows. Bind off 12[12:13] sts at beg of next 2 rows. Leave rem 52[52:58] sts on a spare needle.

2 Front
Work as for back from * to *. Work even in patt until armhole meas 7[7½:7¾]in, ending with a WS row.
Shape neck
Next row: Patt 46[46:48] sts and turn, leaving rem sts on a spare needle. Keeping armhole edge even, dec 1 st at neck edge on every row until 34[34:35] sts rem. Work a few rows even until front matches back to shoulder ending with a WS row.
Shape shoulder
Bind off 11 sts at beg of next and foll alt row. Work 1 row. Bind off rem sts.
Shape second side of neck
With RS facing rejoin yarn to rem sts, bind off next 28[28:32] sts for the center. Complete to match first side reversing all the shapings.

3 Sleeves
Using size 3 needles, cast on 51[53:55] sts and work in rib as for back for 2¼in.
1st and 2nd sizes only
Inc row: (Rib 1, M1) 6[3] times, (rib 2, M1) 19[23] times, (rib 1, M1) 6[3] times, rib 1. (82 sts.)
3rd size only
Inc row: (Rib 2, M1) 27 times, rib 1. (82 sts.)

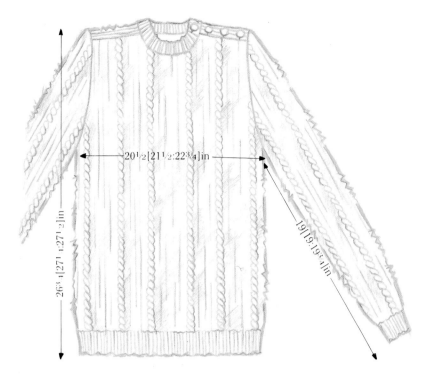

All sizes

Change to size 6 needles and work patt as folls:

1st row: (RS) P2, * K6, (P2, K2) 4 times, P2, rep from * twice more, K6, P2.
2nd row: K2, * P6, (K2,P2) 4 times, K2, rep from * twice more, P6, K2.
3rd row: P2, * sl 3f, (P2, K2) 4 times, P2, rep from * twice more, sl 3f, P2.
4th row: Work as for 2nd row.

Cont working in patt as set, at the same time shape sides by inc 1 st at each end of every 9th[7th:6th] row until there are 106[114:122] sts, taking inc sts into patt. Work even until sleeve meas 19[19:19¾]in, ending with same patt as on back and RS facing for next row.

Shape cap

Bind off 6[7:8] sts at beg of next 2

rows. Dec 1 st at each end of next and every foll alt row until 44[52:60] sts rem. Dec 1 st at each end of every row until 30 sts rem. Bind off.

4 Buttonband

Using size 3 needles, cast on 11 sts and work in rib as folls:
1st row: (RS) K2, * P1, K1, rep from * to last st, K1.
2nd row: P2, * K1, P1, rep from * to last st, P1.
Rep last 2 rows until border reaches across left back shoulder to neck, ending with WS row. Leave sts on a safety pin. Sew in position.

5 Buttonhole band

Work as for buttonband with 3 button holes. The 1st is placed 1¼in from shoulder edge, the 3rd 1¼in from neck edge, and the 2nd in center.
To make a buttonhole, rib 4, bind off 2 sts, rib to end and back casting on 2 sts over those bound off.
End band with a WS row. Leave sts on a safety pin. Sew in position.

6 Right shoulder band

Work as for buttonband.
Sew in position to right shoulder front and back.

7 Neckband

Using size 3 needles, rib across sts from buttonhole border as folls: K2, (P1, K1) 3 times, P1, K2 tog, pick up and K51 sts evenly around front neck, rib across sts from right shoulder as folls, K2 tog, (P1, K1) 3 times, P1, K2 tog, K across sts from back neck as folls: K11[11:14], K2 tog, K2, K2 tog, K18, K2 tog, K2, K2 tog, K9[9:12], K2 tog, K across sts from button border as folls: K2 tog, (P1, K1) 3 times, P1, K2. (127[127:133] sts.) Work in rib as folls:
1st row: (WS), P2, * K1, P1, rep from * to last st, P1.
2nd row: K2, * P1, K1, rep from * to last st, K1.
Rep 1st row once more.
Buttonhole row: Rib 4, bind off 2 sts, rib to end.
Next row: Cast on 2 sts over those bound off in previous row.
Work even until neckband meas 2¼in. Make a further buttonhole to match. Work 3 rows even in rib. Bind off in rib.

8 To finish

Fold neck border in half to WS and sew in position. Join side and sleeve seams, insert sleeves, sew on buttons.

Fair Isle Sweater

Not more than two colors are used in any one row to make this detailed patterned sweater. Choose five contrasting colors to make the Fair Isle pattern.

BEFORE YOU BEGIN
Follow the chart for the Fair Isle pattern. Cross out any portion of the chart you do not require. Mark the graph on completing every row.

Sizes
Chest   40[42:44:47]in
Length   26[26¼:26¾:27]in
Sleeve seam   19in

Note: Instructions for the larger sizes are in brackets [ ]; where one set of figures is given it applies to all sizes.

Gauge
22 sts and 30 rows to 4in meas over St st on size 6 needles.

Choosing your yarn

Recommended yarn

Knit a sample square and check your gauge with that given for the pattern.

Alternative yarns

Check the thickness of alternative yarns against these samples.

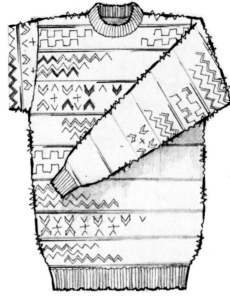

Materials
- Approx 16[16:18:18]oz of knitting worsted weight yarn in main color (m.c.)
- Approx 6[6:6:8]oz in knitting worsted weight 1st contrast (a)
- Approx 4[6:6:8]oz in knitting worsted weight 2nd contrast (b)
- Approx 2[2:2:4]oz in knitting worsted weight 3rd contrast (c)
- Approx 2[2:2:4]oz in knitting worsted weight 4th contrast (d)
- 1 pair each sizes 3 and 6 needles

INSTRUCTIONS
1 Back
Using size 3 needles and m.c., cast on 103[109:113:119] sts and work in rib as folls:
1st row: (RS) K1, * P1, K1, rep from * to end.
2nd row: P1, * K1, P1, rep from * to end.
Rep the last 2 rows for 2¾in, ending with a 1st row.
Inc row: (Rib 3, M1 by picking up the loop before the next st) 10[10:12:11] times, (rib 4, M1) 10[12:10:12] times, (rib 3, M1) 10[10:12:11] times, rib to end. (133[141:147:153] sts.)
Change to size 6 needles and starting with a K row, work 2 rows in St st. Now work in patt from chart reading knit rows from right to left and purl rows from left to right, working extra 6[10:1:4] sts once at beg of K rows and end of P rows.
Rep 24 patt sts 5[5:6:6] times across, working extra 7[11:2:5] sts once at end of K rows and beg of P rows.
Work in patt until back meas approx 16½in, ending with a 20th row of patt.
Shape armholes
Keeping patt correct, bind off 2 sts at beg of next 4[8:10:12] rows, then dec 1 st at each end of the next and every foll 4th row until 117[119:123:125] sts rem.
Work even in patt until armhole meas 9½[9¾:10¼:10½]in.
Shape shoulders
Bind off 37[37:38:38] sts at beg of next 2 rows. Leave rem 43[45:47:49] sts on a spare needle.

2 Front
Work as for back until armhole meas 6¼[6¾:7:7½]in, ending with WS row.
Shape neck
Next row: Patt 49 sts, turn and leave rem sts on a spare needle.
Keeping armhole edge even, dec 1 st at neck edge on next and every foll row 10[10:8:8] times in all then dec 1 st at neck edge on every foll alt row until 37[37:38:38] sts rem.
Work a few rows even until front matches back to shoulder.
Bind off.
Shape second side of neck
With RS facing, rejoin yarn to rem sts, bind off 19[21:25:27] sts loosely and complete to match first side reversing shapings.

3 Sleeves
Using size 3 needles and m.c., cast on

KEY ▨ = mc   ▨ = c   ▨ = a   ▨ = b   ☐ = d

53[57:57:61] sts and work in rib as for back.

Inc row: Rib 4[3:3:2], (M1, rib 3) 15[17:17:19] times, M1, rib to end. (69[75:75:81] sts.)

Change to size 6 needles and work in patt from chart as for 2nd[3rd:3rd:4th] size on back, starting with 55th row, at the same time shape sides as folls:

1st size

Inc 1 st at each end of every 4th row until there are 115 sts taking inc sts into patt.

2nd, 3rd and 4th sizes

Inc 1 st at each end of every [6th: 2nd:2nd] row [2:4:3] times, then 1 st at each end of every foll 4th row until there are [119:125:129] sts, taking inc sts into patt.

All sizes

Work even in patt until sleeve meas 19in, ending with 20th row of patt.

Shape cap

Bind off 2 sts at beg of next 8[10:8:10] rows. Bind off 4 sts at beg of every row until 51[59:61:69] sts rem. Bind off.

4 Neckband

Join right shoulder.

With RS facing and size 3 needles and m.c., pick up and K57[59:61:63] sts around front neck, K across sts from back neck, dec 1 st (99[103:107:111] sts. Work in K1, P1 rib for 2¾in. Bind off.

5 To finish

Join left shoulder and neckband. Fold neckband in half to the WS and sew in position. Sew sleeves in position. Join side and sleeve seams.

Casual Sweater

This man's sweater will look just as good on you as it does on him. Fold the neckband back in half or wear it fastened to the neck.

BEFORE YOU BEGIN
When working the cross stitch pattern always knit into the second and first stitch very loosely, otherwise it becomes very difficult to work into on the following row.

Sizes
Chest   36[38:40:42]in
Length   27½[28:28¼:28¾]in
Sleeve seam 18½[18¾:19¼:19¼]in

Note: Instructions for the larger sizes are given in brackets [ ]; where only one figure is given it applies to all sizes.

Gauge
24 sts and 30 rows to 4in over patt on size 6 needles.

Choosing your yarn

Recommended yarn

Knit a sample square and check your gauge with that given for the pattern.

Alternative yarns

Check the thickness of alternative yarns against these samples.

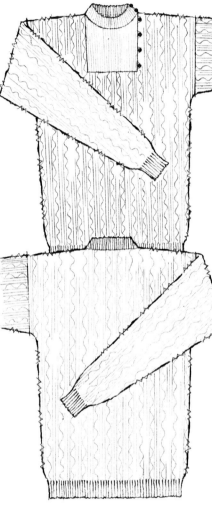

Materials
- ☐ Approx 23[25:25:27]oz of knitting worsted weight yarn
- ☐ 1 pair each sizes 2 and 6 needles
- ☐ Size D/3 crochet hook
- ☐ 6 buttons

INSTRUCTIONS
1 Back
* Using size 2 needles, cast on 121[127:133:139] sts.
1st row: K1, * P1, K1, rep from * to end.
2nd row: P1, * K1, P1, rep from * to end.
Rep these 2 rows for 2¾in.

Change to size 6 needles and work 1 K row. Now work patt as folls:
1st row: (RS) K.
2nd row: P2, * K2, P4, rep from * to last 5 sts, K2, P3.
3rd row: K2, * CR2B (K into back of 2nd st on left-hand needle, then K into the front of first st, slipping both sts off needle together), K4, rep from * to last 5 sts, CR2B, K3.
4th row: P2, * K1, P1, K1, P3, rep from * to last 5 sts, K1, P1, K1, P2.
5th row: K3, * CR2B, K4, rep from * to last 4 sts, CR2B, K2.
6th row: P3, * K2, P4, rep from * to last 4 sts, K2, P2.
7th row: K.
8th row: As 6th row.
9th row: K3, CR2F (K into front of 2nd st on left-hand needle, then K into front of 1st st, slipping both sts off needle together), K4, rep from * to last 4 sts, CR2F, K2.
10th row: As 4th row.
11th row: K2, * CR2F, K4, rep from * to last 5 sts, CR2F, K3.
12th row: As 2nd row.
These 12 rows form patt.
Cont in patt until back meas 17in, ending with a WS row. Place a colored marker at each end of row.
* Now cont even until back meas 24¾[25¼:25½:26]in, ending with a WS row.
Shape shoulders
Bind off 8[8:9:9] sts at beg of next 8 rows, then 9[11:9:11] sts at beg of foll 2 rows.
Bind off rem sts.

2 Front
Work as for back from * to *.
Now cont even until back meas 18[18½:18½:19]in, ending with a WS row.
Shape neck panel
Next row: Patt 41[43:45:47] sts, turn, leave rem sts on a spare needle. Cont on these sts for first side, working even until front matches back to start of shoulder shaping, ending with a WS row.

Shape shoulder

Bind off 8[8:9:9] sts at beg of next and foll 3 alt rows. Work 1 row.
Bind off rem 9[11:9:11] sts.

Shape second side of neck panel

With RS of work facing, rejoin yarn to rem sts, bind off 39[41:43:45] sts. K to end.
Cont on rem 41[43:45:47] sts as for first side, reversing all shapings.

3 Sleeves

Using size 2 needles, cast on 61[61:67:67] sts.

1st row: K1, * P1, K1, rep from * to end.
2nd row: P1, * K1, P1, rep from * to end.

Rep these 2 rows until meas 2½in from beg. Change to size 6 needles and work 1 K row. Work patt as for back, at the same time shape sides by inc 1 st at each end of next and every foll 3rd row until there are 79[89:81:105] sts. Then inc 1 st at each end of every foll 4th row until there are 121[125:129:135] sts. Work even until sleeve seam meas 18½[18¾:19¼:19¼]in. Bind off.

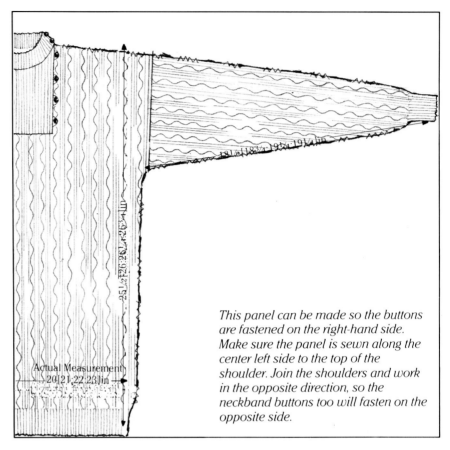

This panel can be made so the buttons are fastened on the right-hand side. Make sure the panel is sewn along the center left side to the top of the shoulder. Join the shoulders and work in the opposite direction, so the neckband buttons too will fasten on the opposite side.

4 Neck panel

Using size 2 needles, cast on 55[57:59:61] sts, and work as folls:

1st row: (RS) Sl 1, * P1, K1, rep from * to end.
2nd row: P1, * K1, P1, rep from * to end.

Rep these 2 rows until work meas 5in, ending with a WS row.

Divide for neck

Rib 14[14:17:17], K2 tog, turn, leave rem sts on a spare needle.
Cont on these 15[15:16:16] sts for first side. Dec 1 st at neck edge on every row until 6 sts rem, then on every 3rd row until 2 sts rem.
Work 2 rows.
Work 2 tog and fasten off.

Shape second side of neck

Rejoin yarn to rem sts, bind off next 23[25:21:23] sts. Work as for first side, reversing all the shapings. Using size 2 needles, cast on 7 sts, work in K1, P1, rib until strip, when slightly stretched, fits along left side of neck to top shoulder. Stitch as you go along. Leave sts on a safety pin.

5 Neck border

Sew panel to front along center up right side to top of shoulder. Join shoulders. Using size 2 needles and RS facing, start at top left corner of panel and K up 23[23:25:25] sts down left side of neck, 24 sts along center front, 23[23:25:25] sts up right side of neck, 50[54:54:58] sts from back and K across 7 sts from facing on safety pin (127[131:135:139] sts.)
Next row: K to form ridge.
Now work in K1, P1 rib as for neck panel until meas 1½in, ending with a WS row. Bind off in rib.

6 To finish

Join sleeve seams and side seams to markers. Insert sleeves.
Make 6 button loops, crochet 6 chains 2in long. Sew at top and bottom of left neck border to form 2 loops. Sew remaining loops along neck panel evenly. Sew on buttons. Press seams.

Fisherman's Rib Sweater

This traditional sweater is still worn by some English fishermen and is knitted in an oiled yarn to give extra warmth and to make it waterproof.

BEFORE YOU BEGIN

When working in fisherman's rib stitch, on every alternate row the knit stitch is worked into the stitch below the next stitch on the left-hand needle. Both the top and new stitch are slipped off the needle together, making one stitch only, producing an elongated knit stitch. Work all the stitches with an even tension.

Sizes

Chest   36[38:40:42]in
Length   26[27¼:28:28¾]in
Sleeve seam   18in

Note: Instructions for the larger sizes are in brackets [ ]; where there is one set of figures it applies to all sizes.

Choosing your yarn

Recommended yarn

Knit a sample square and check your gauge with that given for the pattern.

Alternative yarns

Check the thickness of alternative yarns against these samples.

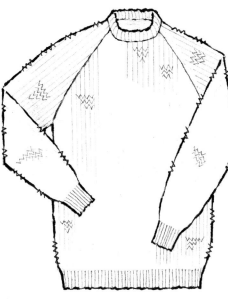

Gauge

19 sts and 28 rows to 4in over patt on size 8 needles.

Materials

☐ Approx 32[34:36:37]oz of Aran tweed-type yarn
☐ 1 pair each sizes 6 and 8 needles

INSTRUCTIONS

1 Back

* Using size 6 needles, cast on 93[97:101:105] sts.
1st row: K1, * P1, K1, rep from * to end.
2nd row: P1, * K1, P1, rep from * to end.
Rep these 2 rows for 2½in.
Change to size 8 needles and patt as folls:
1st row: (RS) K.
2nd row: P1, * K1B (K into st on row below next st, letting above st drop off needle in the usual way), P1, rep from * to end.
These 2 rows form the patt. Cont in patt until work meas 17[17¼:17¾:18]in from the beg, ending with a 2nd row.
Shape raglan
Keeping patt correct, bind off 2 sts at the beg of next 2 rows.

Next row: K2 tog, tbl, patt to last 2 sts, K2 tog.
Work 3 rows even.
Cont to dec on every 4th row 4[4:5:6] times more. *
Now dec on the next and every alt row until 33[35:37:39] sts rem, ending with a WS row.
Leave rem sts on a spare needle.

2 Front

Work as for back from * to *.
Dec 1 st on the next and every alt row until there are 47[49:51:53] sts rem, ending with a WS row.
Shape neck
Next row: K2 tog tbl, K16, turn.
Cont to dec at raglan edge as before, at the same time dec 1 st at neck edge on the next 10 rows.
Cont to dec at raglan edge on every alt row until 1 st rems. K1. Fasten off.

Shape second side of neck

With RS of work facing, sl center 11[13:15:17] sts onto a spare needle, join in the yarn, patt to last 2 sts, K2 tog. Now work as for the first side of neck, reversing all the shapings.

3 Sleeves

Using size 6 needles, cast on
43[45:47:59] sts.
Work in rib as for back for
3in, ending with a WS row.

Inc row: Rib 3[5:7:9], * inc into next
st, rib 4, rep from * 7 times more.
(51[53:55:57] sts.)
Change to size 8 needles and patt as
for back.
Inc 1 st at each end of the foll 11th
row, and every foll 8th row until there are
71[73:75:77] sts.
Cont even on these sts until work
meas 18in from the beg, ending with
a WS row.

Shape raglan

Keeping patt correct, bind off 2
sts at the beg of the next 2 rows.

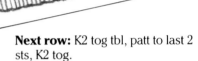

Next row: K2 tog tbl, patt to last 2
sts, K2 tog.
Work 3 rows even.
Dec 1 st at end of every 4th row
4[4:5:6] times more.
Now dec 1 st at each end of next and
every alt row until 11 sts rem, ending
with a WS row.
Leave these sts on a spare needle.

4 Neckband

Join front and left back raglan seams.
With RS facing and using size 6
needles, K33[35:37:39] sts across the
back neck sts, K11 from sleeve and
pick up and K13 sts down left neck edge,
K11[13:15:17] sts from front neck
edge, pick up and K13 sts up right edge,
K11 sts from sleeve. (92[96:100:104]
sts.)
Work 13 rows in K1, P1 rib.
Bind off loosely in rib.

5 To finish

Join remaining raglan seam.
Join side and sleeve seam.
Join neckband seam.
Fold neckband in half on to WS and
slip stitch down.

*Knitted in a novelty yarn this ribbed
sweater can look just as good on a
girl as it does on a man. Wear it loose
with trousers and accessorize with a
belt and scarf.*

Patterned Sweater

Make this striped ribbed sweater in natural colors for the winter days ahead.

BEFORE YOU BEGIN
When working thin stripes of even colors, it is not necessary to cut and join in the threads each time the color is changed. Twist the yarns up the right-hand edge.

Sizes
Chest   36[38:40:42]in
Length   26[26½:27¼:27½]in
Sleeve seam 18[19:19¼:19¼]in

Note: Instructions for the larger sizes are in brackets [ ]; where there is only one set of figures it applies to all sizes.

Gauge
19 sts and 44 rows to 4in over patt on size 5 needles.

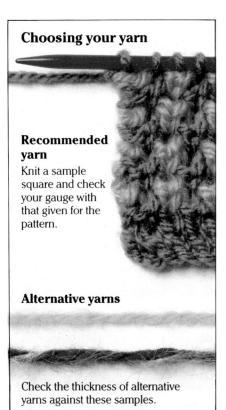

Choosing your yarn

Recommended yarn
Knit a sample square and check your gauge with that given for the pattern.

Alternative yarns
Check the thickness of alternative yarns against these samples.

Materials
☐ 8[8:10:10]oz of Pingouin Pingo-france in main color (m.c.)
☐ 6[6:6:8]oz of Pingouin Pingo-france in 1st, 2nd and 3rd contrast colors (a, b and c)
☐ 1 pair each sizes 2 and 5 needles

INSTRUCTIONS
1 Back
**Using size 2 needles and m.c., cast on 104[112:118:124] sts and work in K1, P1 rib for 2¾in, ending with a RS.
Next row: Rib 6[1:2:5], work 2 tog, (rib 7[7:6:6], work 2 tog) 10[12:14:14] times, rib 6[1:2:5]. (93[99:103:109] sts.) Change to size 5 needles and work patt as folls:
1st row: Using a, K1, * K1B, K1, rep from * to end.
2nd row: K in a.
3rd row: Using b, K2, * K1B, K1, rep from * to end.
4th row: K in b.
5th row: Using c, K1, * K1B, K1, rep from * to end.
6th row: K in c.
7th row: Using m.c., K2, * K1B, K1, rep from * to end.
8th row: K in m.c.

These 8 rows form the patt, cont in patt until work meas 16½in, ending with a WS row.
Shape armholes
Keeping pat correct, bind off 4[4:4:5] sts at beg of next 2 rows. Dec 1 st at each of next and every alt row until 73[75:79:81] sts rem.**
Cont even in patt until work meas 6¼[6¾: 7½:7¾]in, ending with a WS row.
Shape shoulders
Bind off 7 sts at beg of next 2 rows. Then 6[6:7:7] sts at beg of foll 4 rows. (35[37:37:39] sts.) Work on these sts for 2¼in, ending with a WS. Leave sts on a spare needle.

2 Front
Work as for back from ** to **.
Work even in patt until 2 rows less than on back have been worked to start of shoulder, ending with a WS row.
Divide for neck
Next row: Patt 23[23:25:25] sts, turn and leave rem sts on a spare needle. Cont on these sts for first side. Shape shoulder, at the same time as shaping neck.
Next row: K2 tog, K to end.
Next row: Bind off 7 sts, patt to last 2 sts, K2 tog.
Next row: K2 tog, K to end.
Next row: Bind off 6[6:7:7] sts, patt to last 2 sts, K2 tog.
Next row: K
Bind off rem 6[6:7:7] sts.
Second side of neck
With RS facing, slip center 27[29:29:31] sts onto a spare needle. Rejoin yarn to rem sts and work as for first side, reversing all the shapings.

3 Sleeves
Using size 2 needles and m.c., cast on 54[56:58:60] sts and work in K1, P1 rib for 2¼in, inc 1 st at end of last row. (55[57:59:61] sts.) Change to size 5 needles, work in stripe patt as given for back. Inc 1 st at each end of 7th and every 14th row until there are 75[77:79:81] sts.
Work even until sleeve meas

approx 19[19:19¼:19¼]in, ending with the same color row of patt as back and front.

Shape cap

Keeping patt correct, bind off 4[4:4:5] sts at beg of next 2 rows.

3rd and 4th sizes

Dec 1 st at each end of next row. Work 5 rows even. Rep last 6 rows [0:2] times more.

All sizes

Dec 1 st at each end of next row. Work 3 rows even. Rep the last 4 rows until 35[35:31:31] sts rem, ending with the 4th row.

1st and 2nd sizes

Dec 1 st at each end of next and every alt row until 31 sts rem.

All sizes

Work even on these 31 sts until strip fits along shoulder edge, ending with a WS row.

Left sleeve: Bind off 16 sts, work to end.

Right sleeve: Work 15 sts, bind off rem sts.

Leave rem sts on spare needle.

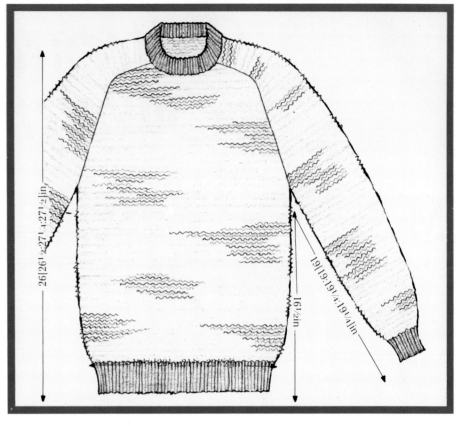

4 Neckband

Join shoulders to saddle strips, leaving left back shoulder open, join bound off edge of right saddle strip to extra rows at top of back.

Using size 2 needles and m.c., starting at center of left sleeve saddle, K15 from saddle inc 2 sts, pick up and K4 sts down left side of neck, K across the 27[29:29:31] sts from front inc 3 sts across these center sts, pick up and K4 sts up right side of neck, K15 sts from right saddle inc 2 sts, and then K35[37:37:39] sts from back inc 5 sts evenly. (112:[116:116:120] sts.) Work in K1, P1 rib for 3¼in.

Change to size 5 needles and bind off loosely in rib.

5 To finish

Do not press. The stitch is a ribbed stitch and will lose all elasticity if pressed. Join left back shoulder to saddle strip, join bound off edge of left saddle strip to extra rows at top of back. Join neckband, fold in half to WS and stitch down. Set in sleeves. Join side and sleeve seams.

Argyll Sweater

This classic Argyll pattern originated in Argyll, Scotland. The first designs were made into socks for sportswear. The design was then transferred to sweaters made in soft natural colors. Nowadays Argyll designs are worn in many variations of styles and colors by both men and women.

BEFORE YOU BEGIN

This sweater is made in three small man's sizes, and would also suit a woman. Use separate balls of yarn when working from the chart. Twist the yarns together when changing color to avoid holes.

Sizes

Bust/Chest   32[36:38]in
Length   23¼[24:24½]in
Sleeve seam   17[17¼:17¼]in

Note: Instructions for the larger sizes are given in brackets [ ]; where one figure is given it applies to all sizes.

Choosing your yarn

Recommended yarn

Knit a sample square and check your gauge with that given for the pattern.

Alternative yarns

Check the thickness of alternative yarns against these samples.

Gauge

28 sts and 36 rows to 4in over St st on size 3 needles.

Materials

☐ Approx 13[14:16]oz sport weight yarn in main color (m.c.)
☐ Approx 2oz each in contrast colours (a and b)
☐ 1 pair each sizes 2 and 3 needles

INSTRUCTIONS

1 Back

Using size 2 needles and m.c., cast on 106[120:130] sts and work in K1, P1 rib for 2¼in.
Inc row: Rib 3[5:5], M1, (rib 10[11:12] M1) 10[11:10] times, rib to end. (117[131:141] sts.)*
Change to size 3 needles and starting with a K row work in St st until work meas 15¼in, ending with a WS row.

Shape armholes

Bind off 3[4:4] sts at beg of next 2 rows. Dec 1 st at each end of every foll row until 103[109:115] sts rem, then at each end of every alt row until 95[103:109] sts rem.
Work even until work meas 23¼[24:24½]in, ending with a WS row.

Shape shoulders

Bind off 10 sts at beg of next 4 rows.
Bind off 8[10:12] sts at beg of foll 2 rows.
Leave rem 39[43:46] sts.

2 Front

Work as for back to *.
Change to size 3 needles, joining in colors, work in patt as from the chart. Rep the 78 sts twice working the extra sts at each side in St st.
Foll chart work until front matches the back to armhole shaping, ending with a WS row.

Shape armholes and divide for neck

Keeping patt correct, cont as folls:
Next row: Bind off 3[4:4], patt 53[59:64], K2 tog, turn and leave rem sts on a spare needle.
Cont on these 54[60:65] sts for first side. Work 1 row.
Dec 1 st at armhole edge on every foll row, at the same time dec 1 st at neck edge on next and every foll alt row until 46[52:57] sts rem.
Now dec 1 st at armhole edge on every alt row, cont to dec at neck edge on every 3rd row until 41[44:46] sts rem.
Cont to dec at neck edge only on every 4th row until 28[30:32] sts rem.
Work even until front matches back to start of shoulder shaping, ending with a WS row.

Shape shoulder

Bind off 10 sts at beg of next and foll alt row. Work 1 row.
Bind off the rem 8[10:12] sts.

Shape second side of neck

With RS facing, sl center st onto a safety pin. Rejoin yarn to rem 59[65:70] sts, K2 tog tbl, patt to end.
Complete to match first side reversing all the shapings.

3 Sleeves

Using size 2 needles and m.c., cast on 54[58:60] sts and work in K1, P1 rib for 1½in.
Next row: Rib 2[4:5], M1, (rib 5, M1)

10 times, rib to end. (65[69:71] sts.)
Change to size 3 needles and starting
with a K row, work in St st and at the
same time, shape sides by inc 1 st at
each end of the 4th and every foll
8th[7th:7th] row until there are
95[103:107] sts. Work even until

sleeve meas 17[17¼:17¼]in, ending
with a WS row.
Shape cap
Bind off 3[4:4] sts at beg of next 2
rows. Work 1 row.
Dec 1 st at each end of next and
every foll alt row until 37[39:41] sts

rem, then at each end of every row
until 17 sts rem. Bind off.

4 Neckband
Join right shoulder seam. With RS
facing and using size 2 needles and m.c.,
pick up and K64[70:74] sts down left

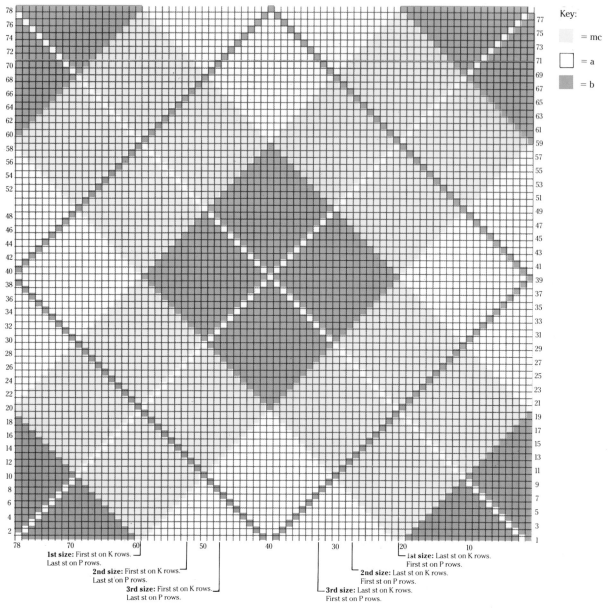

Key:

⬜ = mc

☐ = a

⬛ = b

1st size: First st on K rows.
Last st on P rows.

2nd size: First st on K rows.
Last st on P rows.

3rd size: First st on K rows.
Last st on P rows.

1st size: Last st on K rows.
First st on P rows.

2nd size: Last st on K rows.
First st on P rows.

3rd size: Last st on K rows.
First st on P rows.

side, K st from safety pin and mark with a colored thread, pick up and K64[70:74] sts up right side of neck, K39[43:45] sts from back, dec 3 sts evenly (165[181:191] sts.)

1st row: Work in P1, K1 rib to within 2 sts of marked st, P2 tog, P1, P2 tog tb1, starting with K st work in rib to end.

2nd row: Work in K1, P1 rib to within 2 sts of marked st, P2 tog, K1, P2 tog tb1, K1, starting with a P st work in rib to end.

Rep these 2 rows 3 times more, then the 1st row again.

Bind off in rib, still dec as before.

5 To finish

Press according to ballband instructions. Join left shoulder and neckband. Join side and sleeve seams. Insert sleeves.

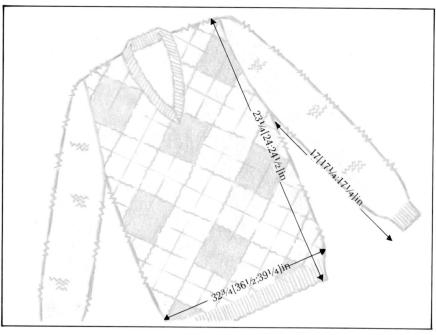

23¹/₄[24:24¹/₂]in

17[17¹/₄:17¹/₄]in

32³/₄[36¹/₂:39¹/₄]in

Heavy Cable Sweater

Knit yourself a hardwearing sweater, which looks just as good on her as it does on him.

BEFORE YOU BEGIN
Work the two stitches from the pattern panel immediately in front and behind the cable stitches fairly tightly, otherwise they will slacken and spoil the pattern panel.

Sizes
To fit Bust/chest 34[36:38:40:42]in
Length 25¼[25½:26:26½:26¾]in
Sleeve seam 19[19:19:19¼:19¼]in

Note: Instructions for larger sizes are in brackets [ ]; where there is only one set of figures it refers to all sizes.

Gauge
22 sts and 30 rows to 4in over St st on size 6 needles.

Materials
☐ Approx 16[18:20:21:23]oz of Knitting worsted weight yarn
☐ 1 pair each sizes 3 and 6 needles

Choosing your yarn

Recommended yarn
Knit a sample square and check your gauge with that given for the pattern.

Alternative yarns

Check the thickness of alternative yarns against these samples.

INSTRUCTIONS
1 Panel patt
1st row: (WS) K2, P3, K4, P6, K4, P3, K2.
2nd row: P2, K3, P4, sl next 3 sts onto cable needle and hold at back of work, K3, then K3 from cable needle (called C6B), P4, K3, P2.
3rd and every alt row: K all the P sts of previous row and P all the K sts.
4th row: P2, sl next 3 sts onto cable needle and hold at front of work, P1, then K3 from cable needle (called C4FP), P2, sl next st onto cable needle and hold at back of work, K3, then P1 from cable needle (called C4BP) twice, P2.
6th row: P3, C4FP, C4BP, P2, C4FP, C4BP, P3.
8th row: P4, sl next 3 sts onto cable needle and hold at front of work, K3, then K3 from cable needle (called C6F), P4, C6B, P4.
10th row: P3, C4BF, C4FP, P2, C4BP, C4FP, P3.
12th row: P2, (C4BP, P2, C4FP) twice, P2.
14th row: P2, K3, P4, C6F, P4, K3, P2.
16th row: As 4th row.
18th row: As 6th row.
20th row: P4, C6B, P4, C6F, P4.
22nd row: As 10th row.

24th row: As 12th row.
25th row: As 3rd row.
Rep rows 2-25 inclusive.
These 24 rows form the patt.

2 Back
Using size 6 needles, cast on 94[100:106:112:118] sts.
Next row: Sl 1, (K1, tbl) to end.
Rep this row 16 times more to end with a WS row.
Work in K2, P2 rib for 4 rows. **
Next row: K into front and back of next st to inc 1, rib 45[48:51:54:57], inc 1, rib 46[49:52:55:57], inc 1. (97[103:109:115:121] sts.)
Now work in flat rib patt as folls:
1st row: (WS) P8[11:14:1:4], (K1, P15) 5[5:5:7:7] times, K1, P to end.
2nd row: K8[11:14:1:4], (P1, K15) 5[5:5:7:7] times, P1, K to end.
These 2 rows form the flat rib patt.
Rep these 2 rows until work meas 15¼in from cast-on edge, ending with a WS row. Place a marker at each end of last row for gussets. Now cont in flat rib patt until work meas 17¼in, ending with a WS row. Place a marker at each end of last row for sleeves.
Cont in flat rib patt until work meas 24¾[25¼:25¼:26:26]in from cast-on edge, ending with a WS row.
Shape shoulders
Keeping patt correct, bind off 6[6:7:7:8] sts at beg of next 8 rows.
Now bind off 7[9:7:9:7] sts at beg of foll 2 rows. Leave rem 35[37:39:41:43] sts on a stitch holder.

3 Front
Work as given for back to **.
Next row: Inc 1, rib 5[8:11:14:18], inc 1, rib 1, inc 1, [rib 2, inc 1] 5 times, rib 22, inc 1, rib 46[49:52:55:57], inc 1.(104[110:116:122:128] sts.)
Now work in flat rib patt as given for back, placing panel patt as folls:
1st row: (WS) P8 [11:14:1:4], (K1, P15) 4[4:4:5:5] times, work 1st row of panel patt, P8[11:14:15:15], K0[0:0:1:1], P0[0:0:1:4].
2nd row: K0[0:0:1:4], P0[0:0:1:1],

113

K8[11:14:15:15], work 2nd row of panel patt, (K15, P1) 4[4:4:5:5] times, K8[11:14:1:4].

These 2 rows establish the position of the panel patt. Cont in this way working in flat rib and panel patt as set until work meas 15¼in from cast-on edge.

Place a marker at each end of last row for gussets.

Cont in flat rib and panel patt until work meas 17¼in. Place a marker at each end of last row for sleeves.

Cont as set until 10[10:10:12:12] rows less than back have been worked to beg of shoulder shaping, ending with a WS row.

Divide for neck

Next row: Patt 46[48:50:54:56] sts, K2 tog, turn, leaving rem sts on a spare needle. (47[49:51:55:57] sts.). Cont on these sts only for right side of neck, dec 1 st at neck edge on every row until 38[40:42:44:46] sts rem, ending with a WS row.

Shape shoulder

Keeping patt correct, bind off 6[6:7:7:8] sts at beg of next and foll alt row.

Next row: Patt to last 6 sts, (P2 tog) 3 times.

Next row: Bind off 6[6:7:7:8] sts, patt to end.

Next row: Patt to last 8 sts, (P2 tog) 4 times.

Next row: Bind off 6[6:7:7:8] sts, patt to end.

Next row: Patt to end.

Bind off rem 7[9:7:9:7] sts.

With RS of work facing return to sts on spare needle.

Sl next 15[17:19:17:19] sts at center front onto stitch holder, rejoin yarn to next st and work on these sts for left side of neck.

Next row: K2 tog tbl, patt to end. 40[42:44:48:50] sts.

Now dec 1 st at neck edge on every row until 31[33:35:37:39] sts rem, ending with a RS row.

Shape shoulder

Keeping patt correct, bind off 6[6:7:7:8] sts at beg of next and foll 3 alt rows. 7[9:7:9:7] sts.

Work 1 row.

4 Sleeves

Using size 3 needles, cast on 50[50:54:54:54] sts.

Work in K2, P2 rib for 2¾in, ending with a WS row.

Next row: Rib 3[3:1:1:1], inc 1, (rib 2[2:4:4:4], inc 1) 14[14:10:10:10] times, rib to end. (65 sts.)

Change to size 6 needles and work in

Be in fashion with this nautical look sweater. Wear it loosely over jeans or trousers. Sizes start at medium and the sweater is ideal for the fuller figure.

19[19:19:19¼:19¼]in

25¼[25½:26:26½:26¾]in

17½[18¾:19¾:20¾:22]in

flat rib patt as folls:

1st row: P8 (K1, P15) 3 times, K1, P to end.

2nd row: K8 [P1, K15] 3 times P1, K to end.

At the same time inc 1 st at each end of 10th[6th:8th:7th:7th] row and then every foll 12th[10:8th:7th:6th] row until there are 81[85:89:93:97] sts.

Cont even in flat rib patt until work meas 17[17:17:17¼:17¼]in from cast-on edge, ending with a WS row.

Place a marker at each end of last row for gusset. Now work even until sleeve measures 19[19:19:19¼:19¼]in.

Bind off.

5 Gusset (make 2)

Using size 6 needles, cast on 2 sts.

Beg with a K row, work in St st, *at the same time* inc 1 st at each end of the 2nd[2nd:2nd:1st:1st] row, then every foll alt row until there are 16[16:16:18:18] sts.

Work 4[4:4:2:2] rows even. Now dec 1 st at each end of the next and every foll alt row until there are 2 sts.

Work 1[1:1:0:0] rows.

Bind off.

6 Neckband

Join right shoulder seam.

Using size 3 needles, with RS facing pick up and K24[24:26:28:30] sts down left side of neck, K15[17:17:17:19] from stitch holder at front neck dec 1 st at center front, now pick up and K24[24:26:28:30] sts up right side of neck and K35[37:39:41:43] from stitch holder at back neck dec 1 st at center back. (94[100:106:112:126] sts.)

Work 10 rows in K2, P2 rib.

Bind off in rib.

7 To finish

Join side and sleeve seams to gusset markers. Join bound-off edge of sleeves to back and front. Insert gussets between markers.

Sweaters For The Family

Family Fair Isles

This traditional Scottish sweater design can be worked in sizes for all the family. The attractive band of pattern can be worked in subtle natural colors for a classic man's style, or in rainbow colors for younger children. Using the color code system, you can devise any combination of shades to suit your own taste.

BEFORE YOU BEGIN

Circle in red all the figures for the size you require before commencing.

Wind a small amount of yarn of each color, not including the main color, onto a separate piece of cardboard to avoid the yarns tangling.

Alternatively, you can leave the main color as a complete ball, but avoid the colored strands knotting by using a kitchen colander. Wind all the contrasting colors in small balls, then thread through separate holes, with the colander resting like a basket at your side or on your lap while knitting.

Choosing your yarn

Recommended yarn

Knit a sample square and check your gauge with that given for the pattern.

Alternative yarns

Check the thickness of alternative yarns against these samples.

 If you have difficulty making up the garment with bulky yarn, buy a matching ball of thinner yarn so that you can join the seams smoothly.

Sizes

Bust/chest	26[28:30:34:36:38:40: 42:44:46]in
Length	20[20¼:20½:23½:24: 24½:24½:24¾:27½:28: 28]in
Sleeve seam	12½[12½:12½:15¼: 15¼:15¼:15¼:15¼: 18:18:18]in

Note: Instructions for larger sizes are in brackets [ ]; where there is only one set of figures this applies to all sizes.

Gauge

18 sts and 17 rows of 4in over Fair Isle pattern chart A on size 9 needles.

Materials

- ☐ Approx 25[25:25:29:29:29:32:32:32:36: 36]oz of bulky weight yarn in color (a)
- ☐ Approx 3[3:3:3:3:7:7:7:7:11:11]oz of colors (b) and (c)
- ☐ Approx 3oz of color (d)
- ☐ 1 pair each sizes 7 and 9 needles
- ☐ 1 ball thinner matching yarn

INSTRUCTIONS

1 Back and front alike

Using size 7 needles and a, cast on 64[68:72:76:80:88:92:96:100:104:108] sts. Work in K2, P2 rib for 2in, inc 1 st at each end of last row. (66[70:74: 78:82:90:94:98:102:106:110] sts.)

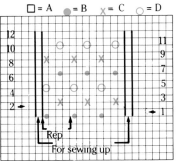

Chart A

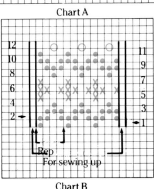

Chart B

Starting the pattern

Change to size 9 needles and commence Fair Isle patt chart A. Cont in this way for approx 10½[10½:10½: 13¼:13¼:13¼:13¼:13¼:16:16:16]in, ending with a 12th patt row.

Change to Fair Isle chart B and work a further 2in, ending with a P row.

Shaping armholes

Keeping Fair Isle patt correct, bind off 4[4:4:5:5:5:6:6:7:7:8] sts at the beg of next 2 rows. Dec 1 st at each end of the next and every alt row until 52[56:60:64:68:72:72:76:76:80:80] sts rem, ending with a P row. Cont in patt until armholes meas 5[5:6:6:6:6¼: 6¼:6¾:6¾:6¾:6¾]in from beg of shaping, ending with a P row.

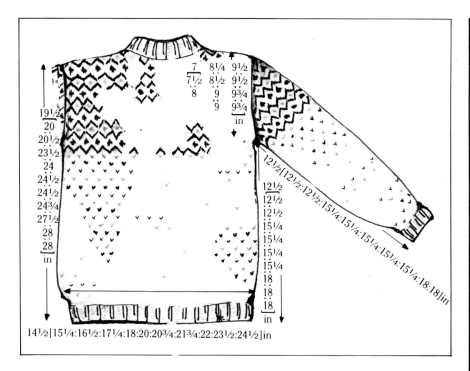

14½[15¼:16½:17¼:18:20:20¾:21¾:22:23½:24½]in

Shaping neck

Patt 20[22:22:25:27:29:29:29:29:31:31] sts and turn, leaving rem sts on a spare needle. Dec 1 st at neck edge on every row until 17[18:19:21:22:22: 24:24:26:27] sts rem. Cont even until armholes meas 7[7½:8:8¼:8½: 9:9:9½:9½:9¾:9¾]in from beg of shaping, ending at armhole edge.

Shaping shoulders

Bind off 6[6:6:7:7:8:8:9:9:9] sts at beg of next and foll alt row. Work 1 row. Bind off the rem 5[6:7:7:8:8:8:9:8:8:9] sts. With RS facing, return to sts on spare needle, slip center 12[12:16:14: 14:14:14:18:18:18:18] sts onto a st holder. Join in yarn to next st, patt to end. Now complete to match first side of neck, reversing all the shapings.

2 Sleeves

Using size 7 needles and a, cast on 32[36:36:36:36:40:40:44:44:48:48] sts and work in K2, P2 rib for 2in, inc 1 st at each end of last row. (34[38:38: 38:38:42:42:46:46:50:50] sts.) Change to size 9 needles and commence Fair Isle chart A. Inc and work in patt 1 st at each end of 2nd [2nd:2nd:6th:6th:6th:6th:6th:6th:6th: 6th] row and then every foll 4th[4th: 3rd:4th:3rd:4th:3rd:3rd:4th:4th:4th] row until there are 50[54:58:58:62: 62:66:70:70:74:74] sts. When sleeve meas approx 10½[10½:10½:13½:13½:13½: 13½:13½:16:16:16]in from cast-on edge, ending with a 12th patt row, change to Fair Isle chart B and work a further 2in, ending with a P row.

Shaping cap

Bind off 4[4:4:5:5:5:6:6:7:7:8] sts at the beg of the next 2 rows. Dec 1 st at each end of next and every foll alt row until 34[38:40:36:40:38:42:40:36: 42:38] sts rem, then dec 1 st at each end of every row until 14[14:16:16:16: 18:18:20:20:22:22] sts rem. Bind off.

3 Neckband

Join right shoulder seam. With RS of work facing, using size 7 needles and a, pick up and K 11[13:11:13:13:15: 16:15:15:17:17] sts down left side of front neck, K12[12:16:14:14:14:14:18: 18:18:18] sts from front st holder, pick up and K11[13:11:13:13:15:16:15:15: 17:17] sts up right side of front neck, 11[13:11:13:13:15:16:15:15:17:17] sts down right side of back neck, K12[12: 16:14:14:14:14:18:18:18:18] sts from back st holder; pick up and K11[13: 11:13:13:15:16:15:15:17:17] sts up left side of back neck. (68[76:76:80:80: 88:92:96:96:104:104] sts.) Work 4in in K2, P2 rib. Bind off loosely in rib.

4 To finish

Press on WS using a warm iron (at wool setting) over a damp cloth. Join left shoulder, neckband, side and sleeve seams with a flat stitch. Fold neckband in half onto WS and stitch down with herringbone stitch.

HELPING HAND

Stranding yarn

When using two colors or more, the yarn color not in use passes in loose strands across the back of the work behind the contrasting stitches until it is needed again. Be careful not pull the color not in use too tightly on the wrong side of the work, which causes puckering.

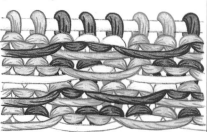

Since only two colors are used per row it is possible to control one with each hand. If you are right-handed you will probably prefer to use this hand to control the most often-used color.

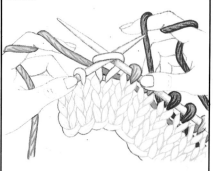

When the right-hand color is being used, the left hand holds the other color out of the way. When the left-hand color is being used, the right hand holds the other contrast color.

These diagrams show stranding at the back of the work on a knit row. It is possible to adapt this method effectively for purling stitches with the strands in front.

Striped Raglan Tops

The neckband and collar version of the raglan top can both be made following the same set of instructions. Sizes start for a ten-year-old to a young adult. Choose six contrasting colors for both versions.

BEFORE YOU BEGIN

When working in the stripe pattern, the yarns not in use can be woven loosely up the side of the work. This will save many hours work when finishing off the garment pieces.

Sizes

Bust/chest   30[32:34:36:38]in
Length   21[21¾:22½:23½:24½]in
Sleeve seam   15¼[17:17:18:18]in

Note: Instructions for the larger sizes are in brackets [ ]; where there is one set of figures it applies to all sizes.

Choosing your yarn

Recommended yarn
Knit a sample square and check your gauge with that given for the pattern.

Alternative yarns

Check the thickness of alternative yarns against these samples.

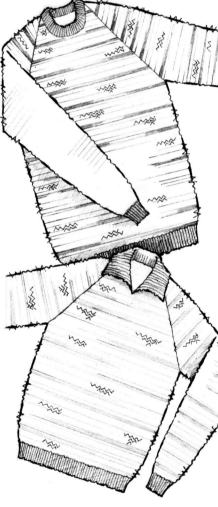

Gauge

22 sts and 30 rows to 4in over St st on size 6 needles.

Materials

Both garments are made in knitting worsted weight yarn.
For sweater with neckband
☐ Approx 3[3:5:5:5]oz in (m.c.)
☐ Approx 2[2:3:3:3]oz in each of 5 contrast colors (a, b, c, d and e)
For sweater with collar
☐ Approx 3[3:5:5:5]oz in (m.c.)
☐ Approx 2[2:3:3:3]oz in each of 5 contrast colors (a, b, c, d and e)
☐ 1 Pair each sizes 3 and 6 needles

Instructions for neckband version

1 Back

* Using size 3 needles and m.c., cast on 84[88:94:100:106] sts. Work in K1, P1 rib for 2in.
Inc row: Rib 8[5:7:7:11], M1 (by picking up loop before next st and working into back of it), * rib 17[13:16:17:21], M1, rep from * to last 8[5:7:8:11] sts, rib to end. (89[95:100:106:111] sts.)
Change to size 6 needles and join in contrast colors when required.
Starting with a K row, work in St st as folls:
Using a, work 2 rows.
Using b, work 2 rows.
Using c, work 2 rows.
Using d, work 2 rows.
Using e, work 2 rows.
Using m.c., work 2 rows.
These 12 rows form the patt.
Cont in patt until work meas approx 13¼[13¾:14¼:14½:15]in, ending with 4th[6th:10th:12th:2nd] row of patt.
Shape raglans
Keeping patt correct, bind off 4 sts at beg of next 2 rows. Dec 1 st at each end of next row. Work 3 rows.
Rep last 4 rows 1[0:0:1:0] times more. (77[85:90:94:101] sts.)*
Now dec 1 st at each end of the next and every alt row until 29[31:32:34:35] sts rem, ending with RS facing for next row.
Leave rem sts on a spare needle.

2 Front

Work as given for back from * to *.
Cont working as for back until front is 17[19:19:23:23] rows shorter than back to shoulder shaping, ending with RS row.
(45[49:50:56:57] sts.)
Shape neck
Next row: Patt 15[17:17:20:20] sts, turn.

119

Next row: Patt to last 2 sts, K2 tog.
Still keeping continuity of patt and
raglan shaping, dec 1 st at neck edge
on the next 3 rows. Dec 1 st on the
next and every foll alt row until
6[6:6:7:7] sts rem. Keeping neck edge
even, cont raglan dec as before
until 2 sts rem, ending with RS facing
for next row.
Next row: K2 tog and fasten off.
Shape second side of neck
Sl next 15[15:16:16:17] sts onto a
spare needle.

Rejoin yarn to rem sts and patt to end
of row.
Now work as for first side of neck
reversing all the shapings.

3 Sleeves (both versions)
Using size 3 needles and m.c., cast on
40[42:42:48:50] sts and work in K1, P1
rib for 2in.
Inc row: Rib 4[6:6:4:5], M1, * rib
8[10:10:10:10], M1, rep from * to last
4[6:6:4:5] sts, rib to end.
(45[46:46:53:55] sts.)

Change to size 6 needles, joining in
contrast colors as required.
Work as stripe patt for back
starting with 11th[1st:5th:9th:1st] row
of patt.
Work 12[10:8:8:8] rows in patt as
given for back. Keeping patt correct,
inc 1 st at each end of next and
every foll 12th[11th:10th:9th:9th] row
until there are 59[64:66:77:79] sts.
Work even until sleeve seam meas
approx 15¼[17:17:18:18]in, ending
with same row of patt as on back

before start of raglan shaping, ending with a WS row.

Shape raglans

Keeping of patt correct, bind off 4 sts at beg of next 2 rows.

Dec 1 st at each end of next and every foll 4th row until 39[46:46:61:63] sts rem. Work 3 rows even.

Now dec 1 st at each end of the next and every foll alt row until 7[8:8:9:9] sts rem, ending with a WS row. Leave these sts on a safety pin.

4 Neckband

Join raglans, leaving left back raglan open.

Using size 3 needles and m.c., K7[8:8:9:9] sts from safety pin at left sleeve, pick up and K14[16:16:20:20] sts down left side of neck, K15[15:16: 16:17] sts from center front, pick up and K14[16:16:20:20] sts up right side of neck K7[8:8:9:9] sts from right sleeve then K29[31:32:34:35] sts at back neck. (86[94:96:108:110] sts.) Work in K1, P1 rib for 2¾in.

Bind off loosely in rib.

5 To finish

Join remaining raglan seam and neckband. Fold neckband in half to inside and stitch loosely in position. Join side and sleeve seams.

Instructions for collar version

1 Back

Work as for version with neckband, but bind off the sts for back neck.

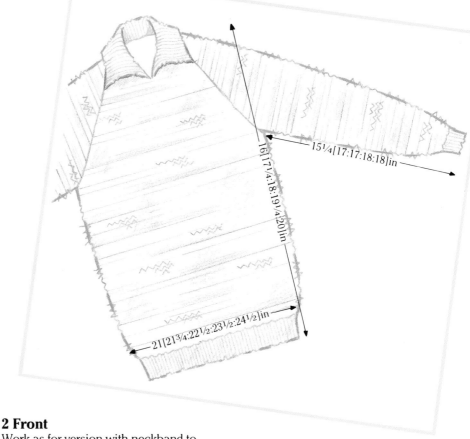

2 Front

Work as for version with neckband to dividing neck shaping. Bind off the center sts. Cont working front as for neckband version.

3 Sleeves

Work as for neckband version, binding off the sts for sleeve cap.

4 Collar

Using size 3 needles and m.c., cast on 105[113:115:129:133] sts.

1st row: K1, * P1, K1, rep from * to end.

2nd row: P1, * K1, P1, rep from * to end.

Rep these 2 rows until work meas 2in, ending with a WS row.

Shape collar

Next row: Rib to last 10[11:11:12:13] sts, turn.

Next row: Rib to last 10[11:11:12:13] sts, turn.

Next row: Rib to last 20[22:22:24:26] sts, turn].

Next row: Rib to last 20[22:22:24:26] sts, turn.

Cont to rib 10[11:11:12:13] sts less on each row until the row 'rib to last 50[55:55:60:65] sts' turn, has been worked twice, work until narrow edge meas 4¾in. Bind off evenly in rib.

5 To finish

Sew cast-on edge of collar to neck edge, starting and finishing at center front.

Join raglans, side and sleeve seam.

Matching Jacket And Slipover

Make this matching jacket and slipover for yourself and your daughter. The slipover is worked in a pattern of bobbles and Fair Isle.

BEFORE YOU BEGIN

Following the pattern from the chart, work the squares marked with a cross in Fair Isle and the squares marked with a circle as a bobble. To work a bobble, knit into the stitch 5 times, turn and knit 5 stitches, turn and purl the 5 stitches, turn and pass the 2nd, 3rd, 4th and 5th stitch over the 1st stitch. Work the next row tightly over these stitches.

Sizes
Jacket
Bust/chest   26[28:30:32:34:36:38]in
Length   21[22:23¼:24½:25½:
                     26¼:26¾]in
Sleeve seam   16¼:[17:17¾:18½:
                     19¾:19¾:20]in

Slipover
Bust/chest   26[28:30:32:34:36:38]in
Length   19¼[20½:21¾:22¾:
                     23½:24½:24¾]in

Choosing your yarn

Recommended yarn
Knit a sample square and check your gauge with that given for the pattern.

Alternative yarns

Check the thickness of alternative yarns against these samples.

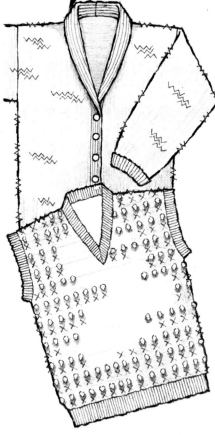

Note: Instructions for the larger sizes are in brackets [ ]; where there is only one set of figures it applies to all sizes.

Gauge
22 sts and 28 rows of 4in over St st on size 6 needles.

Materials
For the jacket
- ☐ Approx 11[13:14:16:18:20:21]oz of knitting worsted weight yarn
- ☐ 1 pair each sizes 3 and 6 needles
- ☐ 6[6:6:7:7:8:8] buttons

For the slipover
- ☐ Approx 6[6:7:7:9:11:13]oz in main color (m.c.)
- ☐ Approx 2[2:2:2:2:4:4]oz in 1st contrast color (a)
- ☐ Approx 2[2:2:4:4:6:6] 2nd contrast color (b)
- ☐ 1 pair each sizes 3 and 6 needles

Instructions for jacket
1 Back
Using size 3 needles, cast on 82[88:94:102:108:114:118] sts. Work 10 rows in K1, P1, rib. Change to size 6 needles and starting with a K row, work 13¼[14¼:15:15¾:16½: 17:17¼]in in St st ending with a WS row. Mark the beg of next row with a colored thread. Cont in St st until back meas 20½:[21¾:22¾:24:25¼:26:26½]in from beg, ending with a WS row.

Shape shoulders
Bind off 12[13:15:16:18:19:20] sts at beg of the next 4 rows.
Bind off rem 34[36:34:38:36:38:38] sts.

2 Right front
Using size 3 needles, cast on 40[42:46:50:52:56:58] sts. Work 10 rows in K1, P1 rib.
Change to size 6 needles and starting with a K row, work 11[12¼: 13: 14¼: 14½: 15¼:15¾]in from beg, ending with a WS row.

Shape neck
Dec 1 st at beg of next and at the same edge on every foll 3rd row until 24[26:30:32:36:38:40] sts rem. Work even until front matches back to beg of armhole, mark with colored thread then cont even to shoulder shaping, ending with a RS row.

Shape shoulder
Bind off 12[13:15:16:18:19:20] sts at beg of next and foll alt row.

3 Left front
Work as for right front reversing all the shapings.

4 Sleeves
Using size 3 needles cast on 62[66:70:74:78:84:84] sts. Work 2¼ [2¼:2¾:2¾:3¼:3¼:3¼]in in K1, P1 rib. Change to size 6 needles and starting with a K row, work in St st inc 1st at each end of next and every foll 9th row until there are 78[82:88:92:96:102:102] sts. Cont even until sleeve meas 16¼[17:17¾: 18½:19¾:19¾:20]in from beg. Bind off loosely.

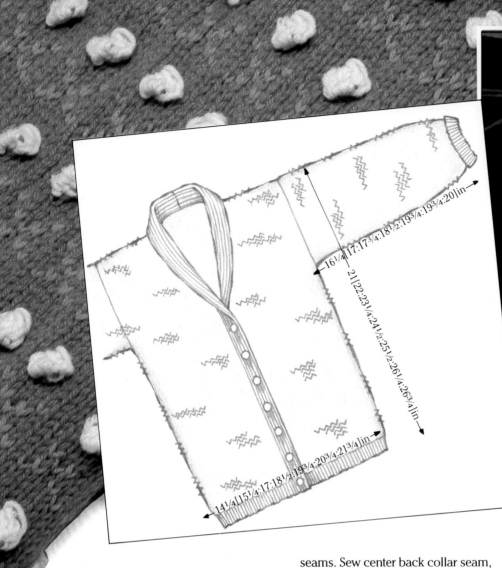

16¼[17:17¾:18½:19¾:19¾:20]in

21[22:23¼:24½:25½:26¼:26¾]in

14¼[15¼:17:18½:19¾:20¾:21¾]in

5 Right front band and collar

Using size 3 needles, cast on 8 sts, work in K1, P1 rib for 4 rows.

Buttonhole row: Rib 3, bind off 2, rib to end.

Next row: Rib casting on over bound off sts. Cont in rib making a buttonhole every 1¾in until there are 6[6:6:7:7:8:8] buttonholes. Cont even until band meas 9¾[11:11¾:13:13½: 14¼:14½]in when slightly stretched, ending with a RS row.

Shape collar

Still working in rib, inc 1 st at the beg of next row then 1 st at same edge on every foll row until there are 26[28:28:30:30:32:32] sts. Work even in rib until collar and band meas 24½[[26:26¾:28¾:29½:30¾:31]in when slightly stretched. Bind off.

6 Left band and collar

Work as for right front omitting buttonholes.

7 To finish

Press lightly with a cool iron over a dry cloth. Join side seams to contrast thread marker, join shoulder and sleeve seams. Sew center back collar seam, mark center back neck, place collar seam to this mark. With a flat stitch sew bands and collar in place. Set in sleeves. Sew on buttons.

Instructions for slipover
1 Back

Using size 3 needles and m.c., cast on 72[78:84:90:96:102:108] sts. Work 2[2:2:2¼:2¼:2¼:2¼]in in K1, P1 rib.
Inc row: Rib 3[6:9:8:2:5:8], * inc into next st, rib 3[3:3:3:4:4:4], rep from * ending rib 4[7:10:9:3:6:9].
(89[95:101:109:115:121:127] sts.)
Change to size 6 needles, starting with

a K row work 2 rows in St st. Foll patt on chart until back meas 12¼[13:13¾: 14½:15:15¼:15¾]in from cast-on edge ending with a P row.

Shape armholes

Bind off 4[4:4:5:5:5:5] sts at the beg of the next 2 rows. **

Cont on these sts until back meas 6¾[7:7½:8:8¼:8¾:8¾]in from beg of armhole shaping.

Shape shoulders

Bind off 11[12:13:14:15:16:17] sts at beg of the next 2 rows, then 12[13:14:15:16:17:18] sts at beg of the foll 2 rows. Leave rem 35[37:39:41:43:45:47] sts on a spare needle.

2 Front

Work as for back to **.
Work 2[4:6:8:8:10:10] rows.

Shape neck

Patt 40[43:46:49:52:55:58], leave these sts on a spare needle. K1, and sl this st onto a safety pin, patt to end. Cont working on this set of sts dec 1st at neck edge on next and every foll alt row until 23[25:27:29:31:33:35] sts rem. Cont on these sts until front matches back to beg of shoulder shaping, ending with a RS row.

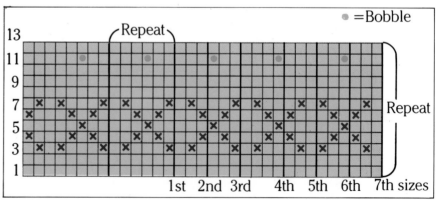

=Bobble

Repeat

Repeat

1st 2nd 3rd 4th 5th 6th 7th sizes

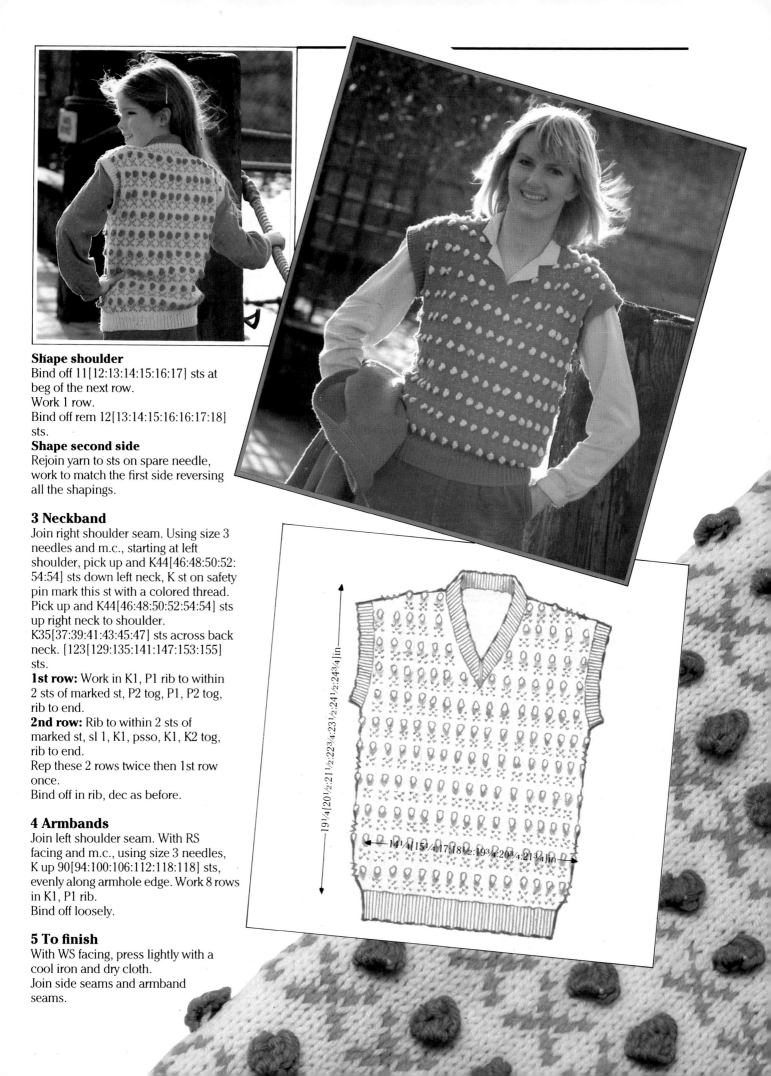

Shape shoulder
Bind off 11[12:13:14:15:16:17] sts at beg of the next row.
Work 1 row.
Bind off rem 12[13:14:15:16:16:17:18] sts.

Shape second side
Rejoin yarn to sts on spare needle, work to match the first side reversing all the shapings.

3 Neckband
Join right shoulder seam. Using size 3 needles and m.c., starting at left shoulder, pick up and K44[46:48:50:52:54:54] sts down left neck, K st on safety pin mark this st with a colored thread. Pick up and K44[46:48:50:52:54:54] sts up right neck to shoulder. K35[37:39:41:43:45:47] sts across back neck. [123[129:135:141:147:153:155] sts.

1st row: Work in K1, P1 rib to within 2 sts of marked st, P2 tog, P1, P2 tog, rib to end.

2nd row: Rib to within 2 sts of marked st, sl 1, K1, psso, K1, K2 tog, rib to end.

Rep these 2 rows twice then 1st row once.
Bind off in rib, dec as before.

4 Armbands
Join left shoulder seam. With RS facing and m.c., using size 3 needles, K up 90[94:100:106:112:118:118] sts, evenly along armhole edge. Work 8 rows in K1, P1 rib.
Bind off loosely.

5 To finish
With WS facing, press lightly with a cool iron and dry cloth.
Join side seams and armband seams.

19¼[20½:21:21½:22¾:23½:24½:24¾]in

14¼[15¼:17:18½:19¾:20¾:21¾]in

Know How

This step-by-step knitting guide is ideal for beginners and for experienced knitters who want to refresh the skills they already have. All the basic knitting stitches and methods are covered, and each set of diagrams is clearly numbered and easy to follow.

Know How

Casting on

The first method uses two knitting needles and is called the cable method. It produces a strong but elastic edge and is widely used for thicker yarns such as those used for cable sweaters.

The second method is called the thumb method. It uses only one needle with the thumb of the left hand acting as the second needle. It produces a finer, more elastic edge.

Cable method

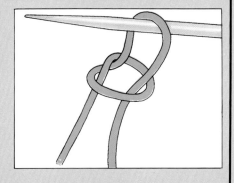

1 *Make a slip loop about 4in from the end of the yarn. Place the loop on the needle. Pull the short end to tighten the stitch. Hold this needle in your left hand.*

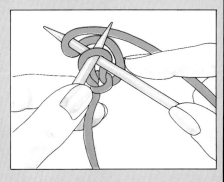

2 *Insert the right-hand needle into the loop so that it rests under the left-hand needle in a crossed position. Take the yarn under and over the point of the right-hand needle.*

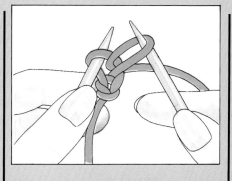

3 *With the right-hand needle draw the yarn through the stitch on the left-hand needle to make a new stitch on the right-hand needle. Work loosely on these stitches.*

4 *Transfer the stitch on right-hand needle on to the left-hand needle. Always make sure each loop is facing the same direction otherwise the edge will look uneven.*

5 *Insert the right-hand needle between the two stitches on the left-hand needle, from front to back. Take the yarn under and over the point of the right-hand needle.*

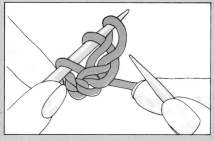

6 *Draw the yarn through between the stitches to make a new stitch. Repeat steps 4 to 6 until you have the necessary number of stitches, keeping your work as even as possible.*

Thumb method

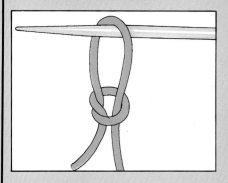

1 *Allowing approximately ³⁄₄in for each stitch to be cast on, make a slip loop that distance from the end of the ball of yarn.*

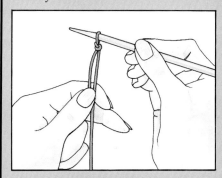

2 *Place the loop on the needle and pull the shorter end to tighten the stitch. Allow ³⁄₄in per stitch for casting on with average yarn.*

127

Know How

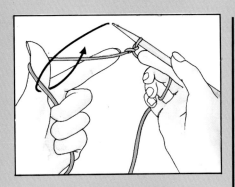

3 *Hold the needle and the yarn from the ball in the right hand. Wind the shorter end around the thumb of the left hand.*

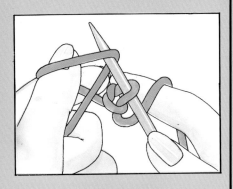

4 *Insert needle through the loop on the thumb, holding this taut in your left hand with the thumb at least ³/₄in away from the needle.*

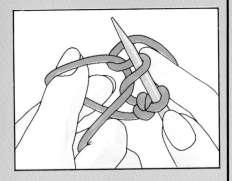

5 *Take the yarn from the ball under and over the point of the needle and draw it through the loop on the thumb to make a stitch.*

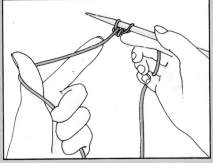

6 *Slip the loop off the thumb. Pull the shorter end to tighten the stitch. Repeat steps 2 to 6 until you have the necessary number of stitches.*

Yarn and needle positions

The yarn is wound around one finger and then over and under the remaining fingers in order to control the flow of the yarn. Right-handed knitters hold the yarn in the right hand and also the needle containing the stitches which have been knitted. The left hand holds the stitches to be knitted. These positions are reversed for left-handed knitters. There are only two basic stitches in knitting – the knit stitch and the purl stitch. Even the most complicated pattern is only made from a combination of these two stitches. Once these simple techniques are mastered, the knitting possibilities are unlimited.

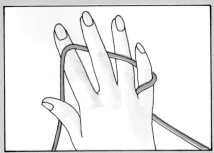

1 *Wind the end of the yarn completely around the little finger and then over and under the remaining three fingers. (First method).*

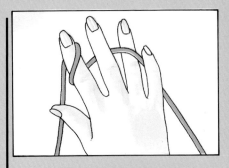

2 *Beginning with the little finger, wind the yarn under and over three fingers and then completely around first finger. (Second method).*

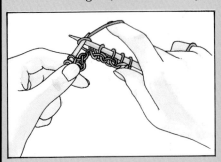

3 *The left hand holds the needle firmly over the top with the thumb at the front and the fingers at the back.*

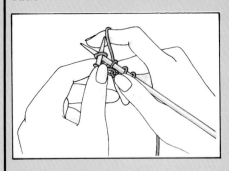

4 *The right-hand needle rests at the base of the thumb and first finger and the hand slides towards the needle point as each stitch is knitted.*

Know How

Basic stitches

Knit and purl stitches can be combined in a variety of ways to produce many different patterns.

When every right-side row is knitted and every wrong-side row is purled and the two are worked alternately the fabric is called stockinette stitch. The right side is smooth and the wrong side is ridged. This is probably the most common of all the patterns.

When every right-side row is purled and every wrong-side row is knitted the fabric is called reverse stockinette stitch. Here the right side is ridged and the wrong side is smooth. This is often used for a bouclé or similar yarn.

Where every stitch on every row is knitted the fabric is called garter stitch. It is often used for hems and borders because the edges lie flat.

The knit stitch

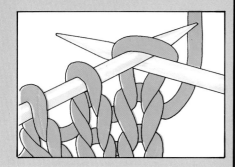

1 *Take the needle holding the stitches in your left hand and the empty needle in your right hand. Keep the yarn at the back of the work. Insert the right-hand needle from right to left through the front of the first knit stitch.*

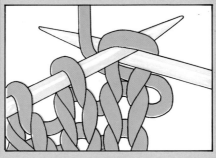

2 *Using your index finger take the yarn under and over the point of the right-hand needle.*

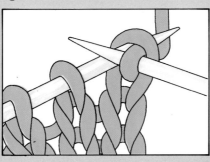

3 *Draw the yarn on the right-hand needle through the stitch on the left-hand needle.*

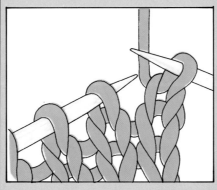

4 *Slip the stitch off the left-hand needle thus completing the knit stitch. Repeat steps 1 to 4 for every stitch.*

The purl stitch

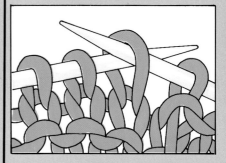

1 *Take the needle holding the stitches in your left hand and the empty needle in your right hand.*

2 *Insert point of right-hand needle from right to left through front of first stitch; take yarn over and under point of right-hand needle.*

3 *Draw yarn on right-hand needle through the stitch on the left-hand needle, from back through to front.*

Know How

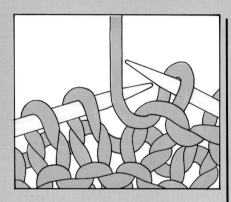

4 *Slip the stitch off the left-hand needle on to the right-hand needle, thus completing the purl stitch. Repeat steps 1 to 4 for every knit stitch.*

Binding off

When binding off, care must be taken to keep the edge loose, otherwise the work will be distorted and the stitches could break if the knitting is pulled. This is most important on a neckband.

The following steps show how to bind off on a knit row but often it will be necessary to bind off on a purl row. To do this, keep the yarn at the front of the work and purl each stitch instead of knitting it.

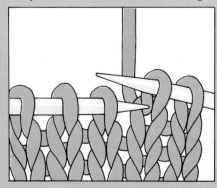

1 *To bind off knitwise keep the yarn at the back of the work. Knit the first two stitches on the left-hand needle in the usual way, working them fairly loosely.*

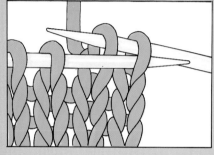

2 *Insert the point of the left-hand needle through the front of the first stitch knitted and lift it over the second stitch knitted, then off the needle. One stitch has been bound off.*

3 *Knit the next stitch on the left-hand needle in the usual way. Lift the second stitch knitted over it and off the needle. Two stitches have now been bound off.*

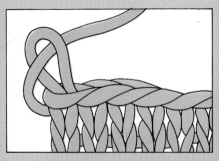

4 *Repeat step 3 until all the stitches have been worked off the left-hand needle and one stitch remains on the right-hand needle. Cut the yarn leaving at least 4in and thread the end through the remaining stitch. Pull end to tighten the stitch.*

Increasing and decreasing

It is often necessary to increase the width of the knitting on the needles. There are various ways of doing this depending on the stitch pattern and how many stitches are required. Here we show the simplest method, worked into a knit stitch. This is used when a pattern reads "increase one stitch" usually abbreviated as inc 1st, or "knit into the front and back of the next stitch".

This method of increasing can be worked into any stitch of the row. Occasionally, where a great amount of fullness is required, it may be necessary to increase into every stitch on a row. This is called a mass increase.

On most knitting patterns it will be necessary to reduce the width of the knitting, for example on neck shaping or on the cap of a sleeve.

As with increasing there are several ways of decreasing and on the right we show the simplest method, knitting two stitches together, usually abbreviated as "K2 tog".

This decrease can be worked in any position on a row. A mass decrease is worked by decreasing into each pair of stitches across the row.

Simple increasing

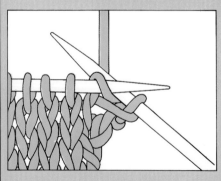

1 *Insert the right-hand needle knitwise into the front of the stitch on the left-hand needle and knit the stitch in the usual way, but do not slip the stitch off the left-hand needle.*

Know How

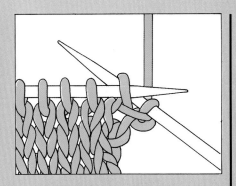

2 *Insert the right-hand needle knitwise into the same stitch, through the back of the loop this time, and knit this stitch.*

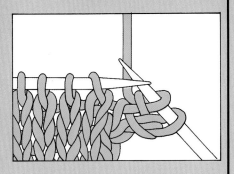

3 *Slip the stitch left from the left-hand needle. You have now made two stitches from one stitch.*

Simple decreasing

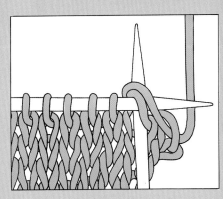

1 *Insert the right-hand needle knitwise through the second stitch then first stitch on the left-hand needle, at the same time.*

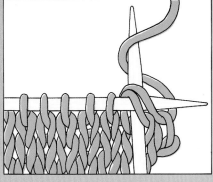

2 *Take the yarn under and over the point of the right-hand needle and draw the yarn through both the first and second stitches.*

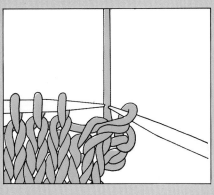

3 *Drop the first and second stitches off the left-hand needle thus decreasing one stitch.*

Slipping stitches

When a stitch is passed from one needle to the next without being knitted, it is called slipping a stitch. When the stitch is slipped onto the next needle, it pulls the stitches either side of this stitch together and produces a stronger fabric. Often the stitches at each end of every knit row are slipped; this makes a neat strong edge and is a good selvedge. When sewing up the garment, it is easy to pick up the alternate slipped stitches on the seams. On raglan shaping and neckbands, a stitch is slipped in the decreasing border to make the edge strong.

Stitches are slipped for many lacy patterns. On cable patterns, stitches are slipped on to a cable needle and held at the front or back of work until they are required. A stitch can be slipped from a striped row to produce a Fair Isle effect without having to strand the yarn across the back of work. This is much easier than darning in loose ends.

Slipping stitches: knitwise

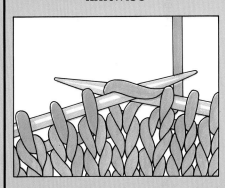

1 *To slip the stitch knitwise, insert the point of the right-hand needle through the next stitch on the left-hand needle, from the front of the loop through to the back. Leave the yarn at the back of the work.*

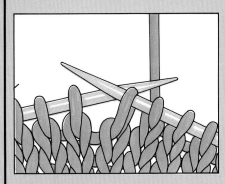

2 *Without wrapping the yarn around the needle, slip the stitch off the left-hand needle on to the right-hand needle. Hold the yarn gently at the back of the work. Keep the yarn at the back of the work if the next stitch is a knit stitch.*

Know How

Slipping stitches: purlwise

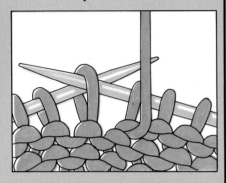

1 *To slip the stitch purlwise, insert the point of the right-hand needle through the next stitch on the left-hand needle from the front of the loop.*

2 *Slip the stitch on to the right-hand needle, holding the yarn in front of the work gently. If the next stitch is to be purled, keep the yarn at the front.*

Picking up dropped stitches

Even the most experienced knitter drops stitches. But do not ignore them or your garment will become unravelled. On a stockinette stitch fabric, for example, where a single stitch has been dropped down one row, it can easily be picked up using knitting needles. Where a ladder has run down the knitting, use a crochet hook to pick up the stitches. For garter stitch, turn the work with each picked up stitch.

Stockinette stitch

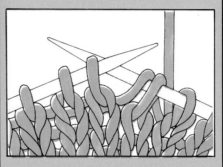

1 *On a knit row, insert the right-hand needle through the dropped stitch from front to back and under the strand of yarn.*

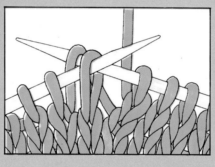

2 *Insert the point of the left-hand needle through the dropped stitch from back to front and lift the stitch over the strand of yarn. Replace the stitch on to the left-hand needle. Continue to knit this row in the usual way.*

3 *On a purl row insert the right-hand needle through the dropped stitch from back to front and then under the strand of yarn.*

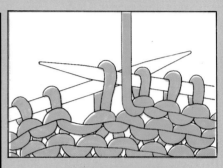

4 *Lift the stitch over the strand of yarn, then transfer the stitch on to the left-hand needle, and continue to purl in the usual way.*

5 *Where a stitch has dropped down several rows forming a ladder, use a crochet hook to pick up the stitch. Firstly slide the stitches away from the needle points, to prevent further loss of stitches.*

6 *No matter which row you were working on, turn the work so the knit side is facing. Insert the crochet hook through the dropped stitch, from the front to back and under the first strand.*

Know How

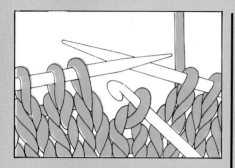

7 *Draw the strand through the stitch. Continue in this way to the top of the ladder, taking care to work up the strands in the correct order. Replace the stitch on to the left-hand needle and continue the row.*

Garter stitch

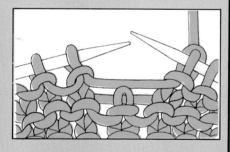

1 *On a garter stitch fabric the method is a little more complicated: turn the work for each stitch you pick up so that the first strand lies behind the dropped stitch, rather than in front of it.*

2 *Insert the crochet hook from the front to back through the stitch and under the first strand. Draw the strand through the dropped stitch.*

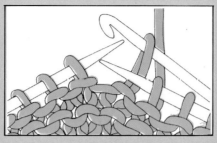

3 *Turn the work and carefully remove the crochet hook. Work from step 1, making sure the strand lies behind the dropped stitch. Continue in this way to the top of the ladder. Replace stitch on the appropriate needle, and knit in the usual way.*

Left-handed knitting

Although knitting patterns are written for right-handed knitters, this should make little difference to the left-handed knitter. Remember that on a pattern for a jacket or a cardigan, when the instructions for the left front are knitted the resulting piece will be right front and vice versa. Providing you realize that the fronts will be reversed the pattern shouldn't cause any difficulties.

Holding the yarn

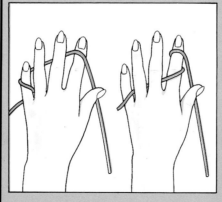

Choose either method. Wind yarn around one finger, then over and under the other fingers of the left hand to control the flow of yarn.

Holding the needles

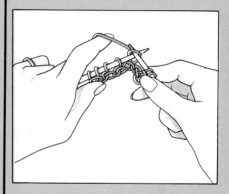

The left hand holds the needle with the stitches which have been worked on, and the right hand holds the needle with the stitches ready to be knitted. Hold both needles with the thumb at the front of the work and the fingers at the back.

Casting on: cable method

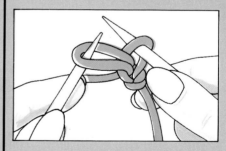

For the cable method, make a slip loop, place the loop on needle and tighten. Hold this needle in right hand. Insert left-hand needle through front of loop. Take yarn under and over left-hand needle and draw yarn through loop to make a new stitch on left-hand needle. Slip this stitch onto right-hand needle. Insert left-hand needle from front to back between the two stitches. Take yarn under and over left-hand needle and make a stitch as before. Continue in this way until the required number of stitches has been cast on.

Know How

Casting on: thumb method

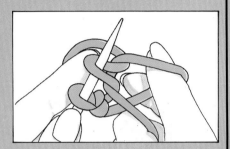

Allowing approximately ³/₄in for each stitch to be made, make a slip loop that distance from end of ball. Place slip loop on needle. Hold needle in left hand. Wind shorter end around thumb of right hand. Insert needle into loop. Take yarn from ball under and over needle and draw it through the loop on thumb to make a new stitch. Slip loop off thumb and pull shorter end to tighten stitch. Continue in this way until the required number of stitches have been cast on.

The knit stitch

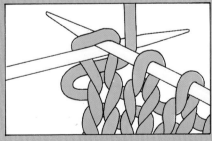

Take the empty needle in your left hand and the needle with the stitches in your right hand. With yarn at back of work, insert left-hand needle through front of first stitch. Take yarn under and over left-hand needle and draw yarn through stitch on right-hand needle. Slip stitch off right-hand needle to complete the knit stitch. The left hand is the working hand and holds the needle that actually creates the stitches. The left hand holds the yarn and guides it.

The purl stitch

Take the empty needle in your left hand and the needle with the stitches in your right hand. With the yarn at the front of work, insert the left-hand needle through the front of the first stitch. Take yarn over and under the left-hand needle and draw yarn through the stitch on right-hand needle. Slip stitch off right-hand needle to complete the purl stitch.

Binding off knitwise

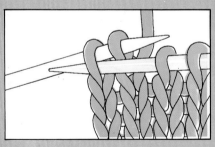

Keep yarn at back of work. Knit first two stitches from right-hand needle. Insert point of right-hand needle through the first stitch knitted and lift over second stitch knitted and off needle. One stitch has been bound off. Knit next stitch on right-hand needle. Lift second stitch knitted over it and off needle. Continue in this way until one stitch remains on left-hand needle. Cut yarn and thread end through stitch. Pull yarn to secure.

Joining yarns

It is easier to join in new balls of yarn at the beginning of a row, so that when the garment is made up the ends can be sewn into the seam. This is far easier than having to darn in the ends.

The following steps show a method which is neat and safely secures a new yarn in the patterns where the old color will be used again in the same row. This method is used when following a pattern such as Fair Isle.

Joining in new yarns

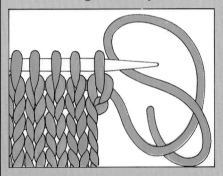

1 *When the remaining length of yarn is insufficient to complete a row, leave a length to darn in at the edge of the work. The recommended length is approximately 6in.*

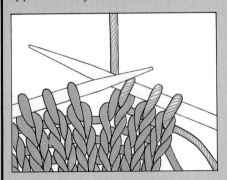

2 *Start knitting with a new ball also leaving a length. With slippery yarns, like chenille and silk, knot the ends together loosely. Untie before darning them into a seam.*

Know How

Splicing

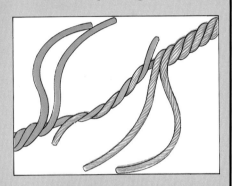

Unravel about 3in of both old and new yarns. Retwist the ends together to make one strand and continue knitting taking extra care over the stitches which immediately follow.

To add a new color

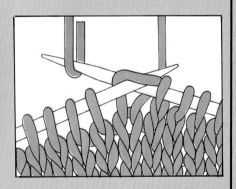

1 Insert the right-hand needle into the next stitch on the left-hand needle. Leaving the old yarn at the back of work, wind the new yarn round the right-hand needle, leaving this end at the back of work.

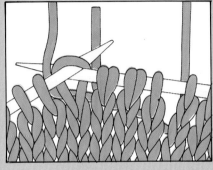

2 Knit the next stitch in the ordinary way with one thread of the new yarn, then knit the next two stitches with the yarn doubled. Leave the short end and continue with the new yarn as required.

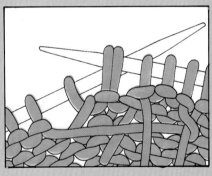

3 The old yarn may be used again in the same row, but do not pull too tightly across the back of work. On the next row, work the two threads as one stitch in the ordinary way.

Ribbing

Ribbing is made from a combination of knit and purl stitches worked alternately. There are many variations from the very simple to the elaborate. By working these two stitches together alternately an elastic fabric is produced which is used mainly for borders, waistbands and neckbands to help keep the garment in shape. Neckbands, cuffs and waistbands particularly are stretched every time the garment is worn, so it is important to work sufficient rows in rib. Some garments, however, are made in rib throughout.

When one stitch is knitted and one stitch purled, this is called a single or plain rib. Usually an even number of stitches are cast on for plain rib. Where two stitches are knitted and two stitches purled, this is called a double rib. It is not as elastic as plain rib and is used mostly for chunky garments. A number of stitches divisible by four are cast on.

Single rib

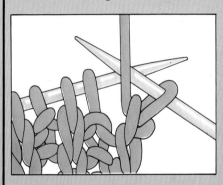

1 Once the cast-on row has been worked, knit the first stitch on the left-hand needle. When the stitch has been worked, and is on the right-hand needle, bring the yarn to the front of the work.

2 Purl the second stitch on the left-hand needle. When this stitch is on the right-hand needle, take the yarn to the back of the work, ready to knit the next stitch. These two steps are repeated.

Know How

Double rib

1 *Once the cast-on row has been worked, the first two stitches of the row are knitted. When these stitches are on the right-hand needle, bring the yarn to the front of the work.*

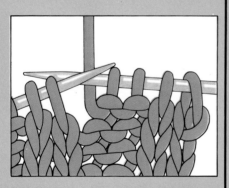

2 *The next two stitches on the left-hand needle are purled. When these two stitches have been worked, take the yarn to the back of the work ready for the next stitch to be knitted.*

Fisherman's rib

1 *Once the cast-on row has been worked, with an even number of stitches, knit a row. Repeat following steps to end of work. Knit the first two stitches of the second row from the left-hand needle in the usual way. Leave the yarn at the back of work.*

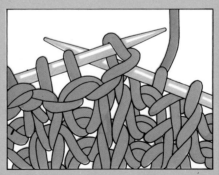

2 *Insert the point of the right-hand needle into the space below the next stitch on the left-hand needle from the front of the stitch through to the back.*

3 *Leaving the top stitch on the left-hand needle, bring the yarn under and over the right-hand needle. Drawing the yarn from back to front of the loop, slip remaining and new stitch off left-hand needle. Knit next stitch. Repeat steps 2 and 3 to end of row.*

Picking up stitches on a curve

It is necessary to pick up the stitches around a curve for neckbands, collars and armbands. The stitches must be picked up neatly and evenly, otherwise it can spoil the appearance of the finished garment.

The best results will be obtained when the shaping has been worked one or two stitches in from the edge, rather than on the edge stitches. This method of shaping is called fully fashioned shaping. The advantage of this method of shaping is that you are left with a straight edge from which to pick up the required stitches.

Where possible it is easier to work on two needles, working forwards and back in rows. However, it is sometimes necessary to use a circular needle or a set of double-pointed needles to work in continuous rounds.

It may help to knit the first row after picking up the stitches. This forms a ridge on the right side of the work which partly covers the picked up stitches to disguise any irregular stitches.

Know How

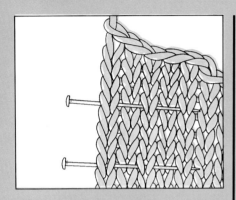

1 *Begin by dividing the work into equal sections using pins. Calculate how many stitches must be picked up from each section. One stitch is picked up from every row.*

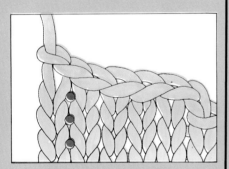

2 *Pick up the stitches one complete stitch in from the edge of the work.*

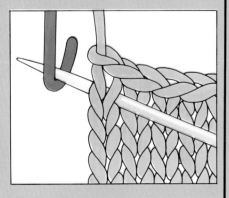

3 *Begin at the right-hand edge and, with right side of work facing, insert needle from front to back through the first row, one stitch in from the edge. Wind yarn under and over the needle.*

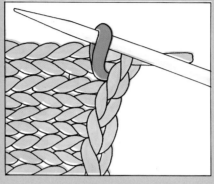

4 *Draw the yarn through the first stitch to the right side of work to make a stitch.*

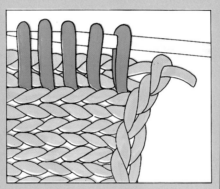

5 *Continue in this way, inserting the needle in the second stitch in every row, until the required number of stitches has been picked up.*

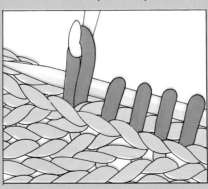

6 *You may find it easier to pick up the stitches using a crochet hook. Using the hook, work steps 3 and 4, then slip stitch from hook on to needle.*

Picking up stitches on the straight

The way in which stitches are picked up on the straight is the same as for a curve. Armbands, pockets, edgings and front bands are all examples of working vertically and horizontally. When actually picking up the stitches follow steps 1 to 6.

Unless the instructions state otherwise, never slip the first stitch of every row. The reason for this is that when the first stitch is slipped, for every two rows knitted you will only have one row at the edge from which to pick up stitches.

When picking up stitches it is essential to pick up the exact number given in the pattern. The designer has carefully calculated this number so that the work is neither too full, nor too tight. To help you pick up the stitches evenly along the edge, either use pins as explained earlier, or count the rows. For example, if you need to pick up one stitch from each of the first five rows and then miss one row.

Stitches which have been bound off, held on a stitch-holder, safety pin or length of yarn, will be worked into horizontally.

Vertically

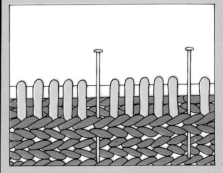

1 *The stitches for a front band are picked up between the first and second stitches from the edge. The pins show where a row of the main piece has not been worked into.*

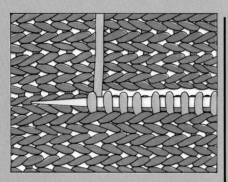

2 *Stitches for a vertical pocket opening are picked up along one side of the opening for the pocket lining. The lining is knitted and bound off. Then stitches are picked up along the other side for the pocket edging.*

Horizontally

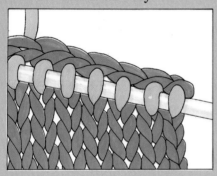

1 *When the stitches have been bound off, insert the needle through the center of the first stitch of the last row and knit the stitch in the usual way, then continue in this way to end.*

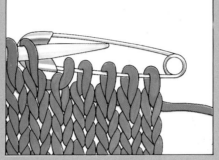

2 *When stitches are held on a stitch holder, safety pin or length of yarn, slip the stitches from left to right on to a needle and then simply work across the stitches as instructed.*

Making buttonholes

The most common fastening for knitted garments is the button and buttonhole. This can be made quite easily in a number of ways. The method used to make the buttonhole will largely depend on the weight and texture of the fabric, and the size and position of the button.

Sweaters, cardigans and jackets usually feature horizontal buttonholes. There is a reinforced version for outdoor, heavyweight garments.

Vertical buttonholes are more likely to pull apart, and are best kept for more decorative positions where they are not under any strain, such as on flaps of pockets.

Fine lacy designs and baby garments only require tiny buttonholes. These are produced by the eyelet method and are the simplest to work.

Vertical buttonhole

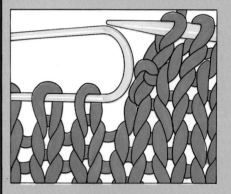

1 *Vertical buttonholes are made by dividing the work to form a split. Knit along the row to the position of the buttonhole and turn. Leave remaining stitches on a stitch holder. Continue on this set of stitches up one side of buttonhole for the required depth, ending at the split edge. Slip the edge stitches on alternate rows for a neat finish. Do not break yarn.*

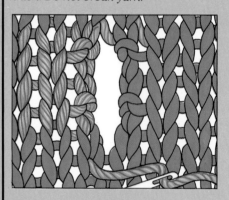

2 *Join in a new ball of yarn to work up the second side of buttonhole. Knit one row less than the first side, ending at the split edge. Break yarn. Take up yarn from first side, and work across last set of stitches. Darn in the loose ends securely.*

Know How

Eyelet buttonhole

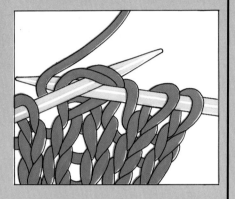

1 *Eyelet buttonholes are worked over one row. Knit along the row to the position of the buttonhole. Bring the yarn to the front of work to make one stitch. Knit the next two stitches on left hand needle together.*

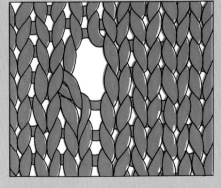

2 *The buttonhole is then complete and the knitting can be continued.*

Horizontal buttonholes

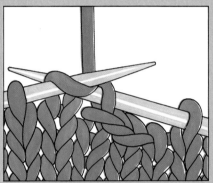

1 *Horizontal buttonholes are worked over two rows. Knit along the row to the position of the buttonhole. Bind off a number of stitches, appropriate to the button size (usually two or three), then continue knitting to the end of the row.*

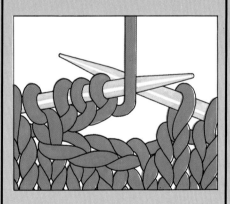

2 *Knit along the next row to the position of the buttonhole. Cast on stitches to replace those bound off on previous row. This is achieved by making a loop on the thumb and slipping it on to the needle. Continue knitting to the end of the row.*

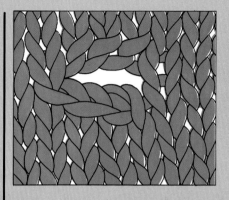

3 *To avoid loose stitches and untidy corners, work into the back of the cast on stitches on the following row. Alternatively, cast on one stitch less than required, and make one stitch on the next row by working twice into the stitch before the buttonhole.*

Stronger horizontal buttonholes

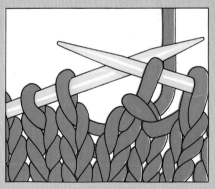

1 *The stronger horizontal buttonhole is made on one row. Knit along the row to the buttonhole position. Bring yarn to the front of work, slip one, take yarn to back of work, bind off without knitting by slipping the next stitch, and passing the first slipped stitch over it. Repeat this until the required number of stitches is bound off. Slip the last stitch back on to the left-hand needle and turn the work around.*

Know How

2 *Take the yarn to the back of work. Cast on stitches onto left-hand needle to replace those bound off, plus one extra but, before placing the last stitch on to left needle, bring yarn to the front of work. Turn.*

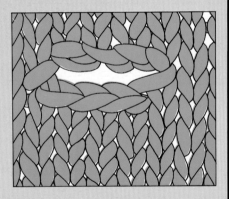

3 *Slip first stitch from left needle to right and pass the extra cast on stitch over it and off needle. Continue knitting to the end of row.*

Blocking and pressing

Correct blocking and pressing, followed by careful sewing up, is the only sure way of producing a well-finished knitted article.

Blocking involves pinning out the knitted pieces to the correct shape and size. Slightly over-large pieces can be eased down and any on the small side can be stretched a little to give a correct final measurement. Ribbing should not be blocked otherwise it looses its elasticity, therefore pin around the inner edge of neckbands and welts.

Before pressing, it is essential to check on the treatment of the yarn used. Most spinners now give a guide on the ball band in symbol form. Also consider the characteristic look of a stitch. Both cable patterns and garter stitch will be spoilt by heavy pressing.

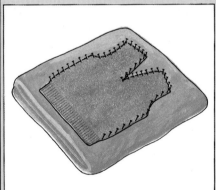

1 *Place the garment pieces right sides down on a springy pad of thick felt covered with an ironing sheet. A blanket folded and covered with an ironing sheet makes a good surface. Pin out to the given measurements, then pin round the shape at ¹/₂in intervals. Take great care that the stitches and the rows are in a straight line. Check all dimensions to be sure they agree with the pattern size instruction.*

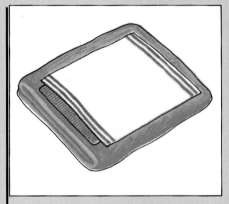

2 *Following the ball band symbols, place a dry cloth or damp cloth, according to the type of yarn, over the work. If the yarn should not be pressed, leave a damp cloth over the work overnight until completely dry. Keep away from direct heat and sunlight.*

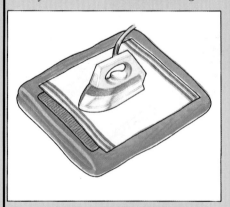

3 *It is the steam created by the iron on the cloth which evens out the knitting, not heavy pressure. Do not use a smoothing action, simply lay the iron on the work lightly and lift off. Continue in this way over all the sections of the article.*

Finishing a sweater

A poor quality seam can spoil the best piece of knitting. Finishing the work needs a lot of care and attention. Patterns often state the type of stitch used in the finishing instructions.

A flat stitch is almost invisible. It is used to give a neat and flat finish on stockinette stitch, garter stitch and on many ribbed sections, such as waistbands. It can be used wherever the shaping has not given an irregular edge to the work.

A backstitch seam gives a firm seam. It is used when joining curved edges such as armholes, or where the seam is sewn across the direction of the knitted stitches as on shaped shoulders. Another commonly used stitch is the invisible seam. A stitch is picked up from each piece of the work on the right side alternately. This can be used on garter stitch and stockinette stitch fabrics for side and sleeve seams. Use a blunt-ended needle with a large eye. The blunted end will slip between the knitted stitches without splitting them.

Flat seam

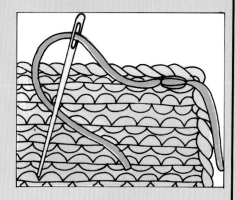

1 Place together the two pieces with the right sides of work on the inner side. Match the pattern stitch for stitch and row for row. Join in the yarn to the right-hand side of one of the completed pieces.

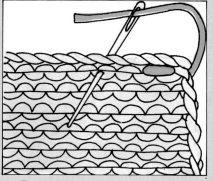

2 Pass the needle through the edge stitch of the wrong side of the under piece, then through to the corresponding stitch on the top piece and pull the yarn through making sure it is secure.

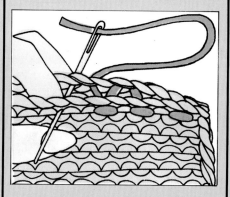

3 Work back through the next stitch on the top piece to the corresponding stitch on the underside piece. Work backwards and forwards in this way until the seam has been completed.

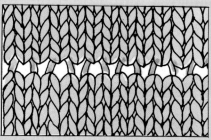

4 Once the seam has been completed, turn the work to the right side. Check the rows have been matched correctly. Press the seam so that the inside edge lies flat.

Backstitch seam

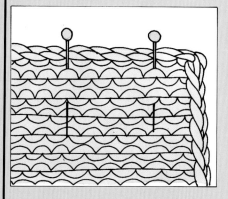

1 Place the right sides of the pieces together. With wrong side of work facing and matching the pattern carefully, pin the pieces together at frequent intervals.

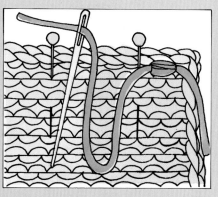

2 Secure the yarn from the right-hand side, making two running stitches on top of the other. With the needle at the back of work, move it one knitted stitch to the left, pull yarn through to the front.

Know How

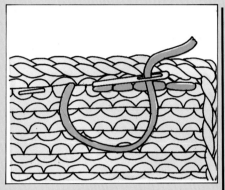

3 *Move the needle across the front of the work to the right, re-insert it through the back where the last stitch was worked. Work in this way until the seam is complete.*

Invisible seam

1 *Place the two pieces of the work side by side with the right side of work facing. Secure the yarn on the wrong side at the lower edge of one piece.*

2 *Bring the yarn to the front of the work. Take the needle over to the other piece, picking up the center bar of the first stitch. Pull the yarn through tightly, making sure it is secure.*

3 *Pass the needle back to the first side and pick up the stitch corresponding to the other side. Pull yarn through. Continue in this way picking up the stitches alternately. Pull each stitch tightly so it is invisible on right side of work.*

Invisible joining

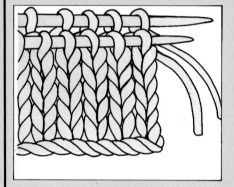

1 *Do not bind the stitches off the needles. Hold both needles back to back, with the right side of the work facing. Space the stitches evenly to correspond with each other. Break the yarn leaving at least twice the seam length.*

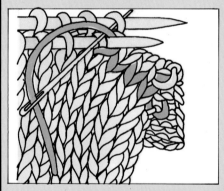

2 *Using a blunt-ended needle insert it knitwise through the first stitch and slip it off the needle. Insert the needle purlwise into the second stitch, keeping it on the needle. Repeat first on one needle, then the next, until the seam is completed.*

Know How

Finishing a garment

At the end of every knitting pattern there are finishing instructions. They state the order in which the different sections of knitting should be joined. Where relevant they will also give the type of seam to be used and whether right sides or wrong sides should be facing when each seam is joined. Pressing instructions will also be included. When the yarn can be pressed, press each seam before joining the next.

To learn how to finish a garment, follow these instructions for finishing a basic jacket, knitted in stockinette stitch with waistbands and cuffs worked in rib. The jacket has front bands, set-in pockets and a collar. These steps can be adapted to suit any style of garment. Remember to darn in all ends for at least 2in. This is particularly important on garments which are to be machine washed.

Shoulder seam: backstitch seam

Place right sides of back and front together, carefully matching each bound off step. Pin at intervals. Beginning at armhole edge, backstitch across shoulder. For a neat seam, stitch in a slanting line from armhole to neck edges rather than following each bound off step. To prevent a heavy garment dropping, reinforce seams with tape which should be sewn in place after the seams have been stitched.

Shoulder seam: grafting

Without binding off and with shoulders together, place front and back horizontally on a flat surface. Thread a darning needle with a long strand of yarn. Weave the needle in and out twice through each stitch to produce an invisible seam. The stitches can also be grafted directly on the two knitting needles if preferred.

Side seams

Begin at lower edge (cast on edge). With right sides facing join rib with an oversewn seam in order to maintain the elasticity of the rib. Oversew corresponding stitches on each piece together. At the top of the rib change to an invisible woven seam (see page 142), to join remainder of seam.

Sleeve seams

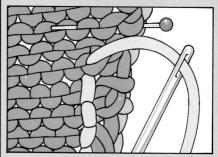

Where the sleeve has increasings at regular intervals up each edge, join the rib as shown in the side seam. Turn work so that right sides are together. Matching increasings, pin the seam to top. Join remainder of seam with a backstitch. Slant the seam rather than stepping around increasings for a neat finish as on the shoulder shaping.

Set in sleeves

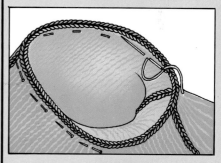

1 *With right sides together, match sleeve seam to side seam and pin. Match center of top of sleeve to shoulder seam and pin. Place pins at regular intervals around remainder of armhole. If necessary gather any fullness in the sleeve cap evenly at shoulder end of armhole.*

Know How

2 *Beginning at underarm seam, backstitch evenly around armhole. When stitching across unshaped edges of back or front take care to follow line of stitches carefully to give a neat result. When joining raglan seams with fully fashioned shaping, use an invisible woven seam.*

Buttonbands

1 *For the bands to fit correctly they should be slightly shorter than the front edges of the garment. With right sides facing, place the band alongside the front. Beginning at lower edge, stretch the buttonband slightly and pin the two sections together, placing the pins horizontally at regular intervals.*

2 *Begin at lower edge. Taking small stitches, oversew the band in place from the right side. Bands can be reinforced by sewing a length of ribbon to the wrong side afterwards.*

Collar

Place right side of collar to wrong side of garment. Match center back neck of each piece and pin. Place side edges to appropriate position on fronts and pin. Pin remainder of collar position. Oversew neatly in place. Press seam and turn collar on to right side of garment.

Pocket linings

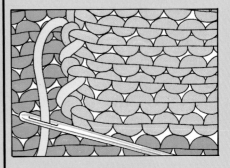

With wrong side of front facing, pin pocket lining in position around both sides and lower edge. Slip stitch lining lightly to front, taking care to sew in a straight line.

Pocket tops

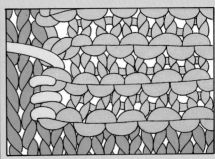

With right side of front facing, pin sides of top edging to front. Slip stitch each side of top edging loosely to appropriate stitch of front.

Know How

Working a V-neckline

There are many variations on working a V-neckline. If the waistband is worked in single rib, the neckband is also worked in a single rib. For this, an uneven number of stitches is required, because an odd number of stitches produces a center stitch. This is marked with a colored thread and decreases are worked either side of the center stitch.

If the waistband has been worked in a double rib, the neckband likewise can be worked in a double rib. This time two center stitches are required, so an even number of stitches is used.

To shape the neck use a third needle to work the first piece. Do not use the original two needles, otherwise the work can break and the stitches stretch. It may be necessary to work the armhole and shoulder shaping at the same time as the neckline, therefore read the instructions very carefully. When the first piece is completed, rejoin the yarn to the inside edge of the second stitch. Work as for the first side reversing all the shapings.

When the neckband is worked, pick up the exact number of stitches recommended in the instructions. This is important as not every stitch is worked into, and too many stitches can cause gathering. Decreases are made next to the center stitch or stitches which produces the V. Once the neckband has been completed, bind off loosely in rib.

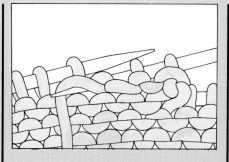

1 *Knit to the center of the row, leaving the remaining stitches on the left-hand needle. Using a third needle, turn the work and purl next row. This is the first side of neck shaping.*

2 *Knit to the last four stitches on the left-hand needle. Knit the next two stitches together, knit the next two stitches in the ordinary way.*

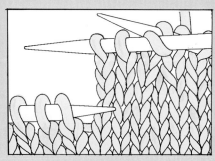

3 *On the following row, purl all the stitches. Work two rows in stockinette stitch without working a decrease on the knit row.*

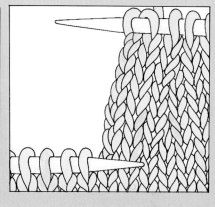

4 *Work as for step 2, decreasing at the neck edge as before. Continue in this way with a decrease on every fourth row, until the required number of stitches are on the needle.*

5 *Work even on these stitches until the neckline shaping is the required length. Work shoulder shaping, binding off the required number of stitches at beginning of the knit rows. Fasten off the last stitch securely.*

Know How

6 *Return to the stitches on the left-hand needle, slip the first stitch off the needle and hold with a safety pin. Rejoin yarn to the inner edge of left-hand needle. Work to end of row.*

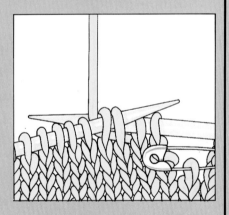

7 *Purl the next row. On the following row, knit the first two stitches in the ordinary way. Knit the next two stitches together through the back of the loop. This produces a decrease which slants towards the left.*

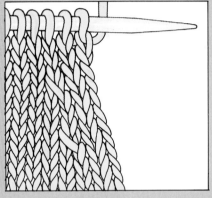

8 *Work in exactly the same way as the previous steps, decreasing on the right side of every fourth row. Continue working until the second side measures exactly the same as the first side, ending with a right side row. Work shoulder shaping and bind off.*

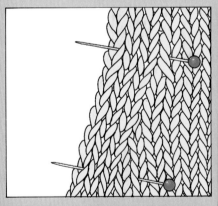

9 *Using several pins calculate how many stitches to pick up down each side of the neck. Do not pick one stitch for every row, or the neckband will be far too loose, but do not pick up too few stitches as this causes puckering.*

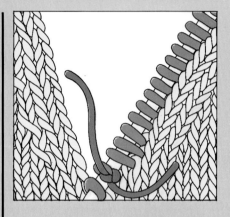

10 *Make sure the total number of stitches for the neckband is uneven. Mark the center stitch with a colored thread. Using the same size needle as all the other welts were worked in, rib to within two stitches of the colored thread.*

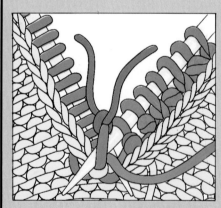

11 *Knit the next two stitches together in the ordinary way. Purl the center stitch and leave a marker. Knit the next two stitches together, work in single rib starting with a purl stitch to the end of row.*

Know How

12 *On the second row of neckband, rib to within two stitches of the colored thread. This time purl the next two stitches together. Knit the center stitch leaving the marker in position, purl the next two stitches together, continue in rib to end of row.*

13 *Steps 11 and 12 form the neckband. Repeat these two rows until the neckband is the required depth, ending with a wrong side row. Bind off loosely. It may be a good idea to use one size larger needle. Decrease on this row as before.*

Working in two colors

Many knitting patterns involve working in several different colors. Geometric and abstract designs for example are often worked in two colors.

To avoid the yarns tangling, a separate ball of yarn or a bobbin is used to work each block of color. Bobbins are made in strong cardboard with notches cut at the top and bottom. The yarn is wound around the cardboard until it is full.

When a row is worked, the bobbins are held at the back of the work, twisting the different colors used each time to avoid a hole.

To make a bobbin

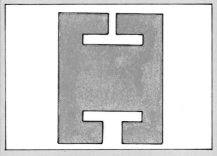

1 *Draw a template on a strong piece of cardboard. Using a small sharp pair of scissors, cut it out.*

2 *Wind the yarn around the bobbin, evenly and in the same direction, until the bobbin is full.*

To twist colors

1 *Using the main color, knit up to the colored pattern. Then, twist the main and the contrast colors together, by taking the main color over the top of the contrast color. Knit the next stitch in contrasting color, pulling the stitch tightly to avoid a hole. Work to end of row.*

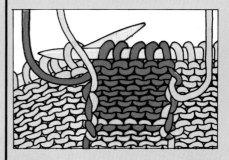

2 *On the following row, work up to the colored panel, and twist the main color and contrast color as before. When the colored panel has been completed, take the contrast color over the top of the main color, pull tightly. Work to end of row.*

Know How

Making and covering buttons

Covered or made buttons provide an attractive way of finishing a knitted garment. They are very practical when a bought button of matching color cannot be obtained.

The knitted cover is worked over a mold which may be a bead or simply an oddment of the same yarn used as a padding for the knitted casing. It is essential that the casing is firmly knitted, so that the stitches do not separate when stretched over the mold, allowing the base to show through. For this reason a much smaller needle size than normal is used.

There are two basic methods of working the casing. The first method is worked using two needles. A small piece of knitting slightly larger than the mold is worked in an octagonal shape, then stretched over the mold. In the second method a set of four double-pointed needles are used to make a flat disc, which in turn is stretched over a mold. The actual method of working a casing is the same, whether it is stockinette stitch, a small textured pattern, or a Fair Isle type of pattern.

Making buttons

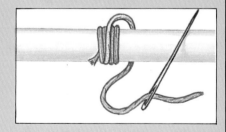

1 *Wind the yarn around a rod, which is slightly smaller in diameter than the required buttons. Leave a long end of yarn and thread on to a needle.*

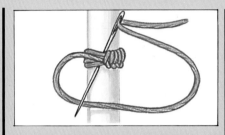

2 *Work around the coil of yarn in a buttonhole stitch, until a complete round has been covered.*

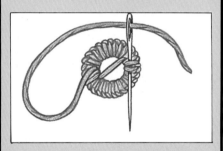

3 *Remove the coil from the rod and using the same needle and thread, pick up a couple of stitches from the opposite side of the ring, then a couple of stitches to one side of the starting point. Pull the yarn through.*

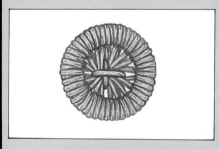

4 *Continue in this way, working around the ring, until all the center has been filled. Work in cross stitch or a few running stitches at the center to secure the diagonal threads.*

Using four double-pointed needles

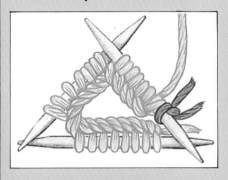

1 *Cast on required number of stitches for the other circumference on to three of the needles. Join stitches into a circle and knit the first round.*

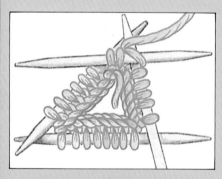

2 *For the next round, knit the next two stitches in the ordinary way. Knit the next two stitches together, repeat these two steps on each of the needles. Work the next round in pattern without working any decreases.*

Know How

3 For the next round, continue to work one stitch less than in previous round and working the next two stitches together, repeat on all three needles. Work a further round of decreasing on next alternate round.

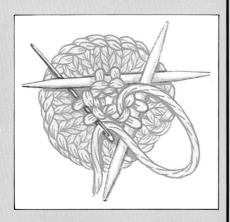

4 Break off the yarn and (using four double-pointed needles) thread through remaining stitches. Place the mold on top of the knitting and draw the stitches tightly together. Fasten off securely.

Using two needles

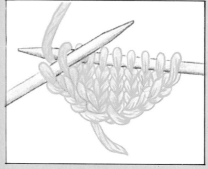

1 Cast on a few stitches and work one knit row. Continue to work in the chosen pattern, increasing one stitch at each end of the row, until the increase edge measures exactly the same as the cast-on edge.

2 Work a few rows without increasing, until the straight edge measures the same as the cast-on edge.

3 Now decrease one stitch at each end of every row until the same number of stitches remains as for the cast-on edge. Bind off remaining stitches. Using the same end of yarn, work a row of running stitches around the edge of the piece of knitting.

4 Place the mold on top of the knitting and pull up the running stitches tightly, thus covering the mold. Fasten off securely.

Know How

Embroidery on knitting

Almost any embroidery stitch can be used on a knitted fabric, and even the most simple stitches can be used to produce a decorative effect. Stockinette stitch makes a good background but embroidery combines equally well with patterned stitches, for example, a small flower in the center of a diamond pattern looks very effective.

Always use a blunt-ended needle when embroidering onto a knitted fabric so the knitted stitches do not split. Almost all thin yarns can be used too. The size of the embroidery needle will depend on the yarn you choose. The needle should always be slightly thicker than the yarn used so it can be pulled through the work smoothly and easily. Be careful not to distort the knitted fabric as the embroidery is worked.

Match the tension of the knitted fabric so the work remains smooth and even. Use the structure of the knitting as a guide to keep the embroidered stitches the same length. This is particularly important for flowers and other symmetrical objects.

Straight chain stitch

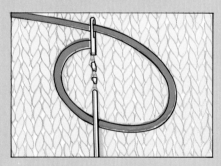

1 *Using a blunt-ended needle and contrasting colored thread, secure the yarn at the back of the work. Bring the needle to the top of the fabric and insert it through to the back. Now bring the needle out to the front of the work a few stitches from the top, but do not pull the needle through.*

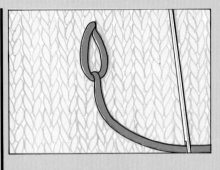

2 *Form the yarn into a loop, holding it down with your fingers. Draw the yarn through the needle, forming one chain stitch.*

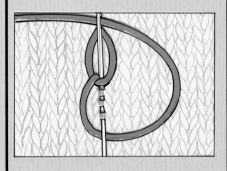

3 *Now insert the needle through the bottom of the same stitch. This is now the top of the second stitch. Work in exactly the same way as in steps 1 and 2.*

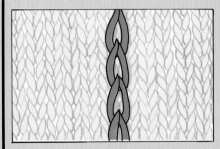

4 *Repeat steps 1-3 until the chain is the required length. Keep all stitches the same length and pull the loop through evenly.*

Flowers

1 *By working several detached chain stitches they can be combined to make flowers. The lazy daisy stitches are worked from the center outwards.*

2 *Work all the detached chain stitches the same length from the center making sure the loop is not pulled too tightly. Work five detached chain stitches for one flower.*

Index

Picture credits

Phil Babb: 147 Berry/Fallon: 49, 75, 78 Steve Campbell: 35, 112, 143 Ray Duns: 35, 109, 148 Terry Evans: 50, 52, 89, 113 Dennis Hawkins: 41, 56, 136 John Hutchinson: 40, 42, 53, 57, 117, 148 Hank Kemme: 130 Tom Leighton: 16, 22 Francis Loney: 104 Jan Mason: 61, 62, 101, 103 Eamonn McCabe: 115 Ray Moller: 133 Coral Mula: 142 Stan North: 7, 9, 13, 15, 17, 19, 21, 23, 25, 27, 28 Spike Powell: 24 Sara Silcock: 39, 124, Jerry Tubby: 10 Peter Waldman: 14 Graham Young: 30, 39 Victor Yuan: 67, 118, 121, 139

Knitting Abbreviations

alt	alternate(ly)	K-wise	knitwise	sp	space(s)
approx	approximately	K1B	knit one below	sl st	slip stitch (knitting)
beg	begin(ning)	M1	make one stitch	ssk	slip one, knit one, pass
ch	chain(s)	meas	measures		slipped stitch over
cont	continu(e)(ing)	P	purl	st(s)	stitch(es)
dc	double crochet	pr	pair	St st	Stockinette stitch
dec	decreas(e)(ing)	patt	pattern	tbl	through back of loop(s)
foll(s)	follow(s)(ing)	psso	pass slipped stitch over	tog	together
gr(s)	group(s)	P-wise	purlwise	tr	treble
g st	garter stitch	rem	remain(ing)	WS	wrong side
hdc	half double	rep	repeat	ybk	yarn back
in	inches	rev St st	reverse Stockinette stitch	yo	yarn over
inc	increas(e)(ing)	RS	right side		
K	knit	sl	slip